LEGALITY'S BORDERS

LEGALITY'S BORDERS

AN ESSAY IN GENERAL

JURISPRUDENCE

KEITH CULVER
MICHAEL GIUDICE

OXFORD
UNIVERSITY PRESS

OXFORD
UNIVERSITY PRESS

Oxford University Press, Inc., publishes works that further Oxford University's objective of excellence in research, scholarship, and education.

Oxford New York
Auckland Cape Town Dar es Salaam Hong Kong Karachi Kuala Lumpur Madrid
Melbourne Mexico City Nairobi New Delhi Shanghai Taipei Toronto

With offices in
Argentina Austria Brazil Chile Czech Republic France Greece Guatemala Hungary
Italy Japan Poland Portugal Singapore South Korea Switzerland Thailand
Turkey Ukraine Vietnam

Copyright © 2010 by Oxford University Press, Inc.

Published by Oxford University Press, Inc.
198 Madison Avenue, New York, New York 10016

Oxford is a registered trademark of Oxford University Press
Oxford University Press is a registered trademark of Oxford University Press, Inc.

Library of Congress Cataloging-in-Publication Data

Culver, Keith Charles, 1969–
    Legality's borders: an essay in general jurisprudence / Keith Culver and Michael Giudice.
        p. cm.
    Includes bibliographical references and index.
    ISBN 978-0-19-537075-1 ((hardback): alk. paper)
    1. Jurisprudence. 2. Law—Philosophy.
    I. Giudice, Michael. II. Title.
    K237.C858 2010
    340–dc22   2009039244

1 2 3 4 5 6 7 8 9

Printed in the United States of America on acid-free paper

Note to Readers
This publication is designed to provide accurate and authoritative information in regard to the subject matter covered. It is based upon sources believed to be accurate and reliable and is intended to be current as of the time it was written. It is sold with the understanding that the publisher is not engaged in rendering legal, accounting, or other professional services. If legal advice or other expert assistance is required, the services of a competent professional person should be sought. Also, to confirm that the information has not been affected or changed by recent developments, traditional legal research techniques should be used, including checking primary sources where appropriate.

(Based on the Declaration of Principles jointly adopted by a Committee of the American Bar Association and a Committee of Publishers and Associations.)

You may order this or any other Oxford University Press publication by
visiting the Oxford University Press website at www.oup.com

For Neil MacCormick

CONTENTS

ACKNOWLEDGMENTS

We owe thanks to many colleagues for their encouragement and valuable comments on various drafts of parts of the book: Julie Dickson, Leslie Green, Neil MacCormick, Dennis Patterson, Brian Tamanaha, and Wil Waluchow. We would also like to acknowledge audiences who participated in discussion at the following events where early chapters of the book were presented: the Atlantic Region Philosophers Association, Fredericton, Canada (October 2006); the Oxford Jurisprudence Discussion Group, Oxford, England (February 2007); a special workshop, 'Legality's Edges', at the meeting of the IVR in Krakow, Poland (August 2007); the Department of Philosophy, McMaster University, Hamilton, Canada (March 2008); the Center for Law and Society, Faculty of Law, University of Edinburgh, Edinburgh, Scotland (October 2008); and the Legal Research Institute, National Autonomous University of Mexico, Mexico city, Mexico (November 2008). We also thank research assistants Jessie Sabbagh, Jessica Duarte, and Emily Gray.

INTRODUCTION

Analytical legal theory has long taken as its central focus the experience of the law-state, and the success of analytical theories of law has been measured by their ability to explain the phenomenon of the law-state. Yet this focus and conception of success may be forced to change as the place of the law-state in our experience of law is changing, from the United Kingdom's devolution of power to Scotland, to integration of European law-states to the point of consideration of a shared constitution, to the rise of super-national legal institutions such as the International Criminal Court. The goal of this book is to revive the tools of analytic jurisprudence for a new set of theoretical challenges posed by the flourishing of novel forms of legal order.

IMBALANCES IN ANALYTICAL LEGAL THEORY'S APPROACH TO PRIMA FACIE LEGAL PHENOMENA

We are far from revolutionary in pointing to a range of social phenomena that challenges the utility of approaches to legality that depart from the law-state as the fundamental instance of legality. Within the analytical approach both H.L.A. Hart and Joseph Raz are aware that the law-state is at the very least an institution with many forms, and that we have not given enough attention to understanding how the idea of "legal system" provides explanatory unity to understanding legality in the law-state and in phenomena not easily dismissed as outliers beyond the scope of our attention. Hart, for example, recognized in the closing chapter of *The Concept of Law* that colonial and post-colonial eras brought unanticipated developments of legal phenomena, raising "fascinating problems of classification" for theorists attempting to understand such devices as "[c]olonies, protectorates, suzerainties, trust territories, confederations"[1]—all variants of sovereignty with associated legal systems or subsystems of various kinds.

---

1. H.L.A. HART, THE CONCEPT OF LAW 220 (1994).

Raz has argued that although an understanding of legal system is crucial to an understanding of law, attention to legal system has been lacking:

> All four problems of the theory of legal system have for the most part been neglected by almost all analytical jurists. It seems to have been traditionally accepted that the crucial step in understanding the law is to define 'a law', and assumed without discussion that the definition of 'a legal system' involves no further problems of any consequence.[2]

Although Raz's remark was made in 1970, we accept its enduring probative value—even though Raz's subsequent writing perhaps inadvertently drew attention away from the problems of legal system and toward individual or constituent aspects of legal systems. He famously argues that legal systems are to be understood as claiming supreme authority to issue norms comprehending the whole of social life, all while remaining open in the sense that complementary social practices can be adopted for special legal purposes.[3] Yet his subsequent work takes up very little of the themes of supremacy, comprehensiveness, and openness, focusing instead on the nature of authoritative reasons for action, often concretized in discussion of the force of particular kinds of norms in practical reasoning.[4] More recently Raz has acknowledged that interest in the identity of legal systems has simply shifted elsewhere since Austin and Kelsen focused on the question:

> John Austin thought that, necessarily, the legal institutions of every legal system are not subject to—that is, do not recognize—the jurisdiction of legal institutions outside their system over them. (I am somewhat reinterpreting his claim here.) Kelsen believed that necessarily constitutional continuity is both necessary and sufficient for the identity of a legal system. We know that both claims are false. The countries of the European Union recognize, and for a time the independent countries of the British

---

2. JOSEPH RAZ, THE CONCEPT OF A LEGAL SYSTEM 24 (1970). Earlier HANS KELSEN expressed a similar view: "Law is not, as it is sometimes said, a rule. It is a set of rules having the kind of unity we understand by a system. It is impossible to grasp the nature of law if we limit our attention to the single isolated rule." GENERAL THEORY OF LAW AND STATE 4, (A. Wedberg trans., 1961).

3. JOSEPH RAZ, PRACTICAL REASON AND NORMS 150–154 (1990).

4. See, e.g., Id. and JOSEPH RAZ, THE AUTHORITY OF LAW (1979).

Empire recognized, the jurisdiction of outside legal institutions over them, thus refuting Austin's theory. And the law of most countries provides counterexamples to Kelsen's claim. I mention these examples not to illustrate that legal philosophers can make mistakes, but to point to the susceptibility of philosophy to the winds of time. So far as I know, Austin's and Kelsen's failures were not made good. That is, no successful alternative explanations were offered. In spite of this there is no great flurry of philosophical activity to plug the gap. Rather, the problem that their mistaken doctrines were meant to explain, namely the problem of the identity and continuity of legal systems, lost its appeal to legal philosophers, who do not mind leaving it unsolved. Interest has shifted elsewhere.[5]

Shifting interests and waning appeal might justify changes in fashion, but they seem rather thin as reasons for analytical legal theorists to ignore important questions raised by new and changing prima facie legal phenomena for understanding of legal systems. The burden of Raz's observation has not been entirely ignored, even though the challenge he offers has not been taken up in any substantial way. Jeremy Waldron recently suggested that:

> Those international lawyers who do bother to read Hart's chapter on international law usually come away with the impression that Hart, like Austin, did not believe there was any such thing as international law. That is not quite correct, but Hart did say that international law is like a primitive legal system—all primary norms and no secondary norms. And that was wrong in 1960 and it is certainly wrong now . . . This is another example of an area where Hart's own carelessness or indifference has been imitated rather than compensated for, by his followers. Those who regard themselves as working to protect and develop Hart's legacy have shown little interest in subjecting Hart's claims about international law to any sort of careful scrutiny or revision. The neglect of international law in modern analytic jurisprudence is nothing short of scandalous. Theoretically it is the issue of the hour . . .[6]

To describe these remarks as strong stuff is likely an understatement. Yet the firm tone of Waldron's remarks is likely justified by the fact

---

5. Joseph Raz, *Two Views of the Nature of the Theory of Law: A Partial Comparison*, in HART'S POSTSCRIPT: ESSAYS ON THE POSTSCRIPT TO THE CONCEPT OF LAW 11 (J. Coleman ed., 2001).

6. Jeremy Waldron, *Hart and the Principles of Legality*, in THE LEGACY OF H.L.A. HART: LEGAL, POLITICAL, AND MORAL PHILOSOPHY 68–69 (M. Kramer et al. eds., 2008).

that so much time has passed from Hart's tentative engagement of borderline phenomena of legality, to Raz's recognition of the shortcomings of analytical approaches to legal system, and to the current situation in which only a few widely read figures such as Neil MacCormick are making real inroads into manifestations of legality at the edges of the familiar model of the law-state.

These observations leave us at a critical turning point. Prima facie legal phenomena give reasons to doubt the adequacy of at least extant analytical explanations of the nature of legal system and the conditions for inclusion or exclusion of social phenomena within particular legal systems or subsystems. Far from this observation arriving as a surprise to analytical theorists, it appears that there is longstanding recognition of the need to account for these troublesome phenomena at legality's borders. What is worse, there is recognition among analytical theorists that for whatever reason they have continued to fail to take up the challenging "issue of the hour" as Waldron puts it. What should be made of this? Here we part ways with Raz's suggestion that the "winds of time" are to blame for analytical legal theory's neglect of the problem of the relation between legality and legal system. Our diagnosis is much less optimistic. What Raz sees as neglect is in fact much worse: it is simply a symptom of an underlying inability of dominant analytical approaches to capture legal phenomena outside the model of the law-state.

Our diagnosis can be framed quite simply. Current analytical approaches to legality and legal system exhibit a kind of explanatory imbalance which deprives those approaches of the capacity to respond to novel law-like social phenomena. Although analytical jurisprudes have constructed rich and deep theories of the distinguishing features of individual legal norms, significantly less attention has been devoted to accounts of legal systems which house individual norms. Two particular aspects of norm-level investigations have exacerbated this imbalance. First, analytical theorists in the Hartian tradition have failed to recognize that accounts of Hart's notion of an official-operated rule of recognition require both structural and functional parts: while we have rich structural explanations of the logical features of the rule of recognition, little attention has been given to whether it can actually function in a way that allows it to carry out the promised task of distinction of valid legal norms of a system from other normative claims. We contend that it does not, and moreover that it cannot, since as we argue in detail in Chapter 1, the official-dependent rule of recognition contains insuperable problems of circularity and indeterminacy in its account of the nature and identity of officials, and these problems deprive the rule of recognition of its promised explanatory power. Legal officials make a special constitutive contribution to the rule of recognition since their practices of norm-creation, application, and enforcement are system-constituting and system-defining practices. Yet without an adequate account of who the legal officials are, and how their identity might change, a necessary precondition for a theory of legality and legal system is unsatisfied. Second, and more generally, the analytical approach contains an imbalance between the descriptive and explanatory parts of its account of legality and legal system. A great deal of effort has been devoted to elaboration of the explanatory part, provided as an account of what is conceptually or logically possible for a system of norms. Much less effort has been given to the descriptive part, understood as the attempt to test conceptual explanations of legal governance against observationally-available evidence. The presence of this imbalance is evident in the paucity of analytical theories' explanation of their connection to observational evidence, and to adjacent areas of inquiry into life under law. As we argue in Chapter 3, employment of evidence tends to proceed without reference to a general account of the nature of evidence, requirements for reliability of that evidence, and so on, required to support the explanatory part of the analytical theory of law. What appeals there are to evidence amount to surveys of data intuitively relevant to elucidation of "our concept" and similarly obscure objects, whose explanation is not clearly connected to moments of greater ambition involving elucidation of more than local practices.

NEW PHENOMENA

Yet the imbalances just identified are perhaps most demonstrable in the failure of analytical legal theory to address prima facie legal phenomena in a variety of emerging contexts. Prima facie legal phenomena fall under four admittedly provisional categories which rely for their utility on their conventional meaning within law, political science, and legal theory.[7] We identify and discuss intra-state legality, trans-state legality, supra-state legality and super-state legality, capturing a range of norms and normative orders often spoken of as international law. It should be emphasized that although we write here of these phenomena as exhibiting "legality," we do so only suggestively, as part of our contention that they exemplify social phenomena which pose a serious challenge to the explanatory adequacy of contemporary analytical legal theory. Conclusive analysis of course awaits the results of our arguments contra contemporary analytical theory, and our positive argument for what we call an inter-institutional theory of legality.

Intra-State Legality

Perhaps the most intuitively challenging instances of prima facie legality are found within the law-state, yet nonetheless appear to be meaningfully independent of the law-state and so deserve recognition as "intra-state" forms of legality. Distributed governance arrangements are likely the most familiar intra-state devices for creation of what are sometimes regarded as subsystems of law, a relinquishing of centralized governance authority that nonetheless stops short of full division of sovereignty. In these arrangements historically core legal institutions distribute their authority to relatively distant legal institutions within the system, whether reformed extant institutions or new institutions. Typically this distribution is undertaken to locate decision-making within institutions best suited to making particular decisions—whether geographically or experientially or financially or in some other way best suited. Shared governance is a less familiar, yet increasingly evident form of governance involving collaboration between traditionally or historically central legal institutions and other social organizations of varying complexity and institutionalization, contributing in various plainly evident ways to formation and variation of legal norms. From shared governance we may now be moving to overlapping, relatively independent legal orders of a new

---

7. For another account, WILLIAM TWINING usefully identifies eight different "levels" of law in GENERAL JURISPRUDENCE: UNDERSTANDING LAW FROM A GLOBAL PERSPECTIVE 70 (2009).

form or kind of order—perhaps sometimes in spite of insistence to the contrary on the part of the central agents in these new orders.[8]

In Canada, for example, federal and provincial governments face complex governance tasks with respect to indigenous "First Nations" peoples, several of whom are still in the process of negotiating land claims treaties, denying Canada's authority and acting in a fashion similar to sovereign states while for the most part remaining *de facto* within the authority of the Canadian law-state. The justice of First Nations claims and the aftermath of colonial practices have left federal and provincial governments very sensitive to the complexity of governance of related issues. One result has been the negotiation of methods of mutual relation between the Government of Canada and First Nations authorities regarding matters such as taxation. For example, the Government of Canada itself acknowledges in the terms of its regulations governing the appointment of commissioners that the newly created First Nations Tax Commission is "a shared governance organization which requires that appointments to the governing body be made by both the Government of Canada and at least one other government or organization."[9] The First Nations Tax

---

8. For an illuminating account of emerging forms of federalism, *see, e.g.,* Robert B. Ahdieh, *From Federalism to Intersystemic Governance: The Changing Nature of Modern Jurisdiction*, 57 EMORY LAW JOURNAL 1–30 (2007).

9. *See First Nations Tax Commissioner Appointment Regulations*, http://www. fntc.ca/en/supporting-legislation/regulations/first-nations-tax-commissioner-appointment-regulations (last visited October 29, 2009) The role of the First Nations Tax Commission (FNTC) is explained as follows:
Specifically, the FNTC was created to
• assume authority for the approval of First Nation property tax laws made under the Act;
• provide professional and objective assessments of First Nation property taxation under the Act;
• prevent and minimize the costs of disputes by providing a mechanism for hearing the concerns of affected parties under the Act and for promoting the reconciliation of the interests of First Nations and taxpayers;
• set standardized administrative practices for First Nation real property tax administrations created under the Act and provide training to ensure standards are achieved;
• provide education in order to raise awareness of the benefits of First Nation taxation between First Nations and the rest of the country; and

Commission aims generally to reform existing divisions of authority, recognize First Nations governments, and reconcile First Nations interests with other Canadian interests. The nature of this relation is complex, yet whatever final analysis reveals, it is worth considering the possibility that new forms of legal order are being forged.

Trans-State Legality

If intra-state practices such as shared governance are the most intuitively challenging instances of potentially non-state legality, perhaps the most surprising unanticipated developments are found in situations in which apparently non-state agents function like state agents in making general agreements outside the state which nonetheless bind citizens within the state. In situations of this kind, norms claiming peremptory, content-independent force[10] arise as a result of practice or convention and are generally recognized as holding that force without reference to authorization of those norms by any particular law-state.

- advise the Minister on policy issues relating to the implementation of First Nation property taxation powers and on any matter or policy put to it by the Minister.

The FNTC is a shared governance organization which requires that appointments to the governing body be made by both the Government of Canada and at least one other government or organization. In the case of the FNTC, nine commissioners are selected by the Governor in Council on behalf of the Government of Canada, with the remaining commissioner appointed by a body established pursuant to subsection 20(3) of the Act. The *First Nations Tax Commissioner Appointment Regulations*, made pursuant to paragraph 140(*a*) of the Act, identify the NLC as the body to appoint the additional commissioner to the FNTC.

Renowned for its expertise in promoting First Nation law, the NLC is a research centre within the University of Saskatchewan. It is responsible for the Program of Legal Studies for Native People. This program has been widely recognized for its role in increasing Aboriginal representation in the legal profession. The NLC also publishes the *Canadian Native Law Reporter* and since 1997, the *First Nations Gazette*. The *First Nations Gazette* is similar to the *Canada Gazette* and has been instrumental in improving the accessibility of First Nation laws, maintaining confidence in First Nation governments, and improving First Nation taxpayer relations.

10. On the peremptory and content-independent character of legal reasons see H.L.A. Hart, ESSAYS ON BENTHAM 243–268 (1982).

Our example is taken from the complex and increasingly important area of ocean resource governance, and more specifically, in governance of fishing of salmon which migrate across state boundaries and international waters. The Greenland Conservation Agreement provides for a seven-year moratorium on commercial, non-subsistence salmon fisheries in Greenland's territorial waters, from the 2007 season forward. This agreement extends the practice established by a 2002 moratorium. The agreement is signed by the "Atlantic Salmon Federation (ASF) of North America, the North Atlantic Salmon Fund (NASF) of Iceland, and the Organization of Fishermen and Hunters in Greenland (KNAPK), three non-governmental organizations" and "has been endorsed by the Greenland Home Rule Government which will help enforce it. . . ."[11] Several aspects of this agreement are relevant to analytical theories of legality, and their inclusion or exclusion of this phenomenon as an instance of legality or part of a legal order.

In assessing whether the moratorium might represent a legal norm or part of a legal order, it is significant that its proponents are neither governmental bodies nor representatives of government; in fact, the independence of this agreement from the law-state and international law goes much further. The Atlantic Salmon Federation draws its membership from both the United States and Canada and as a transboundary non-government organization is beholden to neither government. The Home Rule Government of Greenland is a devolved authority of the Kingdom of Denmark and lacks authority to enter into international treaties. These and the other proponents have entered into an agreement they describe as a "a private contract"[12] growing out of an agreed practice, relying on social pressure within this group for its effectiveness and having no reference to the laws of any state jurisdiction as the laws of the agreement or the legal locus of dispute resolution with respect to the agreement. The agreement nonetheless extends an effective established moratorium on commercial salmon fishing in Greenland's waters, to the extent that

11. "New Atlantic Salmon Conservation Agreement—Safer Ocean Migration Ensured", http://www.asf.ca/news.php?id=99. (Last visited July 27, 2007).

12. Personal communication with the Atlantic Salmon Federation, July 2007.

where ten years ago 600 license holders fished those waters, now there are none.

Supra-State Legality: The Puzzle of the European Union

The preceding example of non-state legality mentioned the familiar feature of international law: that its existence depends largely on the consent of states. This arrangement preserves the sovereignty of states as a fundamental norm of international law while grounding the force of international legal obligations in states. Voluntary agreement of the sort familiar from international law undoubtedly lies at the historic foundation of the European Union; yet as the Union has evolved it has come to claim that it represents a new legal order, neither a super-state nor an intergovernmental association.[13] But what is that legal order? And what is the relation of that order to explanations of legality as fundamentally systemic in a sense best evident in the law-state? Julie Dickson usefully suggests that the puzzling nature of the European Union can be revealed by asking an intuitively but misleadingly simple question: how many legal systems are there in the EU?[14] As Dickson notes, there are several possible answers: one legal system for every Member-State; one legal system for every Member-State plus one additional European legal system; or perhaps only one, super-European legal system. If there is more than one system—i.e. more than just one super-European legal system—how are legal theorists to characterize the relations among the systems? In particular, since both Member-State courts and the European Court of Justice have claimed supremacy of final authority to interpret and apply European law, can we view either Member-State legal systems or a European legal system as in some meaningful sense derivative, subordinate, or part of the other(s)? Or does this puzzle point us back to giving more serious consideration to the possibility that the European Union's claimed "new legal order" really is something new and different, not usefully reduced to talk of legal system?

---

13. Case 26/62 *Van Gend en Loos v. Nederlandse administratie der belastingen* [1963] E.C.R. 1, p. 12.

14. *See* Julie Dickson, *How Many Legal Systems?: Some Puzzles Regarding the Identity Conditions of, and Relations Between, Legal Systems in the European Union* 9–50, 2 PROBLEMA: ANNUARIO DE FILOSOFIA Y TEORIA DEL DERECHO (2008).

Super-State Legality: Claims to Universality in Peremptory
Jus Cogens Norms

In mentioning the role of states' consent in the existence of international law we omitted identification of a further element of international law: the relatively small set of *jus cogens* or peremptory general norms of international law. These norms purport to bind states and their authorities independently of any prior consent: both historic and newly created law-states now appear everywhere subject to a sort of substrate of general, peremptory norms which claim to form part of a universally supreme system.[15] These norms have more recently been employed to bind the leaders of states, who might dispute the norms' application to them, as Slobodan Milosevic, former President of Serbia and Yugoslavia, famously did throughout his trial.[16]

A now-familiar range of jurisprudential questions emerges: is the existence of *jus cogens* demonstration that there is one global legal system, in which each law-state is but a subsystem? What distinguishes one subsystem from another? Or are peremptory international norms part of some non-systemic international legal order instead incorporated universally into otherwise separable state systems, so we have "one" international law inside the "many" law-states? Or something else?

STATE-BASED LEGAL THEORY

Analytical legal theory that takes the experience of the law-state as the standard and measure of legality explains the existence and nature of

---

15. *Jus cogens*, or peremptory norms of general international law, is clearly defined in article 53 of the Vienna Convention on the Law of Treaties (1969):

> A treaty is void if, at the time of its conclusion, it conflicts with a peremptory norm of general international law. For the purposes of the present Convention, a peremptory norm of general international law is a norm accepted and recognized by the international community of States as a whole as a norm from which no derogation is permitted and which can be modified only by a subsequent norm of general international law having the same character.

16. *See, e.g.,* "Milosevic Defiant in Court", http://news.bbc.co.uk/2/hi/uk_news/wales/1420561.stm (last visited Apr. 7, 2008).

non-state types of prima facie legality in the following way: intra-, trans-, supra-, and super-state social phenomena are legal phenomena only to the extent that (i) they share the characteristic features of state law or (ii) are in some way actually supported by or connected to state practice or recognition. Although we shall analyze the quality of state law in detail in subsequent chapters, it is enough at this point to offer a working formulation which combines the views of Hart and Raz: state law exists where there are primary rules of obligation and secondary rules of recognition, change, and adjudication which in combination and in the hands of central law-applying officials claim with a certain degree of success to govern comprehensively, supremely, and openly.[17] On this understanding of the features of state law it is easy to see that other forms of legality must in some way be connected to state practice: if the world is divided without remainder into states which make and practice claims of comprehensiveness and supremacy, little conceptual or normative room is left for novel, state-independent forms of legality to emerge. Yet how well does such a state-based approach actually fare in explaining the novel phenomena sketched above? Here we offer the beginning of a diagnosis which we take up more fully in Chapters 1 and 2.

In examples of intra-state prima facie legality such as the First Nations Tax Commission, application of the state-based approach may be stretched beyond credulity if we say that what marks the legality of this interaction is incorporation of First Nations authorities by Canadian officials' recognition of them. The nature of the relation simply does not bear this out, to the extent that the Government of Canada itself represents the relation as one of shared governance between distinct governments. An adequate theoretical understanding of this situation may need to reach beyond the law-state model of legality and legal system to understand the special characteristics of intra-state legal orders which abut or overlap in various ways the range of other legal orders with which they interact. Put simply, what is the relation between First Nations' legal order and the legal system of Canada? Whatever the answer, it cannot simply presume that First

---

17. We examine in detail the legal theories of H.L.A. Hart and Joseph Raz in Chapters 1 and 2.

Nations' claims and experience must be read through the lens of the extant and dominant Canadian law-state.

A state-based analytical approach also interprets trans-state social practices such as the Greenland Conservation Agreement in a particular way: the agreement-derived obligation applying to all salmon fishers in Greenland's waters is a legal norm insofar as the Greenland Home Rule government has enacted this norm or endorsed it by authoritative certification, out of the urging of non-governmental organizations (NGOs), and under the authority granted it by the Kingdom of Denmark to govern natural resources. The precise contours of this norm can be assessed by observation of how Greenland's officials in fact handle application of the norm. Little more need be said about this situation on the state-based analytical approach, because the NGOs are just that—non-governmental—and so are not parties to an international treaty, and the Greenland Home Rule government is simply exercising its devolved powers. This conventional analytical view of course expresses a plausible understanding of the situation; yet a kind of distorting selectivity of emphasis seems evident, and that selectivity points to shortcomings in an approach that presumes that a justified ascription of legality to some state of affairs must be a statement about membership in a system of norms associated with an authorizing law-state. In seeking a state-based explanation of the phenomena, the conventional view obscures the special formative role of the NGOs in the agreement, and in turn mistakenly underestimates the contribution of the Greenland Home Rule government in reaching an agreement which falls short of an international treaty, yet seems to be something other than simple incorporation into Greenland law of normative content presented by lobbying from NGOs from within and without Greenland. The effectiveness of the moratorium and its independence from law-states resembles the emergence of a legal order or subsystem from practice—even as a description of the situation in these terms might be surprising to some of the participants. This zone of interstitial, transboundary prima facie legality might, of course, be affected by Danish, Canadian, or U.S. governments' activities in international treaties in this area, but this is a familiar matter: not all legal norms are of equal force, nor are all legal orders, systems, and subsystems of equal force.

As with the case of self-governance in Canada, we are left with a puzzle: what is the legality of effective peremptory norms which happen to be reported as "private contracts" despite their being formed by the secondary rules of no particular system? More simply, what tells us whether these social phenomena are legal or non-legal, and if so, what determines their system membership and how that membership matters to their legality? Whatever the answer to these questions, it cannot simply presume that what appear to function as legal norms must have state-based origins.

Answers to questions about the nature of the European Union as a form of supra-state legality also require prior answers to the question of the nature of legal system and the edges of a given legal system. What is also clear, however, is that a search for a state-based explanation of the European Union's legal order will not be of much help. While the expression "European Community" is widespread, there is justifiable reluctance to attribute to it statehood, understood in the conventional way, when it is observed that member-states still retain significant political and legal powers. Yet, it would be equally misleading to suppose that individual state recognition is capable of adequately explaining the existence and nature of the European Union legal order, since on this account *there would be no European Union law at all which governs member-states*, but only a new political source of norms which individual member-states have the discretion of either incorporating or not into their domestic legal systems. Again, such an explanation is required if member-state legal systems are understood to be making meaningful claims of supremacy and comprehensiveness. As will become clear throughout the course of our argument, little ground is gained by simply "bootstrapping" from the presupposition that legality's foundational unit is the state, since such a view is precisely what gives rise to the puzzling aspects of the legality of and within the European Union as we ask whether its new legal order is one or many. Here it seems to us that legal theorists such as Neil MacCormick are right to think that European law is inadequately theorized, and not just because we lack answers to questions regarding its nature, but more importantly because it is likely we lack the theory required to answer them.[18]

---

18. *See* NEIL MACCORMICK, QUESTIONING SOVEREIGNTY: LAW, STATE, AND NATION IN THE EUROPEAN COMMONWEALTH (1999).

State-based legal theory gives much the same explanation—and so faces much the same difficulty—for super-state legality as it does for supra-state legality. But since analytical approaches to law have said so little about super-state legality, there is little merit speculating on how H.L.A. Hart, for example, might renovate the final chapter of *The Concept of Law* in which he concludes that international law exists only in the form of primary rules since no rule of recognition is evident in the practices spoken of and regarded as international law. Indeed, in the next chapter we offer reasons why the core of Hart's view is likely beyond renovation when applied to international law.

RE-BALANCING AFTER IMBALANCE: AN INCREMENTAL ADDITION TO ANALYTICAL LEGAL THEORY

The results of preceding discussion now allow us to state in more detail the goals and course of argument provided in the next and succeeding chapters. We do not take ourselves to be offering fatal criticisms of the analytical approach; rather, we aim to contribute to the cycles of improvement running from Bentham to Austin, to Hart and on through the many contributions undergirding the sophistication of contemporary legal theory's norm-level explanations of legality. Yet we do aim to re-balance the analytical approach by building a better institutional account of legality and legal system, supported by improved descriptive-explanatory elements of an analytical legal theory that aims at continuity between theoretical and empirical accounts of life under law.

We take as our touchstones two characteristic approaches to the novel phenomena we have sketched. State-based theories of Hart and Raz suppose that intra-, supra-, super-, and trans-state legality are only law (and so part of the object of analysis of general jurisprudence) to the extent that they share the characteristic features of state law or are in some way actually supported by or connected to state practice or recognition. As we suggested above and will argue further in subsequent chapters, state-based explanations—with their commitment to the ideas of "official", "hierarchy", and "system"—very likely distort the nature of emerging forms of prima facie legality, forcing as they do all experience of legality through understanding of the law-state. Legal pluralists such as Brian Tamanaha occupy the opposite end of the spectrum of contributions to analytical legal theory which at least purport to recognize and handle novel kinds of social phenomena. Tamanaha rejects entirely state-based legal theory as "analytical imperialism",[19] and urges instead admission that the forms of legality are simply too diverse—with none more theoretically important than others—to continue pursuit of essential features of law. Although legal pluralists are characteristically more sensitive than orthodox Hartians to the diversity and emergence of social phenomena warranting attention from legal theorists, we shall argue that Tamanaha's legal pluralism likely surrenders too readily and too much to a kind of skepticism about the possibility of broad and general understanding of legal order applicable across cultures and times.

The inter-institutional theory of legality we propose in Chapters 4 and 5 is not a panacea, but a modest addition to the line of argument begun by Hart. We aim to secure the explanatory advantages accruing from commitment to morally neutral methods, while advocating a modest universalism in explanation of legality and legal system, much as Hart did in pursuing a style of general jurisprudence which explains law as "a form of social institution with a normative aspect, which in its recurrence in different societies and periods exhibits many common features of form, structure, and content."[20] Although its full meaning can only be delivered in the chapters that follow, our inter-institutional theory offers a descriptive-explanatory picture of legality as variegated combinations of legal institutions, institutions of law, and function-oriented content-independent peremptory norms and associated normative powers. In this picture, diverse kinds of relation of mutual reference among these elements characterize legality, rather than a particular relation to a hierarchical, comprehensive, supreme, and open law-state. To the extent that our inter-institutional account is not based in the law-state, it avoids the explanatory distortions of the approach to legal theory which sees all claims to legality as claims in some way parasitic upon a foundational explanation of legality rooted in the central case experience of the

---

19. Brian Tamanaha, A General Jurisprudence of Law and Society 146 (2001).

20. H.L.A. Hart, *Comment in* Issues in Contemporary Legal Philosophy 36–37 (R. Gavison ed., 1987).

law-state and its typical uses of law. Escape from the historically dominant yet only contingently central experience of the law-state opens the way to explanatory separation of the state from legality. This separation enables better characterization of such blends of legal system and political model as devolved governments, shared governance, associations of international institutions, and many others discussed in the remainder of our argument.

In developing our theory we recognize the importance of the law-state to legal theory, yet we are particularly concerned to provide an account of legality that is minimally attached to the presumption of the law-state as a primary or sole source or model of legality, to avoid prejudicial assessment of the nature of prima facie legal phenomena which seem to be emerging outside the law-state. The inter-institutional theory represents in this way a response to both the meta-theoretical-evaluative challenge of identifying legal theory's object of study, and the task of providing a theoretically illuminating account of that object of study—legality and legal order, whether within or without the long-dominant idea and practice of the law-state. Our conclusion—that we must go beyond theories of law tied to the law-state—is, we think, appropriately unsurprising. Just as we are all now accustomed to a less prominent role for the law-state in life under law, so our theories of law must face their explanatory task without the comforting assumption of a central instance of legality which is the mark and measure against which all other legality is to be understood.

The remaining chapters are organized as follows. Chapters 1 and 2 are preparatory, and investigate the limits to contemporary analytical legal theories as these function in explanation of both the borders of state legal systems and the existence and reaches of non-state instances of prima facie legality. More specifically, in Chapter 1 we analyze the limits to Hart's account of an official-operated rule of recognition as an account of the existence and borders of legal systems. We develop our argument via assessment of the success of the account's solutions to problems of circularity and indeterminacy in the identification of a distinct class of legal officials whose practices constitute the rule of recognition. We aim to show that while the problem of circularity may have been adequately addressed in explanation of state legal systems, its solutions leave intact the problem of indeterminacy and reveal a strong presumption of hierarchy which threatens to run past rather than solve issues at the borders of legality. This is true in explanation of state legal systems, but the difficulties are particularly troubling in explanation of international law, as analysis of Hart's chapter on international law in *The Concept of Law* makes plain.

In Chapter 2 we examine Raz's theory of legal system, which explicitly sets out to overcome difficulties in Hart's account regarding the identity and borders of legal systems by introducing new explanatory elements. Raz claims that legal systems are unique normative systems since they claim, via the activities of a broad range of norm-applying institutions, to govern comprehensively, supremely, and openly the social life of their subjects. Unlike Hart's, Raz's theory is avowedly state-based and state-restricted, as he says it is not meant to be tested against non-state phenomena of legality. Here we argue that there are nonetheless several problems with Raz's theory as a contribution to general jurisprudence. In addition to leaving the problem of indeterminacy unresolved, Raz's theory is unable to explain various types of state legal systems that are comprised of federalist structures as well as shared and distributed governance arrangements. We will also argue that the feature of openness offers a sweeping but distorting account of non-state legality, suggesting as it does that all non-state forms of legality must be in some sense supported or authorized by state institutions and law.

Chapters 1 and 2 examine the limits to two of the most influential contemporary analytical legal theories. In Chapter 3 we consider these limits more generally and return to the method and purpose of analytical jurisprudence. We discuss the way analytical legal theorists have attempted to identify what they claim are necessary features of an admittedly contingent concept of law, and the meta-theoretical-evaluative virtues appropriate to such an explanation. We argue that the problems associated with leaving the issue of indeterminacy unresolved and the lack of specification of the connection to actual social situations demonstrates just how narrowly bootstrapped existing analytical legal theories are. Such theories suppose that adequate data and experience of life under law are in hand such that a general jurisprudence can be advanced. Our conclusion is not that bootstrapping itself is at fault, but only the way it has been carried out. In Chapter 3 we offer a renewed view of the perspective of analytical legal theory that emphasizes the conditions under which bootstrapping must be carried out to achieve a general jurisprudence that is balanced in its conceptual elaboration and descriptive-explanatory responsiveness to situations of life under law.

Chapters 1 to 3 set the challenge to be met by any supplement to analytical legal theory's approach to legality. In Chapter 4 we describe our response to this challenge as an "inter-institutional theory" of legality. Our approach is rooted in an account of content independent peremptory norms, normative powers, institutions, and relations amongst groups of institutions which deserve to be regarded as legal. As we shall argue, these elements of legality can combine in different ways, and at varying levels of intensity, which explains the differing degrees of normative force, scope, and diversity of subject matters that legality covers both within and without the state. The key to our approach is that it makes minimal use of the ideas of legal officials and legal system in explanation of the existence and borders of legality. Where legal officials and legal system are present, these represent particular combinations of norms, powers, institutions, inter-institutional relations, and subject matter, most often focused in the law-state. But the connection between legal official and legal system on the one hand, and legality on the other, is best characterized as contingent. On our inter-institutional view, then, the connection between legality and the state, though historically dominant, is itself contingent. We also show how hierarchy is one among many types of relation between institutions, and by no means exhaustive as a descriptive-explanatory tool in tracing the borders of legality. So although in Chapters 1 and 2 we leave open the possibility that existing accounts may be open to further elaboration in ways that might meet at once both the circularity and indeterminacy challenges in explanation of the law-state, in Chapter 4 we show how the inter-institutional view provides a superior alternative.

Separation of legality from the state is what enables our view to better explain without distortion the various forms of non-state prima facie legality whose emergence is too pervasive to leave outside the scope of a balanced general jurisprudence. In Chapter 5 we return to the prima facie legalities we have identified above, and show fully how freedom from the ideas of legal official, legal system, and hierarchy (and so in general the idea of "chains of validity") is crucial to responsive descriptive-explanation of legality broadly.

In the final chapter we come full circle, and argue how the problems of continuity and identity, declared unsolved by Raz, are fundamentally altered. The old conceptions of the problems are thoroughly state, official, system, and hierarchy-based, and as such are of limited value in facing both old and new challenges to explanation of the existence and borders of legality. We propose a new way of understanding these old problems, here re-characterizing them in terms more suited to the goals of general jurisprudence in facing a much broader range of phenomena than before. In the concluding chapter we also identify some of the next challenges an inter-institutional view faces.

1. LEGAL OFFICIALS, THE RULE OF RECOGNITION, AND INTERNATIONAL LAW

It is only a small exaggeration to say contemporary analytical legal theory began with Hart's contention that we might find the "key to the science of jurisprudence"[1] in the combination of primary and secondary rules. Hart's "practice theory of rules"[2] has influenced a generation of thinking about legal norms, even as Hart himself has conceded defects in the theory. Hart did not, however, surrender the practice theory of rules entirely, and what remains of the theory is arguably its core: the account of the rule of recognition, the special "master" or "ultimate" secondary rule whose intentional practice in the hands of legal officials binds together and gives life to a legal system.[3] For Hart, and indeed for nearly all major contemporary analytical legal theorists, the rule of recognition remains the cornerstone of morally neutral, descriptive-explanatory theorizing of law and legal system; and to the extent that the idea of a legal system bears the mark of legality, the rule of recognition is a key to understanding the idea of legality. It is accordingly crucial to the analytical project that the nature and function of the rule of recognition should be fully explained, with particular attention to the nature and function of the legal officials whose acceptance and practice of the rule of recognition simultaneously constitute the rule and give evidence of its existence and reaches. Here a significant challenge arrives. How exactly are

---

1. H.L.A. HART, THE CONCEPT OF LAW 81 (1994).

2. *Id.* at 254.

3. As Hart puts it in the *Postscript*, ". . . the theory remains as a faithful account of conventional social rules which may include, besides ordinary social customs (which may or may not be recognized as having legal force), certain important legal rules including the rule of recognition, which is in effect a form of judicial customary rule existing only if it is accepted and practiced in the law-identifying and law-applying operations of the courts. . . .," *Id.* at 256.

officials in actual social situations to be identified, such that the existence and borders of legal systems can be determined?

In this chapter we investigate the nature of the limits of Hart's account of legal officials and the rule of recognition in explanation of the borders of law and legal systems. We do so by analyzing two familiar problems the account must face: the problem of *circularity* refers to the burden of identifying legal officials without presupposing a notion of legal validity, which is simply the set of criteria of membership in a legal system practiced by its officials, whereas the problem of *indeterminacy* refers to the burden of identifying which sorts of activities or exercises of power in a legal system distinguish officials from non-officials, and so determine the borders of legal systems. We aim to show that while Hartian analytical legal theories have offered satisfactory solutions to the problem of circularity, they have largely overlooked the problem of indeterminacy and its consequences for (i) identification of legal officials and (ii) characterization of the "functional" part of the rule of recognition qua descriptive-explanatory account of actual experience of life under law.

We should emphasize that our purpose in this chapter is mainly comparative. As we explained in the first chapter, familiar features of theories of state legal systems may be ill-suited to explanation of non-state instances of legality. In explanation of state legal systems, the limits to determinacy in Hart's account of legal officials are more or less tolerable given the restricted focus on explaining the nature of state law (although there is room for more work along lines we suggest, and we take up Raz's account of legal system fully in the next chapter). In explanation of international law, however, we argue that the limits take on new force and become significant shortcomings, and show clearly that new descriptive-explanatory elements—beyond the notion of an official-operated rule of recognition—are needed for a balanced general jurisprudence.

1.1 STRUCTURE AND FUNCTION OF THE RULE OF RECOGNITION

As originally sketched by Hart, the rule of recognition is a criterial device whose operation identifies valid legal norms of some system. He later accepted the suggestion that "the rule of recognition is treated in my book as resting on a conventional form of judicial consensus."⁴ This much, then, is the foundation of the rule of recognition, whose explanatory value is widely accepted by analytical legal theorists. Yet is this an adequate explanation of the role of the rule of recognition in identification of the existence and borders of legal systems? There are reasons to worry about the quality of available answers. As Brian Bix has argued, for example,

> In the course of answering some of Raz's arguments for exclusive legal positivism, Coleman offered clarifications (some might say, modifications) of the legal positivist position regarding the nature and role of the Rule of Recognition within a legal system. The end product may be a more precise theory, and one which arguably offers a more accurate description of our practices, but there are questions about its explanatory force and distinctiveness.⁵

We shall discuss later the descriptive accuracy and the explanatory force of post-Hartian versions of the rule of recognition. For the moment, however, it is worth continuing to follow Bix's summary of Coleman:

> As Coleman pointed out, the Rule of Recognition can serve a variety of purposes within a legal system. It serves a "metaphysical" function to the extent it determines whether norms are valid members of a legal system or not (whether they are or whether they are not "law"). It serves a semantic function to the extent that it helps to specify the truth conditions for general propositions of law ("it is the law that. . . ."). Finally, the Rule can serve two different "epistemic" functions: *validation*, through helping *judges* determine whether official actions are valid; and *identification*, through helping *citizens* determine which norms are binding law for them.⁶

Far from its origins as a criterial device for validation of norms, the rule of recognition as elaborated by Coleman is a multi-purpose entity, even as Coleman is at pains to mark its being addressed to officials, contra Joseph Raz's emphasis on the rule of recognition as a

---

4. HART, *supra* note 1, at 266–7.

5. Brian Bix, *Patrolling the Boundaries: Inclusive Positivism and the Nature of Jurisprudential Debate* (1999) 12 CANADIAN JOURNAL OF LAW AND JURISPRUDENCE 17, 25.

6. *Id.*

validation of norms capable of being obeyed by citizens.[7] Debate over this point of emphasis goes on, as do debates regarding the possibility that the rule of recognition need not (or cannot) be a conventional rule.[8] What remains constant as the conceptual accounts gain detail and precision is the view that the rule of recognition is *chiefly* the product and tool of officials. Raz may be right that the rule of recognition affords citizens an opportunity to identify their legal obligations (and permissions, and so on). Officials, however, remain special insofar as their use of the rule of recognition is taken to be system-constituting, constantly reaffirming and creating the edges of their legal system. Here a much simpler way of understanding the multi-purpose rule of recognition might be introduced, both for clarity in analysis and to assist explanation of what we will later argue are serious problems in the application of the notion of an official-operated rule of recognition to international law.

On the view we propose, the rule of recognition should be understood as having both structural and functional aspects in a descriptive-explanatory account of law and legal system.[9] Our advocacy of this view arises from our observation that analytical legal theorists typically assert simultaneously that legal norms have a special existence distinguishing them from other norms, and further assert that the special existence is revealed in the way those norms are handled by a special class of norm subjects. In its structural aspect the rule of recognition identifies something like the anatomical aspects of a legal system: as explained by Hart, the rule of recognition marks the membership criteria of valid legal norms, and ranks conflicting sources of law. This aspect of the rule of recognition is especially important to analysis of historical systems of law, for example,

---

7. This possibility is a central feature of Raz's "service conception" of authority. *See* Raz, *Authority, Law, and Morality, in* ETHICS IN THE PUBLIC DOMAIN, (1995).

8. *See*, for example, Leslie Green, *Positivism and Conventionalism*, 12:1 CANADIAN JOURNAL OF LAW AND JURISPRUDENCE 35–52 (1999). *See also* Julie Dickson, *Is the Rule of Recognition Really a Conventional Rule?* 27 OXFORD JOURNAL OF LEGAL STUDIES 373–402 (2007) .

9. For a similar view see Lewis Kornhauser, *Governance Structures, Legal Systems, and the Concept of Law*, 79 CHICAGO-KENT LAW REVIEW 355, 375 (2004).

Roman law. Using the rule of recognition for the system of Roman law, it is possible to make findings of Roman law, even though the system's officials are dead. Yet apart from a sort of mechanical derivation of findings from the body of laws we know operated as a legal system, there is little more we can say without looking to the record of how actual officials were identified and how they applied legal norms of the system. So although the existence and identity of a Roman legal system and some of its specific norms might be roughly assessed from an external point of view without reference to officials' actual existence and operations, any "thick" descriptive-explanation of Roman law requires further examination of the identity of officials and their function—much as an understanding of human biology must go beyond the structure or anatomy of the body, and on to its function or physiology. A demand for understanding of the function of legal officials is soon perilously close to a demand for observational evidence, since the general, structural discussion of kinds of norms, analogous to rough biological discussion of "body plans," depends on abstraction from the activities of actual legal officials.

In our view, where contemporary analytical theorists seem to run into trouble—and where we contend more work must be done to substantiate the analytical approach—is precisely in the relation and imbalance between their accounts of structural and functional aspects of the rule of recognition. Although they recognize both aspects of the rule of recognition, analytical legal theorists have much more extensive explanation of its structural aspect than its functional aspect; yet since its structures are identified and distinguished by their use in the hands of officials, it is not an option to deepen the structural account while continuing to populate the functional account via armchair intuition, or selective reading of officials' experiences in specific legal systems. Each part of the account of the rule of recognition must be given independent attention, since each is equally important to a comprehensive explanation of the rule of recognition in its structural and functional aspects, serving, as Coleman says, metaphysical and epistemic purposes in a larger descriptive-explanatory account of law and legal system. Notice, however, that this is not simply a demand for a "verstehen account" of the rule of recognition, looking into its meaning in some way enabled by "deep reproduction" of the meaning of the rule of recognition to those who use it. It is a more general call for recognition that interdependent

parts of a theory need to reflect their interdependence. More specifically, it is a call for an explanation of who counts as a legal official, and
how we are to identify those legal officials as a key part of our knowing where to look in the world for the social experience data fleshing
out the "functional" aspect of the rule of recognition.[10]

1.2 EXPLAINING OFFICIALS' CONTRIBUTION TO THE RULE OF RECOGNITION: FACING CIRCULARITY AND INDETERMINACY

Any adequate deepening of the account of legal officials' functional
contribution to a rule of recognition must address two related problems: the problem of circularity and the problem of indeterminacy.
The problem of circularity refers to the burden of identifying legal
officials without presupposing a notion of legal validity, which is
simply the set of criteria of membership in a legal system practiced by
its officials.[11] The problem of indeterminacy refers to the burden of

---

10. William Twining appears to emphasize a similar distinction between
structure and function in Hartian jurisprudence. He writes "It is sometimes
suggested that Hart's *The Concept of Law* is solely concerned with 'linguistic
analysis' and in this sense is semantic . . . However, Hart's conception of a
descriptive jurisprudence goes far beyond this: it includes both elucidating
concepts and *using* them. Concepts and models (such as the model of law as
a system of rules) are tools of description. *The Concept of Law*, and general
descriptive jurisprudence, go beyond conceptual clarification to describing
the common features of the form, structure and content of legal systems."
[original emphasis, internal notes omitted] WILLIAM TWINING, GLOBALISATION
AND LEGAL THEORY 37 (2000).

11. The literature on circularity, particularly circularity in Hart's theory of
law, is significant and varied. *See, e.g.,* CHARLES SAMPFORD, THE DISORDER OF
LAW: A CRITIQUE OF LEGAL THEORY 35–6 (1990); G.B.J. Hughes, *The Existence
of a Legal System*, 35 NEW YORK UNIVERSITY LAW REVIEW 1001–1030 (1960);
JULES COLEMAN, THE PRACTICE OF PRINCIPLE: IN DEFENCE OF A PRAGMATIST
APPROACH TO LEGAL THEORY 100–1 (2001); Matthew Kramer, *The Rule of
Misrecognition in The Hart of Jurisprudence*, 8 OXFORD JOURNAL OF LEGAL
STUDIES 401 (1988); Kent Greenawalt, *The Rule of Recognition and the
Constitution*, 85 MICHIGAN LAW REVIEW 624n. (1987); BRIAN TAMANAHA,
A GENERAL JURISPRUDENCE OF LAW AND SOCIETY 142 (2001); NEIL
MACCORMICK, H.L.A. HART 136–140, (2008); Ian Duncanson, *The Strange
World of English Jurisprudence*, 30 NORTHERN IRELAND LAW QUARTERLY 267

identifying which sorts of activities or exercises of power in a legal system distinguish officials from non-officials such that the borders of the legal system can be determined. We begin in section 1.2.1 with discussion of the view that officials can be identified via observation of special rules of office and attitudes characteristic of officials' special allegiance to law. In section 1.2.2 we examine speculative social anthropological accounts of the emergence and persistence of officials whose practices constitute the existence of the rule of recognition. We argue that these approaches show that although the problem of circularity has been adequately addressed, the problem of indeterminacy remains incompletely resolved to the extent that it threatens to deprive the rule of recognition of its promised role in identifying the borders of legal systems. In section 1.3 we offer a diagnosis, and argue that the explanatory limits of extant analytical approaches in resolution of the problem of indeterminacy are largely a consequence of a presumption of hierarchy created by Hart's account of the rule of recognition. Hart's account presumes that the set of legal officials as agents of legal systems is structured in a way such that officials can be ranked in terms of their constitutive importance in the determination of borders. This presumption of hierarchy supposes that problems of indeterminacy at the borders of legal systems pose little problem in practice since one need only look up the hierarchy for resolution of borderline cases. We shall argue that the presumption is more or less reliable in explanation of state legal systems, but the presumption is significantly less reliable in explanation of international law.

1.2.1 Officials by Office and Attitude

Hart's theory of law offers many advances over John Austin's command theory of law. Hart showed with exceptional clarity that a theory of law constructed from concepts such as a social rule, the internal point of view, content-independent reason, and union of primary and secondary rules offers a far better explanation of life under law than a theory of law constructed out of the concepts of order, threat, sanction, habit of obedience, and legally unlimited sovereign. In place

---

(1979); Nigel Simmonds, *Legal Validity and Decided Cases*, 1 LEGAL STUDIES 24–36 (1981),; Rolf Sartorius, Hart's Concept of Law, *in* MORE ESSAYS IN LEGAL PHILOSOPHY 131, 156 (R.S. Summers ed., 1971).

of the notion of a legally unlimited sovereign Hart argues we ought to think in terms of rules of office, whereby official positions, with their constitutive duties and powers, enjoy legal authority independently of the particular persons who contingently occupy those positions. Rules of office and rules of succession explain the continuity of legal systems through changes in legislators and governments and also explain the persistence of laws long after their creators have died.

Central cases of legal officials are of course deceptively easy to find. They include judges, lawyers, legislators, police, and immigration officers, among others. There is, however, an immediate problem with an account of officials that does no more than list examples and explain their status as officials by claiming that legal officials are those who occupy their positions by special rules of office, succession, and competence. Rules of office identify who is to count as an appellate judge, state lawyer, police officer, provincial legislator, immigration officer, but not who is to count as a "legal official." This is perhaps to be expected as particular legal systems have an interest in identifying specific legal officials for the specific purposes of those legal systems, but no need for a general account of the nature of officials. Philosophers of law pursuing a general jurisprudence are nonetheless left with a problem: without an account of the shared features that elucidate and explain the genus "legal official," we are left basing what purports to be a comprehensive, general jurisprudence on a fragmented collection of species-level accounts of judicial practices, prosecutorial practices, police practices, and so on.[12]

In Hart's account, however, there is a further element that promises to help with the task of identification of legal officials. Hart famously distinguishes his view from Austin's command theory via the argument that officials of a legal system necessarily "accept" the rules of a legal system, especially its secondary rules, from an internal point of view. Indeed, that the officials of a legal system *accept* the rule of recognition is one of two minimum conditions necessary and

---

12. Peter Morton has remarked that "legal sociology"—the law and society movement—also suffers from lack of critical attention to widely held views. He counts the belief "judges are officials" to be among a set of "ill-considered generalities" that hinder a proper analysis of law. PETER MORTON, AN INSTITUTIONAL THEORY OF LAW: KEEPING LAW IN ITS PLACE 8 (1998).

sufficient for the existence of a legal system.[13] This requirement opens the way to a second, complementary yet separable way to identify officials of a legal system: a descriptive-explanatory theorist might look to see who accepts and practices the secondary rules of recognition, change, and adjudication, conducting this investigation in situations where the difference between officials and private citizens is most likely to be starkly evident. Such situations might include those where the application conditions of rules are unclear and officials might be revealed by their practice of stepping forward to set the application conditions or make determinations of the content of those rules. With this approach, officials' identity and characteristic contribution to a rule of recognition is assessed by detection of the presence of a special normative attitude of commitment to secondary rules, and at least obedience to primary or duty-imposing rules.

Introduction of the idea of the internal point of view does a great deal to give analytical legal theory an explanatory reach which outstrips a bare rules of office approach. Yet even this addition leaves unsolved the problem of determining the class of officials and so determining the borders of legal systems. Two related reasons support this claim. First, social actors ranging from private citizens to lobby groups to

---

13. As Hart puts it in a widely discussed passage:
On the one hand, those rules of behaviour which are valid according to the system's ultimate criteria of validity must be generally obeyed, and, on the other hand, its rules of recognition specifying the criteria of legal validity and its rules of change and adjudication must be effectively accepted as common public standards of official behaviour by its officials. The first condition is the only one which private citizens *need* satisfy: they may obey each 'for his part only' and from any motive whatever; though in a healthy society they will in fact often accept these rules as common standards of behaviour and acknowledge an obligation to obey them, or even trace this obligation to a more general obligation to respect the constitution. The second condition must also be satisfied by the officials of the system. They must regard these as common standards of official behaviour and appraise critically their own and each other's deviations as lapses. Of course it is also true that besides these there will be many primary rules which apply to officials in their merely personal capacity which they need only obey.
Hart, *supra* note 1, at 116–117. It is worth noting that this view survives concessions in the Postscript to critics of the social rule theory of legal rules and the internal point of view.

accountants to supreme court judges can accept secondary rules from an internal point of view, as Hart's own argument makes clear. There is nothing structurally incoherent—or functionally unrealistic—in the idea of a private citizen accepting the constitution of her country as supreme law by invoking a right contained in it to challenge a state or provincial law. So although there is undeniably explanatory value in the distinction between internal and external points of view, the distinction is nonetheless insufficient as a means to practical detection or testing for the borders of legal officials. Questions needing answers remain: do citizens who adopt the internal point of view towards their legal system's secondary rules thereby become officials, even if only low-level or momentary officials? If not, as we might plausibly suppose, why not? If there is no difference in kind between the attitudes of officials and other social actors in legal systems, and the difference is instead to be found in something like an accumulation of practice, is there some "tipping point"? Second, to the extent that this approach augments rather than replaces the rules of office view, it presupposes rather than shows that officials can already be identified by means of rules of office. Since both legal officials and other social actors can accept primary and secondary rules from an internal point of view, it must be that legal officials are those who also occupy a special position in the legal system by virtue of the rules of office.

1.2.2 Speculative Social Anthropological Accounts

It is important to note, however, that Hart's account is not subject to the kind of vicious circularity which would deprive it of all explanatory power. The charge runs as follows. For a rule to count among the rules of a legal system, it must be recognized. Yet recognized by whom? Private citizens may conduct what appear to be acts of recognition, but those acts have at most probationary status, awaiting review by officials. This scenario might occur in a situation in which private citizens apply legal norms as best they can in the absence of relevant officials. So recognition *may* come from citizens, but such recognition is not sufficient for validation, which is necessarily conferred by the officials of the legal system. Legal officials, then, are those who are recognized by the officials of a legal system. So just as a rule requires recognition by officials for its validity, so too officials require official recognition to validate their membership in the body of officials.

Responses to the circularity charge typically try to provide a foundation—often in what might be regarded as a "bootstrapping" approach. Jules Coleman, Kent Greenawalt, and Brian Tamanaha all appear to have taken a route of this sort. Coleman argues, for example, that legal officials emerge as follows:

> First, some group of individuals—we do not call them officials and we need not identify them by reference to laws—choose to have their behavior guided by a certain rule. In other words, they take the rule as giving them good reasons for action. If that rule takes hold in the sense of establishing membership criteria in a system of rules, and if those rules are complied with generally, and if institutions of certain types are then created, and so on, it is fair to say that a legal system exists. If a legal system exists, then that rule which guides the behavior of our initial group of individuals is correctly described as the rule of recognition for that legal system. And those individuals who guide their behavior by that rule are thus appropriately conceived of as "officials." They are, in a sense, officials in virtue of that rule, but they are not officials prior to it (in either the factual or the logical sense). Their behavior makes the rule possible, but it is the rule that makes them officials. [14]

Coleman's story is not that legal officials are those recognized by other legal officials by means of law, but rather that certain conduct gives rise to rules which in turn identify who is a legal official. On this account there is no circle but instead a kind of social fact explanation of legal officialdom—albeit one which does not arrive with specification on the set of social facts from which it is generated. Similarly, in the course of an exercise in applying Hart's notion of the rule of recognition to the United States, Kent Greenawalt supposes the general populace is sufficiently able to identify legal officials that a foundation can be safely presumed:

> At first glance, [Hart's] account may seem to involve a troubling circularity, since officials determine what are the standards of law and they derive their official status from the law. The break in the circle is that one looks to the population at large to see who are recognized as officials. Ordinarily, people's judgments about who are officials may rely on certain assumptions about conformance with legal standards, such as election laws, but people need not understand the complex criteria judges and other officials use to determine what counts as law. [15]

---

14. JULES COLEMAN, THE PRACTICE OF PRINCIPLE 100–1 (2001).

15. Kent Greenawalt, *The Rule of Recognition and the Constitution*, 85 MICHIGAN LAW REVIEW 621–671, n.624 (1987).

Brian Tamanaha also argues that legal officials can be assumed to have a sufficiently determinate existence, conventionally established:

> Remaining with Hart's resort to social practices, the following additional requirement solves the problem of distinguishing legal from non-legal institutionalized systems of normative order: *A 'legal' official is whomever, as a matter of social practice, members of the group (including legal officials themselves) identify and treat as 'legal' officials.* Owing to their recognized status as legal officials, their products (generated pursuant to the secondary rules) are treated as 'law.' Systems of primary and secondary rules that are administered by legal officials—so identified—are 'legal' systems. Systems of primary and secondary rules that are not administered by legal officials may be institutionalized normative systems, but they are not legal.[16]

All three responses meet the charge of circularity, by identifying means by which legal officials can be identified without presupposing the fact of official recognition, but they take us little distance towards positive determination of the class of legal officials whose roles and activities determine the borders of legal systems. Coleman's explanation seems to be close to simply positing a state of normativity as he presumes some historical set of facts corresponding to his description. Does legal order and a cohort of officials in fact arise in the way Coleman supposes? Is this the only way, or can officials ever become officials by request, rather than by creating their own legal power as his analysis seems to suggest? Viewed in this manner, Coleman's way out of the circularity problem depends on unsubstantiated empirical claims, and reduces the account of officials to a hypothetical sociological observation rather than a philosophical theory: "the powerful can sometimes become officials." This looks very much like the speculative anthropology Les Green attributes to Hart, and so marks little advance over Hart's construction of Rex I—a construction in which Hart says explicitly that he does not suppose he is describing any actual historical state of affairs.[17] Yet even if we do accept Coleman's view as a modest advance with respect to a functional aspect of analytical legal theory, that advance is insufficient, since it

---

16. BRIAN TAMANAHA, A GENERAL JURISPRUDENCE OF LAW AND SOCIETY 142 (2001) [emphasis in the original].

17. Leslie Green, *Legal Positivism, in* STANFORD ENCYCLOPEDIA OF PHILOSOPHY, http://plato.stanford.edu/entries/legal-positivism/ (last visited Sept. 17, 2006).

still lacks a general explanation of the nature of officialdom, and how it is to be identified in those other than the "first generation" of officials who create their own legal power. Greenawalt's explanation—that officials are to be identified by seeing who are recognized as such by the population at large—is similarly incomplete. It simply assumes that such recognition occurs and provides no method for resolution of situations in which popular recognition is divided, at odds with officials' self-understanding, or otherwise unsettled. These omissions from Greenawalt's view lead to other troublesome questions. Does the public have the knowledge needed to make this judgment? If the test, to be meaningful, takes as its precondition the existence of a knowledgeable population, what sort of knowledge counts, and how can it be determined if a population is sufficiently knowledgeable? Further, will this actually generate a philosophically satisfying account of officials, or just a snapshot of the perceptions of some group of citizens? Most importantly, are we to conduct some sort of international aggregation in order to reach "the concept of law" as opposed to "American" or "Canadian" or "British" understanding of the nature and identity of legal officials? How are we to avoid parochialism in our theory of law?

Tamanaha's thoroughly conventionalist theory of legal positivism threatens to give up entirely on the pursuit of philosophical explanation of the social foundations of law, giving up on repair of the structure-function imbalance in favor of a nearly entirely functional explanation. Yet if we suppose—as surely we must—that in labeling a group of norm-subjects as legal officials, legal officials and the wider group itself are not doing so willy-nilly, we owe an explanation of the basis of our reasoning. What are the concepts or categories employed, and are they consistent, coherent, and part of an illuminating picture of the social conditions that give rise to law?

Although Coleman's, Greenawalt's, and Tamanaha's explanations might avoid the overt circularity of views that suppose legal officials are simply those persons recognized as such by other legal officials, they leave intact the equally troubling philosophical problem that awaits the speculative anthropological approaches: indeterminacy at the edges of legality and legal officialdom.[18] On Coleman's account,

---

18. *See, e.g.,* CHARLES SAMPFORD, THE DISORDER OF LAW: A CRITIQUE OF LEGAL THEORY 35–6 (1990). Sampford notes that a sociological definition of

which of the non-circularly determined rules identify who is a legal official and *which* sorts of activities demarcate legal officials from private citizens and other social actors? On Greenawalt's and Tamanaha's accounts, according to what non-circularly devised criteria or understanding are legal officials conventionally identified? Are the criteria or understanding coherent, illuminating, and adequate to the task of providing a functional explanation of the borders of legal systems? Most importantly, what costs are incurred by a theory dependent on an account of legal officials when indeterminacy characterizes the theory's attempts to solve at more than an intuitive level the problem of demarcating legal officials from other norm subjects? These unanswered questions suggest that the problem of indeterminacy is to elucidate the philosophical concept of a legal official in a way which provides the means to identify legal officials in actual legal systems, and that it is a problem which runs deeper than the problem of circularity.

1.3 HIERARCHY IN THE RULE OF RECOGNITION

A natural objection at this point is that we have over-emphasized the difficulties for descriptive-explanatory theories of law raised by indeterminacies at the borders of legality. After all, the existence of clear cases of legal officials and legality is consistent with the absence of clear lines of demarcation distinguishing official from non-official activities in law: clear lines should not be sought when they need not or cannot be found. Andrei Marmor offers such a view about the nature of social conventions in general:

> . . . the dividing line between the practitioners, whose practice determines the conventions, and others, who are more or less aware of them, is not a sharp one. To the question, Whose convention is it?, there is rarely a simple answer. What we would normally see is a kind of division of labour: a core of practitioners, whose practices and self-understandings determine, to the greatest extent, what the convention is, and additional groups

---

"official" is needed to overcome circularity, but any such sociological definition would still fail to pick out distinctly "legal" officials. Sampford also cites G.B.J. Hughes, *The Existence of a Legal System*, 35 NEW YORK UNIVERSITY LAW REVIEW 1001–1030, 1029 (1960) for helpful discussion.

of people in outer circles, whose knowledge of the convention is much more partial, and whose influence on its content is relatively marginal. But again, the distinction between the relevant populations is not a hard and fast one; a complex division of labour may obtain, whereby even those groups who are relatively farther removed from the inner circle do affect, albeit in a limited way, the shape and content of the relevant conventions.[19]

Applied to the context of law, Marmor writes that clear lines are unnecessary because we can assume a central case:

> Perhaps the clearest example of this actually obtains in the case of law. Most people are only faintly aware of the rules of recognition of their country, and, mostly, they rely on their lawyers to know what those conventions really are. Even within the legal circles, however, some groups are more important than others. Judges, and perhaps to a similar extent legislators, play the crucial role. The rules of recognition, as noted by Hart himself, are, first and foremost, the conventions of judges, particularly in the higher courts. But in fact, other legal officials can also play various roles in determining the content of the rules of recognition. The practices of police officers, accountants, tax collectors, city councilors, etc., all contribute something to what the rules of recognition are. So once again, the image I suggest is one of a division of labour, taking place in concentric circles; the closer one is to the centre, the greater effect one has on what the convention is; and vice versa, of course.[20]

In the next chapter we will examine Joseph Raz's view of the centrality of norm-applying institutions in explanation of the nature of legal system, which, along with Hart's view that the rule of recognition is first and foremost a judicial practice, no doubt explains Marmor's choice to locate judges in the innermost circle of a legal system. Judges, on this view, are the clearest example of legal official—and so sit in the innermost circle—precisely because their activities have the greatest normative consequences within their legal systems. For now, however, it is necessary to analyze a further feature of Hartian accounts of legal officials that Marmor's argument makes explicit: a strong presumption of hierarchy in the notion of the rule of recognition. The presumption amounts to the view that in practice, problems of indeterminacy at the borders of legal systems, much like problems of

---

19. ANDREI MARMOR, POSITIVE LAW AND OBJECTIVE VALUES 16–17 (2001).
20. *Id.* at 17.

the indeterminacy of legal norms, are resolved by looking up the hierarchy (or towards the center of the system) of officials. For example, one may not know whether an accountant is a legal official or not, but such a problem can be resolved in practice by looking at the practice of those officials who have the authority and jurisdiction to apply and enforce norms about the authority and power of accountants. Similarly, just as one may not know whether a particular interpretation of a legal norm would amount to application of existing content or instead discretionary extension of content, courts do in practice resolve such indeterminacy and render settled what was previously unsettled. In other words, if we can presume a core of officials, such as judges, who sit at the top or center in a hierarchical structure of a legal system, worries about borders become less worrisome, since there is in practice a means of resolving such indeterminacy.

The presumption of hierarchy certainly helps to explain why questions about the determinacy of the class of legal officials persist, and accepted solutions such as those offered by Coleman, Greenawalt, Tamanaha are found tolerable. If anyone can be presumed to be a legal official, surely a supreme court judge is one. We can then measure the distance of other social actors from the top or center of a legal system by means of their similarities and connections to supreme court judges. Yet precisely how reliable is the presumption of hierarchy? We can begin by noticing that the presumption tends to reproduce the imbalance between structural and functional parts to the explanation of the rule of recognition, as the imbalance is perhaps best revealed—rather than remedied—by the near universal attention to judges as the central operators of the rule of recognition, to the extent that virtually no account is offered of how to identify other typical officials in legal systems at more than an intuitive level. Are other norm subjects legal officials only to the extent that they resemble judges?

We should also observe, however, a distinction between two different kinds of hierarchy in Hartian analytical legal theories, a distinction which is often overlooked. Typical modern legal systems include a hierarchy of norms. Constitutional law overrides conflicting statutory law, and supreme court decisions can nullify the decisions of trial courts but not vice versa. For analytical legal theorists who accept a version of the positivist social sources thesis—all law is source-based or entailed by source-based law—it is also thought, as Marmor's "concentric circle" view shows, that a hierarchy of norms likely entails a hierarchy of officials. For example, if a "supreme" court's decisions are weightier or have greater normative consequences than a trial court's decisions, then the supreme court must also be considered a higher cohort of officials. Indeed, common expressions of our institutions confirm this thought: there are "higher" and "lower" courts, "superior" courts and "supreme" courts, and Parliamentary "supremacy." However, is it true that a hierarchy of norms entails a hierarchy of officials?

In any complex legal system, Hart says, the rule of recognition will specify and rank diverse sources of law. For any rule, its membership in the legal system can be revealed by pulling on a chain of validity. Consider Hart's illustration:

> The sense in which the rule of recognition is the ultimate rule of a system is best understood if we pursue a very familiar chain of legal reasoning. If the question is raised whether some suggested rule is legally valid, we must, in order to answer the question, use a criterion of validity provided by some other rule. Is this purported by-law of the Oxfordshire County Council valid? Yes: because it was made in exercise of the powers conferred, and in accordance with the procedure specified, by a statutory order made by the Minister of Health. At this first stage the statutory order provides the criteria in terms of which the validity of the by-law is assessed. There may be no practical need to go farther; but there is a standing possibility of doing so. We may query the validity of the statutory order and assess its validity in terms of the statute empowering the minister to make such orders. Finally, when the validity of the statute has been queried and assessed by reference to the rule that what the Queen in Parliament enacts is law, we are brought to a stop in inquiries concerning validity: for we have reached a rule which, like the intermediate statutory order and statute, provides criteria for the assessment of the validity of other rules; but it is also unlike them in that there is no rule providing criteria for the assessment of its own legal validity.[21]

This example was only intended as an illustration, but it is nonetheless inadvertently misleading. While Hart describes the test of validity as a "familiar chain of legal reasoning," the different links in the chain represent the interaction of several distinct officials. The Oxfordshire County Council and Ministry of Health mutually refer to each other; the Council exercises powers granted to it by the Ministry.

---

21. Hart, *supra* note 1, at 107.

The Ministry of Health in turn interacts with Parliament in a similar way. The sources of legal validity are therefore not foundational in the sense that there is an ultimate criterion—such as "whatever the Queen in Parliament enacts is law"—which gives all the other subordinate criteria and rules their validity. Rather, legal validity, and so legal systematicity, are constituted by the interdependency of the various officials; the interaction of officials is what constitutes legality. The nature of the activities of the Oxfordshire County Council, just as much as the activities of the Ministry of Health and Parliament, give rise to the emergence of law. Legality, in this sense, is to be found within and among the web of interactions of diverse officials, and is therefore not reducible to the activities of any particular group of officials. Notice also that there are several other officials that are suppressed in Hart's explanation; these thicken the web of interactions and also give rise to legality. For instance, in typical legal systems there are also law-applying and law-enforcing officials. Observation of these officials emerges in contexts of dispute and non- or suboptimal compliance. Law-enforcing officials make reference to the bylaws of the Oxfordshire County Council in enforcing its rules, and courts often refer to the provisions of Parliamentary statutes in deciding disputes about the powers of the Minister of Health.

A similar argument was advanced by John Finnis in *Revolutions and Continuity of Law*, and so may help to illustrate our view. In the context of a critical assessment of the capacity of Hart's notion of the rule of recognition to explain the continuity and discontinuity of law, he draws attention to a possible implication of Hart's factual explanation of the existence of the rule of recognition:

> Now if there is, in a system, a rule that does not depend for its existence on present rules of competence, one can raise the question whether perhaps there are other rules similarly independent, existing simply by virtue of the fact of their official acceptance. And one can raise the more radical question whether *any* rule need be regarded as dependent on present rules of competence. Perhaps all rules exist simply by virtue of the fact of their official acceptance?[22]

---

22. John Finnis, *Revolutions and Continuity of Law, in* OXFORD ESSAYS IN JURISPRUDENCE 59 (A.W.B. Simpson ed., 1973).

Finnis's "radical question" is a good one, not least because it emphasizes an under-appreciated feature of Hart's account of the rule of recognition. Sources of law, ranging from ministerial regulations to entrenched constitutional rights or rules, cannot themselves be part of the rule of recognition, i.e., they cannot form part of the explanation of the ultimate existence of law or criteria for membership in a legal system, simply because they all depend on the social fact of recognition. In a sense, the rule of recognition, as part of the functional explanation of the social existence of law, is empty. It consists only of official recognition.[23] Any attempt to give it content, e.g., conformity with a fundamental provision of a constitution, is to mistake what is recognized as a source of law with what ultimately gives rise to a source of law. In other words, recognition, by its very nature, must ultimately come from social actors, not constitutions, statutes, precedents, or any other rules. Once again, it seems to us that to identify a single rule that sits at the foundation of a legal system is to be drawn back to a norm-level explanation of legality and legal system, ignoring that "legal system" may need different treatment and explanation. Consider Hart's explanation of the rule of recognition:

> The existence of such a rule of recognition may take any of a huge variety of forms, simple or complex. It may, as in the early law of many societies, be no more than that an authoritative list or text of the rules is to be found in a written document or carved on some public monument. No doubt as a matter of history this step from the pre-legal to the legal may be accomplished in distinguishable stages, of which the first is the mere reduction to writing of hitherto unwritten rules. This is not itself the crucial step, though it is a very important one: *what is crucial is the acknowledgement of reference to the writing or inscription as authoritative, i.e., as the proper way of disposing of doubts as to the existence of the rule.* Where there is such an acknowledgment there is a very simple form of secondary rule: a rule for conclusive identification of the primary rules of obligation.[24]

On Hart's account what ultimately determines legal validity is the "acknowledgment" or recognition of an authoritative text, such as a

---

23. For a fuller account of this interpretation of the rule of recognition, see Michael Giudice, *Existence and Justification Conditions of Law*, 16 CANADIAN JOURNAL OF LAW AND JURISPRUDENCE 23–40 (2003).

24. Hart, *supra* note 1, at 94–95 (emphasis added).

constitution or more loosely, a precedent, and not what that authoritative text, i.e., its rules, may require. Without the acknowledgment or recognition, there is no legal validity or law. Yet most importantly, the acknowledgment or recognition necessary to sustain a legal system likely spreads far beyond the recognition or acknowledgment of those whom we might consider intuitively as the legal system's top-ranking officials. A country's highest legislature, which practices and recognizes its constitutional rules, would be unable to create any binding decisions (and would no doubt not exist, or not exist for long) if its statutes were not recognized by courts, lawyers, civil servants, police, accountants, city councilors, and so on. Similarly, it is often supposed, and certainly suggested by Hart and others, that supreme courts are supreme in the hierarchy of legal officials. Yet again, if the decisions of courts, supreme or otherwise, were not recognized as binding or as sources of law by lawyers, police, bailiffs, customs officers, legislatures, accountants, and so on, neither would their decisions be binding.[25] Above we said that it might make sense to locate judges, especially supreme court judges, at the top of the hierarchy or in the center of legal officialdom because their activities *have* the greatest normative consequences. Yet as Hart's own explanation makes clear upon analysis, the activities of judges only have great normative consequences because they are *given* great normative consequences by supporting officials' recognition and acknowledgment. If recognition is what counts in creating, sustaining, and determining the borders of legal systems, its identification may not be straightforwardly hierarchical. A similar worry would no doubt arise for any attempt to raise the status of any other particular type of official as supreme.

At this point it is important to be clear about what the preceding discussion has and has not shown. First, identification of the limits to determinacy in the analytical accounts we have examined is not meant to be a fatal criticism, such that we need to abandon the ideas of legal officials and the rule of recognition in explanation of state legal systems. Instead, the examination has shown the extent to which

---

25. For an illuminating account of why the judiciary (particularly federal courts) have persisted in the United States, *see* John Ferejohn & Larry D. Kramer, *Judicial Independence in a Democracy: Institutionalizing Judicial Restraint, in* NORMS AND THE LAW (John N. Drobak ed., 2006).

a focus on a single rule of recognition as a shared practice of judges (as no doubt an important but still only a special class of legal officials) has resulted in an imbalanced account of legal system. Little work has been done to meet the theoretical challenges that still remain to functional explanation of the borders of legal systems, as such borders are revealed by the practices of all legal officials within a particular system and not just its judges. It is significant to note that in work after *The Concept of Law* Hart himself acknowledged several ways precisely in which his account of recognition would need to be elaborated and refined to give it greater determinacy on important questions regarding the identity and borders of legal systems.[26] These further tasks Hart describes as among the "unfinished business for analytical jurisprudence."[27] We take this as a call and motivation for renewed attention to problems of determinacy, borders, and identity, and most importantly as reason for exploring the limits of existing analytical theories and developing new analytical tools to meet emerging challenges to understanding the nature of law.

Second, identification of the limits to the presumption of hierarchy, understood as a justification for allowing an otherwise intolerable degree of indeterminacy at the borders of legal systems, is meant to show the extent to which the problem of indeterminacy remains unsolved. Here, however, we are not suggesting that hierarchy of norms and officials is not at all present in state legal systems. The extent of hierarchy in a particular state legal system is surely a matter of degree. But this observation alone is significant, as it also points to the extent to which the problem of indeterminacy cannot be presumed solved. For the purposes of explanation of state legal systems in which the goal is provision of explanation of the existence of a foundational rule of recognition, the presumption of hierarchy as a means of resolving the problem of indeterminacy is likely acceptable. However, we shall now argue that the reliability of the presumption is likely not acceptable and seems most out of place in explanation of the foundations of international law.

---

26. H.L.A. HART, *Kelsen's Doctrine of the Unity of Law, in* ESSAYS IN JURISPRUDENCE AND PHILOSOPHY (H.L.A. Hart ed., 1983).

27. *Id.* at 310.

1.4 THE RULE OF RECOGNITION AND INTERNATIONAL LAW

Preceding argument has attempted to demonstrate the significance of the problems of circularity and indeterminacy within established, familiar instances of municipal legal systems. In this section we argue that the problems take on new force in attempts to understand the phenomena of international law. In bringing this criticism against Hart and his followers we are doing exactly what Hart thought he need not do in criticizing Austin, and we suppose that we gain further theoretical reach than Hart did by taking this path. So although Hart supposed he could criticize Austin and usefully expand the reach of general jurisprudence via analysis of "familiar features of municipal law in a modern state" we will do what he thought unnecessary and unprofitable to a broad and general understanding of law, to "invoke (as earlier critics have done) international law or primitive law which some may regard as disputable or borderline examples of law"— albeit in our case to implicate Hart, not Austin.[28]

As we explore the analytical approach to international law, it is worth noting that we are engaging Hart's arguments not out of exaggerated respect for his arguments or ignorance of other analytical theorists, but out of recognition that in many ways his discussion of international law in Chapter 10 of *The Concept of Law* is still the best available analytical examination of this topic.[29] Indeed, as Waldron has observed, it is something of an "embarrassment" for analytical legal theory that it has failed to examine the rise of what is at least spoken of and regarded as international law. This failure becomes more acutely embarrassing for those who take themselves to owe at least their point of departure to Hart's conception of the task of legal theory—a conception expressed in the mid 1980s in unashamedly universal terms. Writing in response to Dworkin, Hart argued that

> [T]here is a standing need for a form of legal theory or jurisprudence that is descriptive and general in scope, the perspective of which is not that of a judge deciding 'what the law is,' that is, what the law requires in

---

28. Hart, *supra* note 1, at 79.
29. With the possible exception of Kelsen, whose writings on international law are far more extensive than Hart's. We take up some of Kelsen's view in section 1.4.4. below.

particular cases . . . but is that of an external observer of a form of social institution with a normative aspect, which in its recurrence in different societies and periods exhibits many common features of form, structure, and content.[30]

Within this broad and general vision of the task for legal theory, the rule of recognition plays a central role, underwriting Hart's assertion that what is spoken of and regarded as international law is upon reflection best regarded as a set of rules and not a system. The centrality of the account of the rule of recognition to Hart's concept of law is underscored by its application to both complex developments such as international law, and societies only beginning to depart their pre-legal form of organization. As Hart puts it,

> The existence of such a rule of recognition may take any of a huge variety of forms, simple or complex. It may, as in the early law of many societies, be no more than that an authoritative list or text of the rules is to be found in a written document or carved on some public monument. No doubt as a matter of history this step from the pre-legal to the legal may be accomplished in distinguishable stages, of which the first is the mere reduction to writing of hitherto unwritten rules.[31]

Although we are concerned here primarily with Hart's extension of the account of the rule of recognition into assessment of what is called international law, we should note that some post-Hartian positivists do not share his universal view of the scope of the account of the rule of recognition. For example, Tamanaha writes:

> Shorn of its essentialist overtones, another way to view Hart's analysis is that he is really just asserting that primitive law and international law lack some of the core traits state law possesses, and they possess traits that state law lacks. A less misleading title to his classic text *The Concept of Law* would have been 'The Concept of State Law' or 'The Elements of State Law.'[32]

In Tamanaha's view, Hart's idea of a rule of recognition is misplaced in thinking about international law, which might simply possess different characteristics. Unfortunately, Tamanaha does not specify

---

30. H.L.A. Hart, *Comment in* ISSUES IN CONTEMPORARY LEGAL PHILOSOPHY 36–37 (R. Gavison ed., 1987).

31. Hart, *supra* note 1, at 94–5.

32. Tamanaha, *supra* note 16, at 151.

what these different characteristics might be, motivating us to return to his otherwise intriguing view only in later chapters, since his rejection of Hart amounts here to destruction without subsequent reconstruction of a renewed positivist view. For now it is sufficient to observe that Tamanaha's view raises a tempting avenue for post-Hartian theorists: Hart's account of state law—understood through the lens of an official-operated rule of recognition—is properly restricted to explanation of state law, and so is inapplicable to explanation of international law. The trouble with this view, as an interpretation of Hart's account of international law, is that Hart did in fact apply his theory of a state legal system as a union of primary and secondary rules to international law (though largely, we shall argue, because he had little else to use).[33] Application, in his view, of course turned up a negative finding—no international legal system for international law—but this is application just the same; application and rejection is still application.[34] Nor did Hart suppose in his 1961 view that explanation of international law might in fact require a different theory of law or new descriptive-explanatory tools, for he suggests that *only a change in the facts* might someday warrant altering our conclusion about the quality of international law, such that it might someday become more like a state legal system:

> Perhaps international law is at present in a stage of transition towards acceptance of [a rule of recognition] and other forms which would bring it

---

33. For a recent discussion of Hart's account of international law, see David Lefkowitz, *(Dis)solving the Chronological Paradox in Customary International Law: A Hartian Approach*, 21 CANADIAN JOURNAL OF LAW AND JURISPRUDENCE 129–148 (2008). Lefkowitz identifies three earlier theorists who argued that Hart misapplied his own conceptual account of legal system in explanation of international law, though Lefkowitz shows how these criticisms have been largely misguided: Anthony A. D'Amato, *The Neo-Positivist Concept of International Law*, 59 AMERICAN JOURNAL OF INTERNATIONAL LAW 321; THOMAS FRANCK, THE POWER OF LEGITIMACY AMONG NATIONS (1990); and G.J.H. VAN HOOF, RETHINKING THE SOURCES OF INTERNATIONAL LAW (1983). We take up Lefkowitz's view in section 1.4.3. below.

34. Indeed, it is important not to confuse (a) the view that we must not expect to find a rule of recognition in international law (this was the variety of mistake Hart attributed to Kelsen) with (b) the view that we must not apply the account of the rule of recognition to understanding (even if only negatively) international law in the first place. Hart held (a) but not (b).

nearer in structure to a municipal system. If, and when, this transition is completed the formal analogies, which at present seem thin and even delusive, would acquire substance, and the sceptic's last doubts about the legal 'quality' of international law may then be laid to rest.[35]

There is little suggestion here that an alternative theoretical account is needed to explain the nature of international law.[36] Instead, it is further evidence of the explanatory ambitions of the account of the rule of recognition to go beyond explanation of state legal systems. Our question becomes: is the account of an official-operated rule of recognition adequate as an explanatory device to be used to assess—positively or negatively—international social practices properly regarded as legal, and possibly warranting the title of legal system?

1.4.1 Not a System but a Set

In the final, much ignored chapter in *The Concept of Law*, Hart proceeds cautiously, setting aside in turn three mistaken reasons for denying the title "international law" to what is spoken of and regarded as international law. He rejects denial rooted in the absence of centrally

---

35. Hart, *supra* note 1, at 236–7.

36. It is interesting to note that in *Kelsen's Doctrine of the Unity of Law*, Hart, *supra* note 26, at 339–342, Hart somewhat changed his mind, there remarking that he likely lacked an adequate account of "recognition" for use in explanation of international law:

> I have spoken of recognition by the law-identifying and law-enforcing agencies effective in different territories. This obviously envisages arrangements of modern municipal legal systems where there are courts and special agencies for the enforcement of law. But we cannot leave out of sight more primitive arrangements: there may be no courts and no specialized enforcement agencies, and the application of sanctions for breach of the rules may be left to injured parties or their relatives, or to the community at large. International law, at least according to Kelsen, is itself such a decentralized system. Presumably, in such cases we shall have to use as our test of membership the notion of recognition by the society or the community, and certain problems in defining what constitutes sufficient recognition will have to be faced.

This later view, earlier expressed in the essay as part of the "unfinished business for analytical jurisprudence," does not suppose that all we can do is wait and see if the facts of international law change such that it might come to resemble a state legal system, but instead indicates that further theoretical work remains to be done.

organized sanctions, arguing that this criticism relies tacitly on the discredited command theory of law.[37] Hart similarly rejects the view that international law is conceptually impossible insofar as it requires a sacrifice of autonomy on the part of states for whom autonomy and existence are one and the same.[38] This view, Hart responds, carries an unwarranted presumption that the existence of a state requires absolute autonomy, a requirement neither asserted nor found historically or in 1961, as varieties of states and styles of independence and interdependence have long flourished. Finally, Hart rejects as a false dichotomy the view that international law, lacking the features typical of municipal law, must be supposed to be a kind of moral order. International law differs from morality in several respects: arguments of international law are source-based arguments, rules of international law often contain levels of detail and choice which can only be viewed as arbitrary from a moral point of view, and rules of international law can be altered by deliberate change.[39] Yet rejection of these arguments against international law does not result in straightforward admission of its existence. Rather, Hart sees in international law not a sophisticated, ultimate flourishing of legal order above individual states, but instead an echo of the experience of simple societies reaching toward the complex interweaving of primary and secondary legal rules characteristic of enduring municipal systems of law. Hart appears to regard international law as holding an intermediate position between a patchwork of individual norms, and a fully populated system of laws, calling what is regarded as international law a "set" but not a "system" of laws. He grounds this claim in description, charging that there is little to be gained in a Kelsenian approach which simply asserts the necessity of an underlying basic rule for international law. Whether there is international law is a matter of fact, not *a priori* presumption, according to Hart. In Hart's words,

> What is the actual character of the rules as they function in the relations between states? Different interpretations of the phenomena to be observed are of course possible; but it is submitted that there is no basic rule providing general criteria of validity for the rules of international law, and that the rules which are in fact operative constitute not a system but a set of

---

37. Hart, *supra* note 1, at 217–8.
38. *Id.* at 220–6.
39. *Id.* at 227–32.

rules, among which are the rules providing for the binding force of treaties.[40]

So there are international legal rules, but not an international legal system, because there is no basic rule of recognition. Remarkably, a generation of analytical legal theorists seems to have taken this argument as a license to give international legal phenomena very low priority within their investigations of law, despite Hart's tantalizing description of international law in 1961 as a "set" of rules not amounting to a system yet at least amounting to a set. In this hedged assessment of international law, we see the first indication of the distortion generated by reliance on an official-based rule of recognition as the central explanatory tool of not just legal system, but legality more broadly, to the extent that the heart of the distortion is bound up with presumption of the primacy of a particular hierarchically organized model of the law-state, captured by the bootstrapped rule of recognition. We explore in the next chapter the problems generated by a hierarchical model of the law-state; here we turn to identification of the distortions we have so far asserted in quite general terms.

1.4.2 International Rules of Change and Adjudication

The first distortion comes from the assertion of the absence of a systemic quality to international law. System, on Hart's view, requires the unificatory power of a rule of recognition, and there is no such rule. That rule, on Hart's view, is a special kind of secondary rule. Yet its absence seems unlikely given that Hart has written that a "set" of rules—not systemic yet not without unifying principle—exists in what is spoken of and regarded as international law, and more importantly, he has admitted the existence of "rules providing for the binding force of treaties."[41] These last rules are clearly rules about rules, rules about the force of particular treaty rules. That is, these are secondary rules of international law about the conditions under which particular treaties are binding. Beyond Hart's own recognition of what are surely secondary rules in international law, it seems that Waldron is right to say that some of Hart's view was "wrong in 1960

---

40. *Id.* at 236.
41. *Id.* at 236.

and it is certainly wrong now"[42] to the extent that there are rules of introduction, change, elimination, and adjudication easily visible in the practices of states interacting with one another, and those rules are moreover referred to as legal rules. In addition to rules regarding the formation, ratification, and implementation of treaties, conventions, and the like, there are rules regarding conditions of submission of disputes to the International Court of Justice and World Trade Organization, and many other secondary rules in diverse areas of international law.

It is worth noting, however, that in Hart's own words, international law has no secondary rules of change or adjudication at all:

> For, though it is consistent with the usage of the last 150 years to use the expression 'law' here, the absence of an international legislature, courts with compulsory jurisdiction, and centrally organized sanctions have inspired misgivings, at any rate in the breasts of legal theorists. The absence of these institutions means that the rules for states resemble that simple form of social structure, consisting of only primary rules of obligation, which, when we find it among societies of individuals, we are accustomed to contrast with a developed legal system. It is indeed arguable, as we shall show, that international law *not only lacks the secondary rules of change and adjudication which provide for legislature and courts*, but also a unifying rule of recognition specifying the sources of law and providing general criteria for the identification of its rules.[43]

It is difficult to resist the interpretation here that Hart makes the following assumption: since international law lacks a central legislature and courts with compulsory jurisdiction, it must also lack secondary rules of change and adjudication. But surely central legislatures and courts with compulsory jurisdiction are only particular forms of law-creating and law-applying institutions, and so do not exhaust the possibilities of institutions capable of practicing secondary rules of change and adjudication. To suggest otherwise is to make an unwarranted claim from the specific experience of the law-state.

Yet Hart's argument enables his supporters to reply that the mere presence of secondary rules of the kind discussed above is insufficient

---

42. Jeremy Waldron, *Hart and the Principles of Legality, in* THE LEGACY OF H.L.A. HART: LEGAL, POLITICAL, AND MORAL PHILOSOPHY 68 (M.H. Kramer et al. eds., 2008).

43. Hart, *supra* note 1, at 214. [Emphasis added]

to constitute systemic legality. Legality requires, in this view, that a rule of recognition is evident to the detached observer who notes its emergence from a particular kind of use of secondary rules, a use which defeats the static, uncertain, inefficient character of a regime composed solely of primary rules, or perhaps a combination of primary rules and a few, relatively unrelated secondary rules. One critical indication of the presence of a rule of recognition uniting a set of primary and secondary rules is the means to rank the various sources of rules which emerge, or determine if they are legal rules at all. Yet here it seems that Hart's argument contra the existence of an international legal system commits a version of the error he imputed to Kelsen's supposition of a basic rule underlying international law. As Hart urged his readers in responding to Kelsen, what matters here is whether in fact international law demonstrates the defects of a set of solely primary rules or whether those defects are overcome. If we return to the key matter of validity criteria, it seems to us that close attention to the facts reveals that worries about uncertainty are now something of a red herring. Uncertainty in international law regarding the identity of applicable legal norms seems to us to be no more or less significant than the very similar interpretive problems arising in state law. This similarity is perhaps overlooked because it arises in a context in which there are serious concerns about how to secure states' compliance to those clear and known obligations.[44] In Canada, for example, there is often little doubt about what is entailed by treaty obligations, as detailed policy documents guide participation in treaties from negotiation to implementation,[45] and particular treaties may have detailed provisions for adjudication of disputes regarding the content of the obligations they impose. The North American Free Trade Agreement, for example, provides for a Secretariat, which describes itself as "responsible for the administration of the dispute settlement provisions" contained in Chapter 20 of the agreement, which provides for a range of dispute resolution from a commission of trade ministers to arbitral panels and scientific review boards

---

44. For an early articulation of this view, see W.M. Reisman, *The Enforcement of International Judgements*, 63 AMERICAN JOURNAL OF INTERNATIONAL LAW 1, 1–9 (1969).

45. http://www.treaty-accord.gc.ca/procedure.asp (last visited Oct. 30, 2009).

which assist panels in determining factual matters.[46] The North American Free Trade Agreement is not an outlying example: it is itself formed consistent with the requirements of the Vienna Convention on the Law of Treaties,[47] and contains reference to similar other treaties with which it interacts in various ways, including certainty-providing solutions to problems of priority among norms. Article 103 ("Relation to Other Agreements"), for example, provides that:

1. The Parties affirm their existing rights and obligations with respect to each other under the *General Agreement on Tariffs and Trade* and other agreements to which such Parties are party.
2. In the event of any inconsistency between this Agreement and such other agreements, this Agreement shall prevail to the extent of the inconsistency, except as otherwise provided by this Agreement.

Not all treaties, of course, are so specific in their provision of secondary rules and specification of their relations to other norms of international law, or so successful in terms of actual compliance with their provisions, leading to a diminished status for those treaties to the extent that their ratification is not always followed by thorough implementation in domestic legislation. Even, however, the existence of these less thoroughly implemented treaties is little reason in itself to question the presence and operability of certainty-providing secondary rules in these situations. It is a familiar feature of state law that general norms containing stipulations for sharpening of their provisions in more specific primary norms are not in fact always developed into those sharpened norms.

It is also important to note that in addition to sources of international law that do not appear to be marked by uncertainty, secondary institutions exist capable of adding certainty and determinacy to states' obligations under international law. Commenting on a recent Supreme Court of Canada case dealing with Canada's international obligations under the U.N. Convention Against Torture, Oonagh Fitzgerald offers a helpful example that highlights the fact that issues

---

46. http://www.nafta-alena.gc.ca/en/view.aspx (last visited Oct. 30, 2009).

47. *Vienna Convention on the Law of Treaties, in* BASIC DOCUMENTS IN INTERNATIONAL LAW 270–297 (I. Brownlie, ed., 2009, sixth edition).

of the relationship between international law and state law typically amount to issues of compliance and not certainty:

> In the *Suresh* case, the Supreme Court of Canada recognized that the international law rule prohibiting return to torture was absolute, but noted that the right in section 7 of the *Canadian Charter of Rights and Freedoms* was not absolute. Rather, section 7 was subject to balancing such that there was a possibility "in exceptional circumstances" for return to torture to be justifiable under the *Charter*, even if it could never be justifiable under the *Convention against Torture*. When Canada was invited to report on its compliance with the Convention, the UN Committee against Torture was unimpressed by Canada's legal conundrum and emphasized that domestic law could not excuse failure to comply with international law obligations.[48]

Here we have not only a tolerably clear international peremptory norm of *jus cogens*–an absolute prohibition on returning persons to torture—but also a certainty-confirming institution of international law: the U.N. Committee against Torture.

From even these limited observations regarding the function of what is spoken of and regarded as international law, it seems there are reasons to doubt Hart's view that the uncertainty of international legal obligations is evidence of the absence of their membership in a system providing validation criteria for member norms. If it is true that international laws amount to just a set and not a system, this claim's truth likely depends on factors other than uncertainty driven by the absence of a special system-constituting, norm-validating practice of a rule of recognition. Further analysis could be undertaken to examine whether international laws are capable of modification and associated with the means to efficient application. That task may be left to the side here, since we believe we have done enough to show at least that (1) uncertainty is not factually obvious, and (2) in the interaction between the Vienna Convention on the Law of Treaties, the North American Free Trade Agreement, and the General Agreement on Trades and Tariffs, there is evidence that uncertainty, stasis, and inefficiency have been overcome. Of course, this analysis does not

---

48. O.E. Fitzgerald, *Understanding the Question of Legitimacy in the Interplay between Domestic and International Law*, in THE GLOBALIZED RULE OF LAW: RELATIONSHIPS BETWEEN INTERNATIONAL AND DOMESTIC LAW 128 (O.E. Fitzgerald ed., 2006) [author's notes omitted].

amount in itself to a positive case for regarding these treaties and structurally and functionally analogous norms as exhibiting systematicity in the sense Hart intends but without the rule of recognition the Hartian analysis leads observers to expect to see. This analysis is a negative case showing merely that certain disqualification triggers have not been tripped—albeit a rather important negative case since it corresponds to a key transition point from a primitive set of legal norms to a developed legal system, and for that reason may prompt an observer to look for a Hartian rule of recognition to explain the situation.

1.4.3 International Legal Officials?

If there is in fact evidence of secondary rules systemically connected in international law, why not simply opt for a conclusion urged by others: Hart's account of legal system is substantially correct, but for whatever reason he misapplied it to international law and turned up a false negative.[49] However, for a positive case to be made, a different argument must be offered, one which builds from an account of legal officials to enable positive identification of where the gap between "set" and "system" lies in officials' operation of secondary rules associated with international legal norms of the sorts we have described. As the situation stands, the rule of recognition seems to obscure as much as it explains: secondary rules are characteristic of a more rather than less developed group of legal norms, yet at some point the secondary rules and their use exhibit a quality that warrants a detached observer's regarding that group of norms as having matured into a system. Hart has claimed that on factual grounds we must withhold from supposing that the "set" of international norms amounts to a system; yet it is far from clear just why the rule of recognition has the meta-theoretical-evaluative force to justify denying the plain fact of a complex form of interaction among norms such as the North American Free Trade Agreement and the General Agreement on Tariffs and Trade. Indeed, to the extent that commitment to the meta-theoretical-evaluative merit of the rule of recognition compels denial of plain facts, this conflict seems reason to investigate the merit of the analytical device and not to change our view of the facts. It seems to

---

49. *See, e.g.*, Franck, *supra* note 33, at ch. II.

us that these concerns about the capacity of the bootstrapped rule of recognition to account for the interconnection of international secondary rules are not reduced by a positive argument regarding the way in which a rule of recognition might be detected or found absent. Advancing prior argument regarding circularity and indeterminacy to the case of officials of what is spoken of and regarded as international law, it seems to us that without an explanation of what sorts of practices of normative power constitute an office of international legal official, it is not possible to conclude that none or any exist. And without knowledge of whether any international legal officials exist, it is impossible to conclude one way or the other whether an international rule of recognition exists. Hart's argument against the existence of an international legal system then fails on its own terms since it cannot express those terms in the non-circular, determinate manner required to capture and distinguish international law and an international legal system from other forms of social order, social norm, and so on.

There is indeed good reason to believe that identification of legal officials of international law is particularly fraught with difficulties of circularity and indeterminacy. One reason stems from the fact that in international law, conventionally understood, states are at one and the same time both the creators and subjects of international law. Circularity is most evident: statehood or state sovereignty in international relations requires recognition from other states. To escape from circularity of course requires a positive account of the practices or legal-normative powers which make states into legal officials, if they are to be viewed as creators of international law. Yet here indeterminacy looms large. It may be easier to distinguish the legal-normative powers that mark officials from citizens in state law, but the very exercise of powers by states that, e.g., create treaties, are the same powers that render them subject to treaty obligations. Are we to view treaties, then, as forms of private contracts, even though the provisions of treaties often bind large populations and indefinite successions of future generations? Or do we keep the idea that the practice of secondary rules of change in the form of treaty rules are akin to the emergent practices of international legal officials, but recognize that an explanation rather than mere presumption is still required? Perhaps more plausibly, does the dual nature of states in international order—as both analogues of citizens and officials in states—show that a distinction between officials and citizens, itself crucial to any adequate functional explanation of the rule of recognition, is misguided when applied to international order?

Although Hart took few steps to address the question of the identification of international legal officials, the force of the problems of circularity and indeterminacy is highlighted in consideration of a recent account of a Hartian approach to understanding a puzzling feature of customary international law. In "(Dis)solving the Chronological Paradox in Customary International Law: A Hartian Approach" David Lefkowitz discusses the familiar problem of the chronological paradox about the creation of customary international law:

> In order to create a new rule of customary international law, states must act from the belief that the law already requires the conduct of the specified rule. Yet until they have successfully created the new rule of customary law, the conduct in question is not legally required. Thus the development of a new rule of customary international law appears to be impossible.[50]

Various solutions have been offered to solve the paradox, but Lefkowitz argues that all are inadequate because they ignore a crucial distinction between (i) the emergence of a customary international *rule* and (ii) its recognition as part of customary international *law*.[51] As Lefkowitz writes,

> Agents' adoption of the internal point of view enables us to distinguish rule-guided behavior from convergent behavior that merely reflects habit or overlapping interests. Yet the existence of a customary (or social) rule is only a necessary, not a sufficient, condition for the creation of a new rule of customary international law. For even if there exist customary rules that govern a particular domain of state conduct, it does not follow necessarily that the customary rules in question are legal ones. For instance, ceremonial salutes at sea and the practice of exempting diplomatic vehicles from parking prohibitions are both governed by non-legal customary rules. Rather, what makes customary rules international law is adherence by

---

50. Leftkowitz, *supra* note 33, at 129. For another account of legal positivism and customary international law, though one not directly concerned with applying a particularly Hartian approach, see David Hutchinson, *Positivism and International Law, in* POSITIVISM TODAY (Stephen Guest ed., 1996).

51. Lefkowitz, *supra* note 33, at 129.

officials in the international legal system to a rule of recognition that takes custom to be a source of valid law (at least with respect to certain domains of conduct).[52]

There is much of interest in Lefkowitz's article, especially his account that although there may be no rule of recognition for all of international law, there is certainly a rule of recognition for an international system of customary law.[53] His account of the difference between legal system and legal order is also valuable.[54] For the moment we leave these interesting claims to the side, for our central concern is with how well Lefkowitz's reliance on the notion of "legal official" fares against the problems of circularity and indeterminacy, as the crucial difference between a customary international rule and a customary international law is that the latter but not the former has been recognized by legal officials of international customary law. The note which accompanies the above passage is important:

> The reader might reasonably wonder how there comes to be specific legal officials in the first place. After all, the existence of such officials are presupposed in the account set out in the text of how a customary rule becomes legally valid, and the concept of an office seems best understood in terms of various normative rules, which at least initially might well be customary rules. Thus the initial creation of a legal office, and so of a legal official, would seem to require the temporally prior existence of some customary legal rules, and so the chronological paradox arises once again. I set this question aside here in order to focus on the question of how new customary norms of international law come to be part of an already existing international legal order (which includes, among other things, international legal officials). For one account of this issue regarding the origins of legal officials (within a Hartian legal positivist account of law and a legal system), see Coleman . . .[55]

In section 1.2.2. we argued that although Coleman's account of the emergence of legal officials offers a satisfactory solution to the problem of circularity, it inadequately addresses the problem of indeterminacy, so those convinced of our argument there will be unpersuaded, as we are, by Lefkowitz's reliance on that account here. However, there

---

52. *Id.* at 134.
53. *Id.* at 129–148.
54. *Id.*
55. *Id.* at 134.

is a special difficulty of indeterminacy in identification of legal officials in international law which makes Lefkowitz's decision to set aside the question of their emergence and identity particularly troubling, and seems to undermine his solution to the chronological paradox. Lefkowitz writes

> Why, then, have so many international legal theorists thought that the creation of new norms of customary international law suffers from the chronological paradox? A likely answer is that they have been misled by the fact that, in the international legal system, states comprise both the primary actors whose conduct and beliefs give rise to the existence of a customary rule, and the vast majority of the officials in the international legal system whose adherence to the rule of recognition leads them to deem that rule legally valid.[56]

There are two key claims here: (i) that customary rules are distinct from customary international laws because laws are recognized by the legal officials whereas rules are not; and (ii) *states are the actors whose practices at one and the same time give rise to both the customary rules and customary laws*. Yet when read in light of the problem of indeterminacy, to claim at one and the same time (i) and (ii) diminishes entirely the force of Lefkowitz's argument: (i) relies precisely on a distinction between international legal officials and non-officials to dissolve the paradox, but (ii) shows that the distinction cannot really be drawn beyond bare presumption. Another way to put it is to say that the *goal* of the distinction between international legal officials and non-officials has been provided—namely the distinction between customary rules and customary laws which dissolves the paradox— but the *argument* for the distinction itself is missing. In his defense, Lefkowitz offers the argument that, as a conceptual matter, there is no reason why officials and citizens *need to overlap*. As he says, "[w]e can imagine, for example, a society whose legal officials live in isolation from their subjects, but subscribe to a rule of recognition that directs them to validate the society's customary rules as law."[57] Although such a society might be possible to imagine, and may even do a good job of explaining some state legal systems whose practices sometimes recognize as law customary practices of non-official citizens,

---

56. *Id.* at 135 [author's notes omitted].
57. *Id.* at 135.

the hypothetical example no doubt fares poorly in explanation of international legal officials of customary law, the very issue the example is meant to illuminate, where there is complete overlap between officials and citizens. Equally important, the example still leaves us without non-circular determinate means of identifying the possible legal officials "who live in isolation from their subjects." Quite simply, what exactly might make someone, some group, some state, or some group of states, an international legal official?

At this point we can also see precisely why the presumption of hierarchy, which in explanation of state legal systems at least puts off worry about indeterminacy at the borders, offers little help to accounts of international law, which, as Hart notes, lacks a central legislature, court with compulsory jurisdiction, and centrally organized enforcement agency. If states are at one and the same time both the creators and subjects of international customary law (and other types of international law), there is no hierarchy to climb onto which might bring determinacy to their membership in a class of international legal officials.

It seems difficult to resist the conclusion that Lefkowitz has simply replaced one conceptual puzzle about customary international law—the chronological paradox—with an equally and quite possibly even more arresting puzzle—the identity of a distinct class of international legal officials. Yet it remains possible, we acknowledge, to continue efforts to identify international legal officials and specify the rule of recognition in a way that might enable it to underwrite distinction of an international set of secondary rules from an international system of secondary rules. We will leave that activity to others, accepting for our part that the weight of evidence against the rule of recognition warrants investigation of the causes of its failure, and development of an explanatory tool adequate to the tasks failed by the rule of recognition, without recourse to confusing talk of "sets" versus "systems" and secondary rules whose generation of a rule of recognition is a mysterious rather than explicitly characterized process.

1.4.4 Kelsen's Account of International Law

Perhaps the best way to avoid the distorting effects of one's theory of law is to resist generalizing from an unduly limited experiential base as Hart does. Hart presumed that experience of the law-state was sufficient evidence for constructing a fully general jurisprudence, such that non-state social phenomena presenting itself as law could be usefully included or rejected as legal phenomena to the extent that they resembled state law or are in some way recognized as law by state officials. The alternative is to avoid presuming that experience of the law-state exhausts the relevant evidence, and theorize instead from a greater range of experience. On this score at least, Kelsen's much discredited account of international law looks much less foolish than Hart makes it appear. Kelsen writes

> Because legal cognition aims to comprehend as law—to comprehend within the category of the valid legal norm—*material characterized as international law, as well as material presenting itself as state law*, legal cognition sets the very same task for itself that natural science sets for itself: to represent its object as a unity.[58]

It is important to distinguish two parts to Kelsen's "epistemological postulate": a presumption that legal theory aims to understand as law both state law and international law, and a presumption that international law must be seen to form a unity with state law. The first part of the postulate is much overlooked but sound. International law, as we have suggested above, enjoys a kind of existence in name *and* practice that makes it difficult to justifiably exclude it from the center of analytical legal theory's attention. While there may be reasons to doubt Kelsen's general account of international law (which he more fully explains as a form of decentralized normative coercive order[59]) and its relation to state law, we need not fault his presumption that international law is a kind of legality and so deserves explanation.

The second part of Kelsen's epistemological postulate is of course subject to fatal criticism, but importantly can be seen to commit the opposite kind of error committed by Hart. Whereas Hart saw no system of international law, Kelsen saw nothing but system. Kelsen famously

---

58. HANS KELSEN, INTRODUCTION TO PROBLEMS OF LEGAL THEORY 111, (B.L. Paulson & S.L. Paulson trans., 1992) [emphasis added]. *See also* HANS KELSEN, PURE THEORY OF LAW 328–9 (Max Knight trans., 1967); HANS KELSEN, PRINCIPLES OF INTERNATIONAL LAW 569–70, (Robert W. Tucker ed., 1966); and HANS KELSEN, GENERAL THEORY OF LAW AND STATE 373 (A. Wedberg trans., 1961).

59. *See generally*, HANS KELSEN, PRINCIPLES OF INTERNATIONAL LAW (Robert W. Tucker ed., 1966) and HANS KELSEN, GENERAL THEORY OF LAW AND STATE 325–327 (A. Wedberg trans., 1961).

was willing to see a system quite capable, on one interpretation, of providing the reason for validity and spheres of validity for all systems of state law as sub-systems of international law.[60] As Hart notes, however, the view that both state law and international law form a single system, where each can be seen to complement each other's norms and provide the reason for the validity of each other's norms, supposes an explanatorily deficient relation between the two legal orders. Here is Hart's illustration to establish the inadequacy of Kelsen's view:

> Suppose the British Parliament (or *mutatis mutandis*, Congress) passes an Act (the Soviet Laws Validity Act, 1970) which purports to validate the law of the Soviet Union by providing that the laws currently effective in Soviet territory, including those relating to the competence of legislative and judicial authorities, shall be valid. The enactment of this Act of Parliament or Congress would not be a reason for saying that English (or American) law together with Soviet law formed one legal system, or for using *sans phrase* any of the Kelsenian expressions such as that Soviet law 'derives its validity' from English law or that English law was 'the reason for the validity' of Soviet law. The reason for refusing to assent to these propositions is surely clear and compelling: it is that the courts and other law-enforcing agencies in Soviet territory do not, save in certain special circumstances, recognize the operations of the British (or American) legislature as criteria for identifying the laws that they are to enforce, and so they do not recognize the Soviet Laws Validity Act, though a valid English (or American) statute, as in any way determining or otherwise affecting the validity of Soviet law in Soviet territory. It is true indeed that the relationship of validating purport holds between that Act and the laws made by the Soviet legislature, which the Soviet courts do recognize; but the division of laws into distinct legal systems cuts across the relationship of validating purport, for that relationship, like the completion relationship examined above, may hold either between laws of different systems or between laws of the same system.[61]

---

60. HANS KELSEN, INTRODUCTION TO PROBLEMS OF LEGAL THEORY 120–2 (B.L. Paulson & S.L. Paulson trans., 1992); HANS KELSEN, PURE THEORY OF LAW 332–3 (Max Knight trans., 1967); HANS KELSEN, PRINCIPLES OF INTERNATIONAL LAW 578–80 (Robert W. Tucker ed., 1966); and HANS KELSEN, GENERAL THEORY OF LAW AND STATE 366–8, (A. Wedberg trans., 1961).

61. Hart, *supra* note 26, at 319.

The criticism is decisive.[62] To employ a distinction introduced at the beginning of this chapter, although Kelsen's account of the relation between national and international law may be *structurally sound*, it fails significantly to provide an adequate *functional explanation* of the relations between legal systems: laws purporting to validate subordinate laws may make sense in the abstract, but whether or not such laws are part of the same system or form one system depends on the actual existence of social practices of recognition by "courts and other law-enforcing agencies" that unite the otherwise unconnected laws. Kelsen's idea of a relation of validating purport is simply unable to function in explanation of actual relations between states or between states and an international legal order.

Despite their radically different conclusions, neither Hart's nor Kelsen's view seems to explain without distortion various phenomena known as international law. Yet there is an important similarity between the epistemological commitments of Hart's and Kelsen's accounts of international law. We have already argued that the idea of legal official is of limited use in serving its function in explanation of the existence and borders of legality, and here we think that in seeing the shortcomings of Hart's and Kelsen's approaches to international law we begin to see the inadequacy of another related theoretical notion: legal system. Both Hart and Kelsen shared the presumption that international law can be usefully viewed through the lens of legal system, a notion which essentially associates legality with a special form of unified normative practice.

In the next chapter we consider the way Joseph Raz responds to the problem of indeterminacy, and argue that his solutions are bound up with a hierarchical view of legal system which—quite apart from the problem of indeterminacy—raise separate questions about the utility of the notion of "system" in accounting for legal order, particularly novel legal orders apart from the law-state.

---

62. Joseph Raz presses similar criticisms in THE AUTHORITY OF LAW 127–129 (1979), and in THE CONCEPT OF A LEGAL SYSTEM 100–105 (1980).

2. THE HIERARCHICAL VIEW OF LEGAL SYSTEM AND NON-STATE LEGALITY

In this chapter we explore an important and influential variation on Hart's attempt to explain legal system on the back of an official-based rule of recognition. Joseph Raz accepts the probative idea of the value of a suitably modified version of the rule of recognition, yet deploys that idea in a significantly different way. Where Hart sought to capture the identity and continuity of a given legal system by its operation of a single rule of recognition, Raz argues instead for the possibility of multiple rules of recognition in a single system, a possibility which demands introduction of new explanatory elements to carry out theoretical tasks Hart left to the unitary rule of recognition. As we explore Raz's view, we will see a new dimension of the problematic assumption of hierarchy we saw in Hart. Where Hart's view embodied a presumption of hierarchy in the relation of norms and officials within a given system, Raz's plural rule of recognition approach avoids an assumption of internal hierarchy yet presumes hierarchy in another way, as he relies exclusively on a particular idea of state legal system as the basis for his contribution to general jurisprudence. This reliance, we aim to show, brings problems for a general jurisprudence with aspirations to universality, or at any rate to more than parochialism.

The chapter is divided as follows. In section 2.1 we identify the ways in which Raz's theory of legal system diverges from Hart's. In section 2.2 we assess the limits to Raz's account in its functional explanation of the borders of legal systems and their variations, here showing how his view leaves the problem of indeterminacy intact and risks parochialism. In section 2.3 we gather preceding argument and identify the precise way in which Raz's theory of legal system is hierarchical, supposing as it does that all legality emanates from state institutions and activities. Finally, in section 2.4 we test Raz's account of legal system in explanation of supra-state and trans-state legal orders, demonstrating just how unbalanced his account is when assessed against standards of a more general jurisprudence. These sections will conclude the critical part of this book and set the stage for development of our positive view which we begin in the next chapter.

2.1 RAZ'S STRUCTURAL ACCOUNT OF LEGALITY

Raz has long expressed misgivings regarding Hart's use of the rule of recognition as the ultimate customary, duty-imposing foundation of a legal system's identity and continuity. In *The Identity of Legal Systems*, published in 1971, he remarked that "Hart's discussion of the rule of recognition falls short of the high standard of lucidity characterizing the rest of his book [*The Concept of Law*] and requires interpretation . . ."[1] In subsequent interpretation Raz argues that a given legal system may have more than one rule of recognition: "Furthermore, there is no reason to suppose that every legal system has just one rule of recognition. It may have more . . . [T]here may be two or more rules of recognition that provide methods of resolving conflicts; for example, the rule imposing an obligation to apply certain customs may indicate that it is supreme, whereas the rule relating to precedent may indicate that it is subordinate."[2] This fact brings various difficulties which come to a head, according to Raz, in Hart's inability to show how the rule of recognition can account for the continuity of legal systems as one ends and another succeeds it.[3] For our purposes here we need to examine Raz's methodological reasoning justifying divergence from Hart's view, followed by assessment of the consequent capacity of Raz's view to evade problems of circularity and indeterminacy while facing up to novel phenomena of legality.

Raz's first modification involves reduced explanatory emphasis on officials' conduct by focusing on the norm-applying institutions within which they reside, thereby avoiding the problem of identification of officials. As he puts it in *The Authority of Law*,

> What are the identifying features of public officials? This is a problem which is both important and difficult. It is, however, a problem which it would be best to avoid here, for though we will find public officials in all

---

1. Joseph Raz, *The Identity of Legal Systems*, 59 CALIFORNIA LAW REVIEW 795, 806 (1971).

2. *Id.* at 810.

3. *Id.* at 811.

legal systems, not all of them must exist in the system if it is to count as a legal system. Instead we should try to identify a subclass of norm-applying institutions, namely those the presence of which is necessary in all legal systems.[4]

In the context of this passage Raz defines the necessary special subclass of "primary" norm-applying institutions as those "institutions with power to determine the normative situation of specified individuals, which are required to exercise these powers by applying existing norms, but whose decisions are binding even when wrong."[5] Typically, those primary norm-applying institutions are courts, and in particular courts of final jurisdiction, although other institutions may be primary in some systems. The life of these institutions provides the key to Raz's explanation of the identity of a legal system. He explains in a note to his assertion of the possibility of a plurality of rules of recognition that in the absence of a unitary rule of recognition to identify a legal system, "It is the fact that a set of laws of recognition are maintained by the practice of the same law-applying organs that indicates they are all part of one legal system."[6]

A second modification to Hart's view is that Raz further avoids emphasis on officials' conduct by identifying as necessary and common to municipal systems' identity their characteristic exhibition of a combination of claims to *comprehensiveness, supremacy*, and *openness*. In exhibiting a claim of *comprehensiveness* a legal-normative social system embodies the claim that there is no sphere of private or social conduct that is immune to the system's claim to authority to regulate in some way, either by prohibition, requirement, or permission. A claim to *supremacy* can be seen in a legal system's claim that its standards take precedence over other sorts of standards in cases of conflict. Finally, a legal-normative social system is *open*: other normative systems are supported by legal systems and their norms are "adopted" or certified by the legal-normative system for special purposes. Law-applying institutions, then, such as provincial or federal courts of appeal, are distinctively *legal* institutions not because they

---

4. JOSEPH RAZ, THE AUTHORITY OF LAW 107 (1979). For recent criticism of Raz's view see Hanoch Sheinman, *The Priority of Courts in the General Theory of Law*, 52 AMERICAN JOURNAL OF JURISPRUDENCE 229–258 (2007).

5. Raz, *supra* note 4, at 109–110.

6. Raz, *supra* note 1, at 810 n.30.

are practiced and recognized by legal officials, but because they figure as part of a normative system that claims (and is to some degree effective in claiming) to be comprehensive, supreme, and open. As Raz states, the features of comprehensiveness, supremacy, and openness serve well to explain the way in which ". . . we feel that legal systems not only happen to be the most important institutionalized system governing human society, but that that is part of their nature."[7] This two-pronged approach allows Raz to identify legality and legal system by examining whether a purportedly legal-normative system claims to be comprehensive, supreme, and open, and whether these characteristic claims are evident in the operation of a special core subclass of its norm-applying institutions.

This, then, is Raz's structural account of legality. To assess how well Raz's account of legality functions in explanation of actual instances of life under law it is first necessary to examine its context to make clear its methodological purpose and limits. Returning to *The Identity of Legal Systems*, perhaps the first and most important observation concerns the nature of "legal system" as a conceptual tool:

> The term "a legal system" is not a technical legal term . . . Therefore, when trying to clarify the notion of a legal system, the legal theorist does not aim at defining clearly the sense in which the term is employed by legislators, judges, or lawyers. He is, rather, attempting to forge a useful conceptual tool, one which will help him to a better understanding of the nature of law.[8]

That conceptual tool, in the context of the problem of the identity and continuity of legal system, is capable of explaining the "formal unity" of legal system, Raz argues, an account not of the "material unity" of a legal system in its particulars, but the "all-pervasive principles and the traditional institutional structure and practices that permeate the system and lend to its distinctive character.[9] An account of the formal unity of legal system is presupposed by "any investigation into its material unity,"[10] which is of course as a matter of practice

---

7. Raz, *supra* note 4, at 116.
8. Raz, *supra* note 1, at 795.
9. Raz, *supra* note 1, at 796.
10. Raz, *supra* note 1, at 796.

ontologically prior to the material account. Yet the formal account is nonetheless just that and not at the same time a "systematic and reasonable account of the limits of a legal system,"[11] an account whose realization would require the theorist to cross the boundary between general and particular jurisprudence. That task is very difficult, Raz admits: "Attempting to formulate criteria of validity based on complex court practices that are in a constant state of change and that are necessarily vague and almost certainly incomplete, involves not only legal perceptiveness and theoretical skill, it demands sound judgment and reasonable value decisions as well."[12] So the gap between the theory of the identity of legal system and specific examples of legal systems is not an easy one to bridge; perhaps Raz was right to limit his later, 1979 examination of legal system and identity to not just the formal side of the story, but to an explicitly limited part of the formal side. In *The Authority of Law* Raz identifies three unargued "assumptions" at the basis of his account of the "identifying features of municipal legal systems."[13] The first assumption regarding the social nature of legal systems may be passed over.[14] The second and third are of much greater interest for the problem of identification of the nature and borders of legal systems. The second assumption

> . . . is the assumption of universality according to which it is a criterion of adequacy of a legal theory that it is true of all the intuitively clear instances of municipal legal systems. . . . It must fasten only on those features of legal systems which they must possess regardless of the special circumstances of the societies in which they are in force. This is the difference between legal philosophy and sociology of law.[15]

The third assumption is in a sense built in to the second assumption of universality: an adequate legal theory need only scope over salient municipal legal systems in order to be sufficiently important to warrant theoretical attention and an independent theory. Raz is

---

11. Raz, *supra* note 1, at 809.

12. Raz, *supra* note 1, at 809.

13. Raz, *supra* note 4, at 103.

14. This is the assumption that "normative systems are existing legal systems because of their impact on the behaviour of individuals, because of their role in the organization of social life." Raz, *supra* note 4, at 104.

15. Raz, *supra* note 4, at 104.

careful, however, to show that this limitation to his theory is not a matter of willful blindness to the existence of other normative systems and the relation of municipal legal systems to those other systems:

> Obviously, in part the investigation of municipal systems is designed to compare and contrast them with other normative systems. Indeed it is to this part that the present essay is dedicated. In pursuing such investigations it may turn out that municipal systems are not unique, that all their essential features are shared by, say, international law or church law. If this is indeed so, well and good. But it is not a requirement of the adequacy of a legal theory that it should be so or indeed that it should not be so. It is, however a criterion of adequacy that the theory will successfully illuminate the nature of municipal legal systems.[16]

A final methodological note warns against expectations of precise boundary-drawing between legal and other normative systems: "It would be arbitrary and pointless to try to fix a precise borderline between normative systems which are legal systems and those which are not. When faced with borderline cases it is best to admit their problematic credentials, to enumerate their similarities and dissimilarities to the typical cases, and leave it at that."[17] Raz's conception of legal system amounts, then, to a highly generalized or "formal" account of the necessary features of all intuitively clear instances of municipal legal systems, finding in those systems a cluster of elements that includes a rule or rules of recognition, whose distinctively legal quality is assessable via the presence of norm-applying institutions whose operations express a combination of systemic claims to comprehensiveness, supremacy, and openness. Questions of course remain regarding the sense in which municipal systems can be "open" to other systems, as Raz's account is explicitly skeptical of the possibility of precise delineation of the borders or identity conditions for other kinds of systems. Interaction seems, then, to be between intuitively clear municipal instances generalized and unspecified others. We shall encounter this question in more detail below. For the moment, let us return to the problems of circularity and indeterminacy.

---

16. Raz, *supra* note 4, at 105.
17. Raz, *supra* note 4, at 116.

2.2 FUNCTIONAL ASSESSMENT OF RAZ'S ACCOUNT OF LEGALITY

2.2.1 Indeterminacy at the Borders

There are two principal sources of doubt about the adequacy of Raz's account in functional explanation of legality. The first source of doubt is familiar, and is the capacity of Raz's account of legality to determine adequately the borders of legal systems that might display characteristic features of comprehensiveness, supremacy, and openness. Bearing in mind Raz's admonition that his theory is both general and limited to municipal systems, it is nonetheless useful to use a "material" example derived from a particular system to illustrate how Raz's "formal" extension of the rule of recognition-based approach attempts to avoid the problem of circularity as initially run against official-based accounts of the rule of recognition. Consider the question of the legality of the decisions of a statutorily empowered president of a public university, decisions that are binding since they determine students' rights and obligations and are enforced by other bodies in the university even if those decisions are mistaken.[18] What can Raz's view tell us about the legality of those decisions?[19] At first glance it seems that the decisions of a university president fall under the description of a primary law-applying institution, despite our likely intuition that university presidents are not legal officials and universities are not legal institutions. Binding decisions of law-applying institutions are those that are legally valid, even when mistaken, and legally binding decisions are those that are recognized as such by law-applying institutions. The decisions of a university president appear on this measure to be binding: a person banned from campus by authority of a university president, for example, may subsequently be charged with trespassing upon returning to campus, so that person's position under law was non-optionally (unlike a contract between private citizens) varied by the president's order under authority of the board of governors, statute, and so on. Yet an equally plausible view would

---

18. This example is inspired by the issues raised in Freeman-Maloy v. Marsden [2005] O.J. No. 1730.

19. Notice that our question is not whether universities are themselves legal systems, but whether their officers and institutions are part of state legal systems.

hold that the decisions of a university president are not legally binding or legal decisions at all, but simply decisions which might be permitted or supported (or not) by law. Universities are, after all, typically autonomous in their creation and practice of academic rules and conferral of degrees, and they cannot, for example, introduce their own criminal laws, which shows they are more akin to private subjects than legal institutions.

This division of views demonstrates that resolution of the question of the legality of the office of university president cannot be found in Raz's account of norm-applying institutions alone without introduction of a prior presumption or argument regarding the question of whether the statutorily created office of president is a legal norm-applying institution. This presumption is necessary, as there is nothing in the idea alone of an institutional power to make binding decisions, even when wrong, that distinguishes legal-normative powers from non-legal normative powers. Such a presumption, however, would amount to a circular account of the characteristic legality of legal norm-applying institutions. The way out of circularity lies in observation of the interaction between legal norm-applying institutions, and their representation of the legal system's claims to comprehensiveness, supremacy and openness. While there may be difficulty, Raz admits, in stating precisely the interaction and borders between legal systems and other normative systems, difficulty at the borders does not mean there are no clear instances of legal system. The answer to the question of the status of the university president lies in assessing the distance of the office of president from the core features of the legal system in which the president is enmeshed. Our university president is an executive officer in a statutorily enacted social institution whose establishment and nature are bound up in a systemic hierarchy of legal norms typical of developed modern municipal systems of law, as captured by Hart's conception of the rule of recognition.

Yet, as we saw in the last chapter, escape from the problem of circularity does not necessarily entail escape from the problem of indeterminacy at the borders of legal systems. The fact of a well-known core set of legal norms and law-applying institutions does not settle the question of which legal norms and law-applying institutions are the *least* authoritative while still remaining legal norms and law-applying institutions of legal officials rather than, say, a community of interest whose knowledge of law enables its leaders to exert suasive force on others via prediction of likely legal consequences of proposed conduct.[20] So although all might agree that the decisions and rules of a university president are further from core institutions and nearer the bottom of any hierarchy of normative institutions and norms in a particular society, this is not dispositive of the question of whether a university president falls within or without the conditions for membership in the group of legal institutions.

There is still in Raz one further device in need of examination that might be used to help avoid the conclusion that we simply cannot say determinately, with conceptual precision and in a non-circular way, just why universities and their presidents are not legal norm-applying institutions and officials. Raz offers a distinction between norms that are members of a legal system and so are legal norms, and norms that are merely adopted by the system for particular purposes. Consider the test offered for determination of whether a norm is or is not part of the legal system:

> Norms are 'adopted' by a system because it is an open system if and only if either (1) they are norms which belong to another normative system practiced by its norm-subjects and which are recognized as long as they remain in force in such a system as applying to the same norm-subjects, provided they are recognized because the system intends to respect the way that the community regulates its activities, regardless of whether the same regulation would have been otherwise adopted, or (2) they are norms which were made by or with the consent of their norm-subjects by the use of powers conferred by the system in order to enable individuals to arrange their own affairs as they desire. The first half of the test applies to norms recognized by the rules of conflict of laws, etc. The second part of the test applies to contracts, the regulations of commercial companies, etc . . . Norms which meet this test are recognized by a system but not part of it.[21]

The test of adoption is an important part of Raz's account of legal system, and will benefit from close attention. As Raz says, the point of the test is to ". . . define with greater precision the character of an open system,"[22] and as such purports to meet the challenge of

---

20. The Canadian Civil Liberties Association and the American Civil Liberties Union are examples of such communities of interest.

21. Raz, *supra* note 4, at 120.

22. Raz, *supra* note 4, at 119.

indeterminacy in explaining the function of legality and legal system. Yet how well does the test accomplish this goal? According to the first part of the test, norms can be adopted when they "are norms which belong to another normative system." But this is fundamentally troublesome. Assertions regarding adoption of norms from other normative systems presuppose an understanding of the general, formal nature of municipal system into which other systems' norms may be temporarily adopted, but often the existence of different, separate systems is precisely in question. We cannot know one way or the other if norms belong to a legal system if we do not know if their originating system is itself part—perhaps a sub-part or co-part—of the legal system. Indeed, the test's focus on the source and home of *norms*, rather than the relation between *systems*, is characteristically symptomatic of the imbalance between explanation of norms and explanation of systems we identified in chapter one. Explanation of the relation between norms too often proceeds without an account of the relation between systems.

The second part of the test also fails to illuminate and resolve the problem of the least authoritative *member institutions* of the legal system, illustrated by the example of the university president. The test supposes that norms do not belong to the legal system if they "were made by or with the consent of their norm-subjects by the use of powers conferred by the system in order to enable individuals to arrange their own affairs as they desire." This condition forces counter-intuitive results such as the denial that provincial laws in a federated state such as Canada are in fact "recognized" rather than merely "adopted" laws, since provincial laws are supported by the federal system through conferred powers set out in a constitution that provides provinces with the facilities for arranging their affairs as they desire. Yet surely such a conclusion is mistaken. Provincial laws are thought of, spoken of, and function as rules of law in Canada, and would be very oddly characterized if explained only as norms capable of being adopted by a federal system. Also, provincial institutions not only create, apply, and enforce provincial laws and regulations; they also apply and enforce federal norms as well. Finally, provincial governments are quite unlike private corporations; provincial governments serve not their own interests but the interests of their citizens. However, without an account of when two separate systems exist, it becomes impossible to say when norms are within or outside a legal system. So, in the Canadian context we need to ask whether there is one legal system or several, and if there are several, can any be meaningfully understood to be making claims of comprehensiveness, supremacy, and openness? Again, when legality is determined by means which provide no "cut off" point, finding a place for particular norms in the hierarchy simply raises again the question of the edges of legal institutions, their operations which constitute legality and legal system, and the nature of the officials conducting those operations. So although the characteristics of supremacy, comprehensiveness, and openness may well have an important explanatory role in understanding the core of legality and legal system, they offer no great advance to determination of the membership criteria of legal institutions of the system and hence the borders of legality.[23]

---

23. One further line of argument against Raz's evasion of indeterminacy deserves our attention. In the midst of his discussion of the interaction of legal norm-applying institutions and claims of comprehensiveness, supremacy, and openness, Raz recognizes the need to say more about the nature of primary norm-applying institutions, which hold "power to determine the normative situation of specified individuals, which are required to exercise these powers by applying existing norms, but whose decisions are binding even when wrong." As we have seen before, difficulties arise when this general account of norm-applying institutions is adapted to legal theory. Raz himself remarks on the need to adapt this definition of primary norm-applying institutions to legal situations. As he says, "[i]t has to be modified to allow for the possibility of appeal, re-trial, etc., and also for the possibility that the determination is binding for one purpose but not for others." Raz, *supra* note 4, at 110. So in order to account for the binding quality of decisions of law-applying institutions which do not possess final and absolute authority, the notion of "binding" must be modified to account for the fact that a lower court's decision is subject to being overruled if it is found to be mistaken. A suitably modified definition, applied to legal contexts, might be formulated as follows:

> Law-applying institutions are institutions with power to determine the legal-normative situation of specified individuals, which are required to exercise these powers by applying existing legal norms, but whose decisions are binding even when wrong *and not overruled or appealed.*

So, a lower court decision which clearly misapplies the relevant legal norms is nonetheless still binding for the parties concerned if it is not overturned or up until it is overturned. Consider again, though, the problem of the legality of the decisions of a university president. Her decisions remain binding, unless or until overturned by a higher institution in the university or possibly,

More generally, it appears to us that Raz's test for adoption has only given the goal of the distinction in expressing the difference between adopted and recognized norms: it is certainly desirable to be able to distinguish legal from non-legal normative systems via some observable characteristic feature of their norms. Yet provision of the goal of the distinction is not the same as provision of the argument for the distinction. In his account of the conceptual structure of legal system Raz has unquestionably gone beyond the roots of the Hartian "monopolistic" rule of recognition view; yet he has done so without sufficient argument about the way the phenomena of life under law compel this kind of thickening of the rule of recognition-based view to provide a better descriptive-explanatory account of the situation. Indeed, Raz's methodological restriction of his view to "intuitively clear" instances of municipal systems seems to us to be a fatal limitation to a project aiming to contribute to general jurisprudence in an era when, as we have demonstrated in the Introduction, the very idea of the "intuitively clear instance" is under challenge. The attempt to resolve the problem of the university president's legality by reference to the interaction of legal norm-applying institutions and their exhibition of claims of comprehensiveness, supremacy, and openness founders, then, on the familiar imbalance between structural and functional accounts of legality. The assumption of the primacy or signal importance of the experience of the municipal legal system,

---

in unfanciful circumstances, by a trial court. Where, in Raz's view, is the basis for distinction of the president's decisions as non-legal, rather than legal and not yet overruled? Yet the problem of indeterminacy runs even deeper. Consider another illustration. A forms a contract with B, and each subsequently meets their agreed obligations, taking themselves to be bound. Suppose, though, that under the law their contract is invalid, perhaps because it is grossly immoral. Suppose, also, that this fact comes to light and a court authoritatively dissolves the contract. What, then, is to distinguish the validity or bindingness of the obligations under the contract between A and B, *before it is dissolved by a court*, from mistaken decisions by lower courts which are later overruled by higher courts? Even on the modified definition of a law-applying institution, there is no non-arbitrary way to draw the line. Yet without a way of distinguishing the legal quality of void contracts between private citizens and mistaken lower courts decisions, it remains unsolved whose practices of law-application constitute legality and where the borders of legal systems lie.

intuitively identified, camouflages a shortage of both structural and functional detail regarding the general, formal nature of such systems, and more importantly, the focus on the experience of municipality rules out by design much concern with the range of variants within the experience of municipality. The trouble with this move comes out most clearly when Raz attempts to state as precisely as possible the nature of the borders between municipal legal systems and other normative systems. With only an intuitively driven sense of municipal system and no account of functional variations, and a formal account of normative system with no account of functional variations, it is extremely difficult to find any argumentative basis in Raz's theory for identifying the "other" normative system from which "adoption" is the only possible relationship of incorporation on the grounds of foreignness. Raz is admittedly rather unambitious in his claims for the "adoption" view and the precision it can bring to demarcation of legal from non-legal normative systems. At the close of "The Identity of Legal Systems" in *The Authority of Law* Raz writes,

> That a norm is identified as one the courts ought to apply by the fact that it is a norm of a certain society, association, or state is no indication whether or not it is part of the system. Legislation by reference is a familiar technique; for example, a statute passed in one country adopting by reference the civil code of another country. No other formal distinction will succeed in drawing a reasonable dividing line. The reasons for enforcing the norm, and the attitude of the courts and the legislature to its enforcement, are the crucial factors.[24]

Returning to the challenge posed by the decision-making authority of the university president, it seems that Raz's view of legality and the scope of legal system has run full circle from rejection of Hart's view to renewed endorsement of its fundamentals. Rejection of an official-based account of legality in favor of an institutional emphasis on primary law-applying institutions is insufficient to distinguish the office and operations of the university president from legal-normative institutions and officials. Addition of the requirement that legal-normative institutions exhibit systematic claims of comprehensiveness, supremacy, and openness serves only to show that the university president's office and decisions might amount to a borderline case of

---

24. Raz, *supra* note 4, at 102.

legality, far down the hierarchical chain of legal norm-applying institutions and their use of recognized and adopted norms. The deepened structural account of legality and legal system offered by Raz in replacement of the practice-oriented, official-based Hartian view must ultimately face the borderline case of the university president via precisely what it proposed to abandon—a view rooted in the characteristic "attitudes" or point of view of officials of norm-creating and norm-applying institutions. This deeper structural account of legal system undoubtedly advances our understanding of municipal legal system in various ways, yet it does not face the indeterminacy problem head-on: it relegates to the status of borderline case of legality and system-membership incapable of further precision what appears to be a fairly simple, ordinary challenge in the case of the office of university president and exercise of the powers of that office. The inability of Raz's view to handle this challenge should shake the confidence of those hoping that the municipally-based theory will be of use in handling the new crop of complex challenges we have identified in the Introduction and explore further below, as well as in succeeding chapters.

2.2.2 Parochialism

The second source of doubt about the adequacy of Raz's account of legal system in functional explanation of legality is the ability of the notion of a legal system as a comprehensive, supreme, and open normative system to explain all instances of legal systems. For example, Finnis argues that the claims of comprehensiveness, supremacy, and openness, while made by positive legal systems, are necessarily unjustified or fictitious, since there are principles of the natural law (of a distinctly international order) which ultimately govern the content and force of any particular national legal order.[25] Even within the

---

25. Finnis writes:
But we must not take the pretensions of the modern state at face value. Its legal claims are founded, as I remarked, on its self-interpretation as a complete and self-sufficient community. But there are relationships between men which transcend the boundaries of all *poleis*, realms, or states. These relationships exist willy-nilly, in manifold and multiplying ways, in three of the four orders: for there is physical, biological, ecological interdependence, there is a vast common stock of knowledge (including

analytical tradition, Andrei Marmor argues that the claim of supremacy is only a contingent, and not a necessary feature of legal systems.[26] He writes

> Those who maintain that the law must, as a matter of its essence, claim such supremacy over other normative domains, face a very serious problem regarding the history of law. It is arguable that medieval legal systems, for example, had no such claims to supremacy. On the contrary: positive law was seen as an exception to customs, traditions, religion, and in general, social practices long in force. Thus the law, as a relatively exceptional normative source, could only intervene within the narrow space left open by these other normative sources.[27]

Marmor's view is shared by Tamanaha, who argues that another problem is that

> . . . it is not clear that even state legal systems today meet Raz's conditions. Many theorists as well as citizens would say that there are protected spheres of private activity which the law has no power over (thus it is not comprehensive), and many would assert that there are normative orders superior to law (like religion or morality). Raz qualifies his account by asserting that what counts is that legal systems *claim* comprehensiveness

---

> knowledge of each other's existence, concerns, and conditions), and there is a vast common stock of technology, systems of intercommunication, ideological symbolisms, universal religions . . . Thus there is no reason to deny the good of international community in the fourth order, the order of reciprocal interactions, mutual commitments, collaboration, friendship, competition, rivalry . . . If it now appears that the good of individuals can only be fully secured and realized in the context of international community, we must conclude that the claim of the national state to be a complete community is unwarranted and the postulate of the national legal order, that it is supreme and comprehensive and an exclusive source of legal obligation, is increasingly what lawyers would call a "legal fiction".

JOHN FINNIS, NATURAL LAW AND NATURAL RIGHTS 149–150 (1980).

26. ANDREI MARMOR, POSITIVE LAW AND OBJECTIVE VALUES 39–42 (2001). *See also* Neil MacCormick, who writes ". . . [states] are apt to seek to redefine all forms of institutional order as existing only by delegation from and permission of the state itself. But philosophical understanding of law and state should not give credence to overweening pretensions of states. States cannot turn their own contingent triumphs into necessary truths." NEIL MACCORMICK, QUESTIONING SOVEREIGNTY 24 (1999).

27. Marmor, *supra* note 26, at 40.

and supremacy. But it is not obvious that legal systems routinely make such claims, especially those systems understood in terms of limited law-making powers obtained by delegation from the people. The notions of comprehensiveness and supremacy are especially dubious when one considers that in many societies today there are several 'legal' systems asserting authority within the same jurisdictions. Consider, for example, that citizens in European countries are subject to national law, the law of the European Union, public and private international law, as well as the direct effect of human rights (i.e. the International War Crimes Tribunal, and the trials of the East German border guards), not to forget other applicable bodies of law like the lex mercatoria and the GATT, as well as various bodies of religious law for adherents. In the context of such various competing and overlapping claims to authority, it makes little sense to give primacy to the features of comprehensiveness and supremacy.[28]

The objections raised by Marmor and Tamanaha are important, and can be compounded if we return to one of the prima facie legalities we identified in chapter one. For example, in explaining intra-state forms of legality—network governance, shared governance, federalism, etc.—there is often a disposition to speak of sub-systems in which legal systems house sub-legal systems. Such a framework preserves the idea that there is a supreme legal system—the state legal system—which supports the practice and existence of subordinate legal sub-systems. On Raz's account, however, only the authorizing, supportive state legal system is a genuine legal system, with all other normative systems providing norms which are capable of being adopted by the supreme state legal system. Here we show how Raz's theory of a legal system distorts rather than illuminates the existence and nature of intra-state forms of legality.

Consider first the various forms of shared governance. Our example in the Introduction was the recent creation of the First Nations Tax Commission, described by the Government of Canada as "a shared governance organization which requires that appointments to the governing body be made by both the Government of Canada and at least one other government or organization."[29] There are of course a

---

28. Brian Tamanaha, A General Jurisprudence of Law and Society 140 (2001).

29. See First Nations Tax Commissioner Appointment Regulations, http://www.fntc.ca/en/supporting-legislation/regulations/first-nations-tax-commissioner-appointment-regulations (last visited October 29, 2009).

variety of ways of interpreting the force of shared governance in this situation and we leave unaddressed for the moment the question of whether First Nations possess sources of law giving them the capacity to participate meaningfully in some kind of sovereignty-like division or shared authority. For now it is enough to note that the commission poses difficulties for Raz's account of legal system as a comprehensive, supreme, and open normative system of law-applying institutions: what exactly is the nature of the First Nations Tax Commission? Is it part of the legal system itself, as a law-applying institution that in combination with others claims to be comprehensive, supreme, and open? Or is it outside the legal system, but nonetheless capable of being supported and its norms and practices adopted by the legal system of Canada? As we argued above, Raz's account leaves intact the problem of indeterminacy at the edges of legal systems, and so is at its core unable to answer these questions. But more importantly, it is likely that framing the key questions in terms of relations between systems may be the wrong approach.

If the view of legal systems as comprehensive, supreme, and open normative systems is adopted to attempt to understand the relation between a Canadian legal system and an aboriginal legal system, we are likely left with a distorting picture of legality. Either (i) we begin from the presumption of the supremacy of the Canadian legal system, and suppose that aboriginal legal systems are capable of being supported as non-legal normative systems, or (ii) we begin from the presumption of the supremacy of aboriginal legal systems, which are capable of supporting or adopting the norms of federal, provincial, and territorial institutions, which, if considered to be law-applying institutions, derive their validity from the aboriginal legal systems.[30] Neither view, however, seems plausible. Interpretation (i) outright ignores the way in which the Government of Canada and indeed the First Nations Tax Commission understand and practice their relation, whereas interpretation (ii) distorts the practices of recognition which

---

30. This is not an entirely fanciful view, since some aboriginal groups have expressed the relation of authority in this way. See, e.g., an account provided in DALE TURNER, THIS IS NOT A PEACE PIPE: TOWARDS A CRITICAL INDIGENOUS PHILOSOPHY 4–5 (2006). See also John Borrows, *Constitutional Law from a First Nation Perspective: Self-Government and the Royal Proclamation*, 28 UNIVERSITY OF BRITISH COLUMBIA LAW REVIEW 1–47 (1994).

are well understood to give rise to Canadian law, whether legitimate or not in the eyes of aboriginal communities. To view the state as a comprehensive, supreme, and open system thus leaves us with an inadequate understanding of shared governance arrangements such as the First Nations Tax Commission, which, if anything else, is better understood to relate or refer to the legal order of Canada rather than depend upon it or even authorize it. Similarly, it makes little sense to suppose that the First Nations Tax Commission itself constitutes a hierarchical legal system that provides the reason for the validity of the larger Canadian legal order. This way of proceeding—supposing that legal systems must make claims of comprehensiveness, supremacy, and openness—yields only a duality of distorting pictures of legality, rather than a unified account free of inadequate presumption. For this reason, we believe it is misguided to ask about the relation between distinct legal systems of the state and First Nations if these are to be understood as comprehensive, supreme, and open normative systems. As we shall argue in later chapters, what is of greater interest is not the possible relations between distinct legal systems that claim to be comprehensive, supreme, and open, but the diverse ways in which distinct institutions coordinate their normative practices and share normative powers.

It is important to note that the issues of self-government raised by the First Nations Tax Commission are situated within a larger context of federal and provincial government practices and policies that aim to recognize and accommodate aboriginal groups in Canada in a way that acknowledges a sharing of sovereignty rather than a delegation of power as a hierarchical model of legal system would suppose. Perhaps the best evidence of widespread and growing shared governance is the conclusion of several comprehensive claims agreements between aboriginal groups and territorial, provincial, and federal governments since 1975. Several aboriginal claims policies have been implemented by the federal government in the last three decades, but perhaps the most interesting is the current "Inherent Right Policy" established in 1995. As Gibran van Ert and Stefan Matiation write,

> In its Inherent Right Policy, the government of Canada recognizes the inherent right of self-government as an existing Aboriginal right under section 35 [of the *Constitution Act, 1982*]. This recognition is based on the view that the Aboriginal peoples of Canada "have the right to govern themselves in relation to matters that are internal to their communities,

integral to their unique cultures, identities, traditions, languages and institutions, and with respect to their special relationship to their land and their resources."[31]

As van Ert and Matiation note, the Inherent Right Policy identifies three lists of powers, some of which may be included in particular comprehensive claims agreements, and others which remain with territorial, provincial, and federal institutions. Yet most importantly for our purposes, the status of the comprehensive claims agreements is typically not understood as a kind of delegated federal or provincial power, or as private, non-official or non-institutional practices that may derive authority or legitimacy from federal or provincial government. In those situations in which the comprehensive claims agreements are practiced, they are understood to be constitutive forms of power-sharing, recognizing at the same time inherent rights of First Nation's peoples and acquired rights of established federal and provincial governments. A hierarchical model of legal system is simply unable to explain accurately this kind of phenomenon. Equally important, such forms of shared governance or power-sharing resist explanation in terms of legal systems that claim to be comprehensive, supreme, and open: a federal government which recognizes distinct spheres of power of self-government for aboriginal groups cannot be understood to be claiming to govern comprehensively since it is precisely recognizing that there are areas of conduct and decision-making that are immune from its legal regulation.

Evidence against the adequacy of the view of legal systems as comprehensive, supreme, and open normative systems can also be adduced from examination more broadly of federal-provincial relations in states such as Canada, Australia, and the US. The distinguishing feature of federated states is of course a constitutional division of power among central and territorial-based governments, each assigned separate and sometimes overlapping spheres of authority. Yet, as we saw above, on Raz's view we are unable to say whether the systems of provincial law form part of the Canadian legal system, or whether these are non-legal systems whose norms and perhaps

---

31. Gibran van Ert and Stefan Matiation, *Labour Conventions and Comprehensive Claim Agreements, in* THE GLOBALIZED RULE OF LAW: RELATIONSHIPS BETWEEN INTERNATIONAL AND DOMESTIC LAW 213 (O.E. Fitzgerald ed., 2006), quoting from DIAND, ABORIGINAL SELF-GOVERNMENT (1995).

institutions are capable of being adopted by an open federal legal system. Alternatively, on Raz's view of legal system we might also be left with a familiar but likely implausible possibility: perhaps one can presume the supremacy of a provincial legal system, perhaps that of Ontario, and conclude that other provincial legal systems as well as the federal legal system derive their validity from Ontario law. This is the inevitable picture that results from a hierarchical understanding of the nature and relation between legal systems.

At this point we should return to a version of an objection to our position which we identified in the last chapter: the objection that we have exaggerated the difficulties facing a particular argument from a particular analytical theorist. We might be faulted here for subjecting Raz's view to criticisms it simply need not meet. Its general and formal focus is on municipal systems, and that limited scope might justify its regarding some problems as outside its explanatory responsibility. As we noted again in this chapter, clear cases of legality and legal norm-applying institutions are compatible with the absence of clear borders between legal and non-legal norms and institutions; and sharp borders should not be sought where they cannot nor need not be had. It is important to see that this objection again misses the mark, since the conclusion it draws is radically premature. There are several reasons for rejecting the objection.

First, as a meta-theoretical-evaluative matter, while it is reasonable to resist demands for precision where it cannot or need not be had, resistance cannot simply stop after reminding readers of the need to accept a tolerable degree of vagueness in accounts of key concepts, and indeterminacy in their application. The reader is owed an account of the appropriate standards of tolerance. What vagueness is acceptable? What indeterminacy? And how does this bear on the drawing of the border between general and particular jurisprudence, formal and material accounts of legal system, and indeed the importance of conceptual tools such as "legal system" in explanation of legality? Specification of such a standard is in conspicuously short supply in dominant analytical accounts of legality and legal system.

Second, we are concerned with borderline cases as explanatory challenges to be met by an adequate general jurisprudence, and not merely as evidence of defects in the approaches of Hart and Raz. Our worry is that "borderline" cases might reveal inadequacies in the very features of the concepts employed in analytical explanations.

If analytical legal theorists have failed to offer adequate dis
criteria for the identification of legal officials or law-apply.
tions, this might not simply reveal that there are borderlir
legal officials or law-applying institutions, but rather that
cepts themselves cannot serve the purpose of explaining the
conditions and borders of legal systems. Perhaps another the
notion is required. Raz notes that his definition of a law-a
institution will need to be *modified* to account for re-trials, a
and courts with non-final authority.[32] Here we can ask abo
extent of the required modifications, and whether these might
surprising conclusions. These are open questions, and raise cond
that run deeper than mere identification of borderline cases. In
view, the presence of borderline cases may be evidence that analyt
legal theory has devoted too much effort to attempts to mitigate cc
signment of particular cases to the category of "inexplicable borde
line instance," failing to recognize that theoretical victory might lie i
finding ways to account for these apparently borderline cases, even
at the cost of a changed conception of what counts as the core
experience to be explained.

Third, by pressing the suitability of theoretical accounts of legal
officials and law-applying institutions at the purported core and
apparent borders, we may find borderline cases where we did not
expect to find them. Indeed, there is something quite odd about an
analytical legal theory that might suggest that the legal systems of
Canada, the United States, and Australia, as federal systems, are borderline instances of legal system. As we have also seen, intuition
might tell us that university presidents, even those authorized by
statute, do not occupy an office properly regarded as legal, whose
decisions are properly regarded as legal norms. Somewhat alarmingly, our best analytical theories seem to have difficulty handling
these sorts of examples, and that difficulty amounts not just to rele-
gating them to the category of "borderline" but whether to relegate
them at all. Indeed, they might even represent a clear case of official
activity constituting legality given existing theoretical resources. If
apparently borderline cases are ultimately too many, too diverse, and
too compelling to ignore, we might be driven by our new understanding

Prof. Zaffar Bugtti, Esq. LL.B. (Hon) LL.M. J.D.
Former Senior Professor & Attorney at Law (UK & USA)
Specialist in Medical & Surgical Law

4 Barclay House
Well Street
London E9 7RA
United Kingdom

E-mail:
profzbugtti@yahoo.co.uk
Skype: profbugtti

Flat 503 Sambara Tower
Thandi Sarak
Hyderabad
Sindh, Pakistan

---

32. Raz, *supra* note 4, at 110. *See also* footnote 23 above.

of the diversity of phenomena needing explanation to give serious consideration to renovation of the central explanatory concepts we have grown accustomed to using under the approaches lumped together, however awkwardly, as analytical legal theory.[33]

These reasons against releasing Raz's view from responsibility for a clearer, more precise account of legality's borders tend to lead us back to one of his foundational assumptions and its effect on his view: the assumption of the primacy of the case of municipal legality as experiential source and explanatory focus of a general jurisprudence of legality and legal system.

2.3 STATE-CENTERED HIERARCHY

In the last chapter we noted two ways in which Hart's view embodies an assumption and argument regarding the hierarchical nature of law. Hart's view identifies a hierarchy of legal norms ranked by the rule of recognition, and in the context of modern municipal systems of law, a hierarchy of officials that establish, vary, and apply those legal norms. Hart famously summarizes the foundation of one possible rule of recognition as "the Queen in Parliament enacts. . . ." Raz's view also depends on a presumption of hierarchy, yet it is a different sort of hierarchy, which appears at a different place in Raz's theory. In place of a chain of validity of the sort familiar from Hart's Oxfordshire Council example, Raz holds something more like a "web" view: law exists when there is a sufficiently connected web of law-applying institutions, which range from courts to police: "[c]ourts, tribunals, and other judicial bodies are the most important example of primary organs. But other officials, such as police officers, may also be primary organs."[34] A plausible reading of Raz would suppose that it is the collective, diffuse practice of these law-applying

---

33. *See generally,* WILLIAM TWINING, GLOBALISATION AND LEGAL THEORY (2000) for the view that shifting legal phenomena—both within but especially between nation-states—calls for re-consideration of the conceptual commitments of classical and contemporary legal positivism. More recently see WILLIAM TWINING, GENERAL JURISPRUDENCE: UNDERSTANDING LAW FROM A GLOBAL PERSPECTIVE (2009).

34. Raz, *supra* note 4, at 110.

institutions or primary organs that gives rise to law, and not the particular status of any one of them, even while the decisions of appellate courts might often be the best guide to understanding the membership and weight of legal norms of the system. The legality of the social situation accounted for in these terms is found in the combination of elements set out, not in the characteristics of any one element. Even as the title of supreme courts tends to support the interpretation that they claim supremacy over everything they survey, it is important to see that Raz does not suppose that comprehensiveness, supremacy, and openness are claims made by particular institutions in legal systems; rather, they are the product of systems of institutions, perhaps usefully regarded as epiphenomenal emergent properties of a system.

Yet Raz's assumption of the importance of the municipal system embodies a different kind of hierarchy, a sort of meta-theoretical-evaluative view that municipal legal experience is sufficiently central to experience of law that reliable inferences might be made from municipal legal system to meaningful, even if in some ways limited, contributions to general jurisprudence. We have asserted in general terms above the worry that the assumption of the importance of municipal legal system might lead to errors of emphasis, omission, inclusion, exclusion, and so on, all distorting the general picture of legality emerging from Raz's analysis. That line of criticism may now be amplified.

The nature of legal system as an epiphenomenal, emergent property of a web of institutions seems fundamentally connected with a hierarchical view in the sense that law, in Raz's view, only emanates from activities of a state that is co-constituted by the legal system,[35] and so conceptually rules out for inclusion within the picture of legal system any prima facie legal social phenomena which do not emerge from the decisions or support of state institutions.[36] In other words, Raz's view supposes that in the order of normative institutional practices—i.e., those practices in which there are institutions capable of making decisions that are binding even if wrong—only those that

---

35. Raz, *supra* note 4, at 99.

36. Such a view has been recently described as "statist." *See* Roger Cotterrell, *Transnational Communities and the Concept of Law*, 21 RATIO JURIS 1–18 (2008).

can be attributed as part of a system that claims to be comprehensive, supreme, and open can be deemed law. All other normative practices and systems, such as sports leagues, universities, corporations, industry-led standards, and perhaps provincial norms, are non-legal to the extent to which they are not part of a comprehensive, supreme, and open normative system. Their practices can be supported by law, but they cannot themselves generate law or be considered legal, and as such they are beyond the scope of a general jurisprudence. As almost any legal pluralist will point out, however, this is a particularly narrow view of the subject-matter of legal theory, as it severely restricts consideration of the range and sources of norms which govern norm-subjects.[37] According to legal pluralists, local, customary, and sub-cultural norms, among others, often compete with and trump official state laws in practice, and as such demand in various ways theoretical attention. We will develop our view in contrast to legal pluralism in later chapters, but at this point we should note our agreement: the set of norms, normative practices, and normative institutions deserving consideration by analytical jurisprudence is far larger than the set of official state norms, normative practices, and normative institutions.

What can we conclude, then, about the descriptive-explanatory use of the concept of a legal system as a comprehensive, supreme, and open normative system in explanation of state legality? Two quite different observations seem clear: first, if the concept is unable to determine the boundaries of actual legal systems, it risks being over-inclusive such that any institution connected to core norms and institutions is part of a state legal system. This, we think, is a significant limitation of the account's capacity to carry out successful functional explanation of the borders of legal systems. We attempted to demonstrate this consequence by arguing that Raz's notion of adoption is incapable of serving the role he attributes to it, of distinguishing member norms and institutions from non-member norms and institutions in legal systems. Second, the concept risks being under-inclusive in severely restricting the range and source of norms and institutions, as well as normative orders, possibly warranting the

---

37. *See, e.g.,* Tamanaha, *supra* note 28. *See also* Sally Engle Merry, *Legal Pluralism,* 22 LAW AND SOCIETY REVIEW 869–896 (1988).

title of "legal." Why should only state norms and institutions be considered legal and so the proper focus of analytical legal theory? As we have argued, these problems are particularly troublesome for adequate functional explanation of state law. We shall now show that they take on new force in explanation of non-state legality.

2.4 NON-STATE LEGALITY

Preceding argument has shown that although Raz's account provides a more sophisticated structural explanation of the identity and borders of legal systems, it is nonetheless still inadequate in functional terms, since the account (i) provides little explanation about how to determine the boundaries between legal norm-applying institutions and non-legal norm-applying institutions, and (ii) it seems to fail to explain accurately several familiar instances of municipal legal systems. It was also argued that part of the reason for the failure of Raz's account on functionalist grounds was that the notion of a legal system as a comprehensive, supreme, and open normative system has built into it a misleading and false picture of hierarchy, in which law-applying institutions are presumed to rank above and support the norms and practices of other normative systems. The argument, however, was largely restricted to the problem of explaining the identity and borders of single municipal legal systems considered in isolation. Yet if a hierarchical understanding of determinate law-applying institutions offers a poor explanation of single municipal legal systems, it becomes critical to consider whether the same is also true in contexts where there may be several systems relating to each other in various ways verging on legal order. In this section we show the additional shortcomings of the view of legal systems as comprehensive, supreme, and open normative systems when attempting to explain relations *between state legal systems and between non-state actors across states.* Like Hart, Raz does not suppose that a state-centered legal theory needs to be tested against other forms of purported legality; but in testing Raz's theory to account for non-state forms of legality we suppose again that we gain further theoretical ground in general jurisprudence than both Hart and Raz all while presuming less about the centrality of the experience of the law-state.

2.4.1 Hierarchy and the European Union

The dominant approach to viewing the relations between legal systems is to presume a supreme legal system that authorizes or provides the validity for subordinate systems, much like a legal system provides support for the creation and enforcement of private contracts. The distorting effects of reliance on this approach can be seen clearly in its application to supra-state normative phenomena such as the European Union. While the goal of the Union is integration, theorists committed to the state idea of legal system must observe that a *systems clash* better describes the relation between member-state legal systems and a European Union legal system.[38] If member-state legal systems are hierarchically-organized and claim to be comprehensive, supreme, and open, it is impossible for them to recognize the authority of superior legal orders and still remain independent legal systems. Similarly, the European Court of Justice has observed that the norms of European Community law are supreme,[39] which in turn means that the European Union's legal system, to be a legal system, must claim supremacy, comprehensiveness, and openness to support the legal-normative practices of member-states. This is a consequence of Raz's theory, but it is also a now familiar Kelsenian issue.[40] As we saw in the last chapter part of Kelsen's epistemological postulate presumes that all valid legal norms must be viewed as a unitary system. In numerous works Kelsen applied his "monistic" view to the

---

38. H.P. Glenn, *Doin' the Transsystemic: Legal Systems and Legal Traditions*, 50 McGILL LAW JOURNAL 863–898 (2005), at 896.

39. Case 6/64 Costa v. ENEL 1964 E.C.R. 585.

40. Some of the literature on Kelsen's theory applied to the EU includes: Ines Weyland, *The Application of Kelsen's Theory of the Legal System to European Community Law: The Supremacy Puzzle Resolved*, 21 LAW AND PHILOSOPHY 1–38 (2002), Catherine Richmond, *Preserving the Identity Crisis: Autonomy, System and Sovereignty in European Law*, 16 LAW AND PHILOSOPHY 377–420 (1997), Neil MacCormick, *Beyond the Sovereign State*, 56 THE MODERN LAW REVIEW 1–18 (1993), Nick Barber, *Legal Pluralism and the European Union*, 12 EUROPEAN LAW JOURNAL (2006), 306–329. For an application of Raz's view to the European Union, see Julie Dickson, *How Many Legal Systems?: Some Puzzles Regarding the Identity Conditions of, and Relations Between, Legal Systems in the European Union*, 2 PROBLEMA: ANNUARIO DE FILOSOPHIA Y TEORIA DEL DERECHO 9–50 (2008).

relation between state law and international law, and always reached the same conclusion: if one begins from the presumption of state law, international law must be viewed as deriving its validity from state law and completing the norms of state law.[41] In this view, state law is superior and international law is subordinate. Alternatively, if one begins from the presumption of international law, each state's law is to be viewed as deriving its validity from international law and the norms of each state's law are understood to complete the international legal norms. In this view, international law is superior and state law is subordinate. However, whether one begins from the presumption of state law or international law is entirely a matter of choice from the perspective of legal theory:

> In our choice between them, we are as free as in our choice between a subjectivistic and an objectivistic philosophy. As the choice between the latter cannot be dictated by natural science, so the choice between the former cannot be made for us by the science of law. In our choice, we are obviously guided by ethical and political preferences. A person whose attitude is one of nationalism and imperialism will naturally be inclined to accept the hypothesis of the primacy of national law. A person whose sympathies are for internationalism and pacifism will be inclined to accept the hypothesis of the primacy of international law. From the point of view of the science of law, it is irrelevant which hypothesis one chooses. But from the point of view of political ideology, the choice is important since tied up with the idea of sovereignty.[42]

A choice certainly seems inevitable, and perhaps serves well to characterize accurately the set of relations between some state legal norms and some international legal norms.[43] But surely the choice is

---

41. Indeed, in this view, one must begin from the presumption of a particular state's law, in which case not only international law but also the law of every other state derives its validity from and completes the norms of the first state's law.

42. Hans Kelsen, General Theory of Law and State 388 (Anders Wedberg trans., 1961). See also, e.g., Hans Kelsen, Principles of International Law 587 (Robert W. Tucker ed., 1966) and Hans Kelsen, Sovereignty, in Normativity and Norms: Critical Perspectives on Kelsenian Themes 535–6 (Stanley L. Paulson & Bonnie Litschewski Paulson eds., 1998).

43. However, Kelsen hedges his bet on this. He writes "[t]he two monistic theories may be accepted or rejected in the face of any empirically given stipulations of positive national or international law—just because they are

only inevitable if one begins with Kelsen's epistemological postulate of unity. In other words, a choice must be made only if one shares Kelsen's monistic view of the world of legal norms. We saw in the last chapter that Kelsen's monistic view of the relation between state law and international law suffers from a decisive flaw, noticeable when one attempts to apply it in descriptive-explanation of the phenomena. As Hart observes, for norms to form part of the same legal system, there must be actual practices of recognition of those norms by systemically-connected law-applying institutions. Otherwise, a cognitive hypothesis of validating purport will distort more than illuminate.

In the context of the European Union, Neil MacCormick offers a rather different criticism of Kelsen's monistic view. MacCormick supposes that it is not an option to argue that in fact the legal systems of member-states and European Community law are unconnected. Evidence of mutual recognition is easily gathered from the practices of member-state courts and the European Court of Justice, and the various union-constituting treaties.[44] Instead, MacCormick advises that we give up the commitment to monism and hierarchy in thinking about the relations between legal systems, and adopt instead a view of juridical pluralism:

> No state's constitution is as such validated by that of any other, nor is it validated by Community law. For each state, the internal validity of Community law in the sense mandated by the 'supremacy' doctrine results from the state's amendment of constitutional and sub-constitutional law to the extent required to give effect and applicability to Community law. On the other hand, the Community's legal order is neither conditional upon the validity of any particular state's constitution, nor upon the sum of the conditions that the states might impose, for that would be no Community law at all. It would amount to no more than a

---

epistemological hypotheses that do not carry any implications in that respect." KELSEN, GENERAL THEORY OF LAW AND STATE 388. Kelsen's view here is perhaps the clearest, most explicit preference for structural over functional explanations of legality to be found in analytical legal theory.

44. The core treaties include the Treaty Establishing the European Steel and Coal Community (1951), the Treaty Establishing the European Economic Community (1957), the Treaty establishing the European Atomic Energy Community (1957), The Maastricht Treaty on European Union (1992), the Treaty of Amsterdam (1997), the Treaty of Nice (2001), the Treaty of Lisbon (2007).

bundle of overlapping laws to the extent that each state chose to acknowledge 'Community' laws and obligations. So relations between states *inter se* and between states and community are interactive rather than hierarchical. The legal systems of member-states and their common legal system of EC law are distinct but interacting systems of law, and hierarchical relationships of validity within criteria of validity proper to distinct systems do not add up to any sort of all-purpose superiority of one system over another.[45]

In MacCormick's view it is nothing less than a failure of imagination to suppose that legal systems must always interact with each other by trying to subordinate the other. There is no logical or sociological necessity for a hierarchical relation between systems. MacCormick writes

> The key question becomes whether there can be a loss of sovereignty at one level without its inevitable and resultant re-creation at another. Is sovereignty like property, which can be given up only when another person gains it? Or should we think of it more like virginity, something that can be lost by one without another's gaining it—and whose loss in apt circumstances can even be a matter for celebration? This book is dedicated to the latter view.[46]

This is a superb and colorful way of putting the question, but although the move away from Kelsen's monistic view may be sound, it is important to be clear in characterization of the move so that its success may be properly assessed. In particular, two related observations about the meta-theoretical value of system can be made. First, MacCormick supposes that we need to dissociate the idea of legal system from the idea of a supreme, comprehensive, and open normative system. A member-state legal system which relinquishes some of its legal-normative power to another legal system can no longer claim to be either supreme or comprehensive. Nor can a European Community legal system claim supremacy or comprehensiveness since it must share, through the principle of subsidiarity, legal-normative power with member-state legal systems. However, if neither member-state legal systems nor a European Community legal system claim to be supreme, comprehensive, and open, in what sense does it still make sense to speak of distinct systems, especially if these

---

45. NEIL MACCORMICK, QUESTIONING SOVEREIGNTY 117–8 (1999).
46. *Id.* at 126.

all interact in that both member-state institutions and European Community institutions must recognize and apply both member-state law and European Community law?[47] Second, the "interactive" nature of the relations between member-state legal systems and between member-state legal systems and a European Community legal system needs careful elucidation. Yet here it appears that MacCormick's own statement of juridical pluralism risks being unable to explain the interaction at all. MacCormick notes that

> It follows also that the interpretative power of the highest decision-making authorities of the different systems must be, as to each system, ultimate. It is for the ECJ to interpret in the last resort and in a finally authoritative way the norms of Community law. But equally, it must be for the highest constitutional tribunal of each member-state to interpret its constitutional and other norms, and hence to interpret the interaction of the validity of EC law with higher level norms of validity in the given state system.[48]

This account raises two rather odd puzzles. First, if the highest decision-making authorities are each claiming supremacy to interpret the relation between member-state law and European Community law, what MacCormick claims are interacting systems look more like two hierarchical systems talking past one another. Each system includes both the norms of member-states and the European Community, but they differ in their view of which norms are supreme

---

47. *See, e.g.*, Ines Weyland, *The Application of Kelsen's Theory of the Legal System to European Community Law: The Supremacy Puzzle Resolved*, 21 LAW AND PHILOSOPHY 1–38 (2002). Weyland writes: "It does not seem plausible to maintain the separateness of an order which, like that of the Community, depends for the operation of basic functions, like law making, application and enforcement, on the institutions of another legal order." *Id.* at 35.

48. MacCormick, *supra* note 45, at 118. MacCormick also writes: "A pluralistic analysis . . . shows the systems of law operative on the European level to be distinct and partially independent of each other, though also partially overlapping and interacting. It must then follow that the constitutional court of a member-state is committed to denying that its competence to interpret the constitution by which it was established can be restricted by decisions of a tribunal external to the system. This applies even to a tribunal whose interpretative advice on points of EC law the constitutional court is obligated to accept under Article 177. Conversely, the ECJ is by the same logic committed to denying that its competence to interpret its own constitutive treaties can be restricted by decisions of member-state tribunals." *Id.* at 119.

and who has supreme authority to interpret the norms. So wherein lies the interaction? Second, if a detached observer can begin from either the perspective of the ECJ, in which case European Community law is supreme, or the perspective of a member-state court, in which case that member-state's law is supreme, we are left with a choice not unlike the choice identified by Kelsen between the primacy of state law or the primacy of international law. Indeed, what MacCormick identifies as juridical pluralism in which distinct legal systems sit in an interactive rather than hierarchical relation in fact looks no different from Kelsen's monism, a view MacCormick is attempting to escape. Kelsen's view is after all pluralist in precisely the same way: epistemologically, there are several ways in which to view the unity of the world of legal norms: these can be viewed by presuming the primacy of state law (with a further presumption in the choice of a particular state's law), or by presuming the primacy of international law. In the context of the European Union, one can begin from the presumption of member-state law or from the presumption of European Community law. [49] How, then, is MacCormick's pluralist view different from Kelsen's monism? Yet more importantly, has MacCormick's view successfully freed legal theory from hierarchical ways of thinking about legality, especially since it appears that his view amounts to a plurality of hierarchies?

Part of the answers to these questions would need to include rejection of the claim that individual decision-making authorities must claim to be supreme or hold ultimate interpretive power. Advancing earlier argument, such a view relies on the mistaken idea that institutions within societies with law must always be arranged in a hierarchy. For example, while the European Court of Justice makes supremacy claims *for European Community law* on some matters (claims which are made also by some member-state courts[50]), in descriptive-explanatory terms it should not make supremacy claims *for its supreme authority*

---

49. Catherine Richmond nicely explains the pluralism in Kelsen's view applied to the context of the European Union in *Preserving the Identity Crisis: Autonomy, System and Sovereignty in European Law*, 16 LAW AND PHILOSOPHY 377, 408–419 (1997). *See also*, Nick Barber, *Legal Pluralism and the European Union*, 12 EUROPEAN LAW JOURNAL 306, 326 (2006).

50. *E.g.*, Factortame Ltd v. Secretary of State for Transport (No. 2) [1991] 1 A.C. 603.

to settle European Community law.[51] If it did, its claims would be best taken as fictions, rather than sound descriptive explanations of legality in the European Union. The explanation draws precisely on our earlier analysis of the misleading hierarchy in Hart's account of the rule of recognition. The existence and content of European Community law depends on the horizontal practice of numerous and diverse European Community institutions and member-state institutions. Interaction emerges, then, when institutions mutually refer to the same set of laws and recognize each other's spheres of power. For example, in an illuminating article on the relation between European Community law and state law, Imelda Maher identifies several instances where European Community directives were implemented by statute by the UK Parliament and related regulatory institutions on issues such as food safety, toy safety, and beer labeling.[52] In some instances, the directives were implemented exactly, whereas in other instances the directives underwent some modification. Here, then, there is mutual reference between member-state institutions and European Union institutions, but the claim of hierarchy would be misplaced since member-state institutions are capable of modifying the directives to suit their purposes and in any case have the bulk of the institutional responsibility to enforce those directives. Successful interaction has also occurred between member-state courts and the European Court of Justice. Observing a conflict between norms on a right to abortion in the Irish constitution and the European Convention on Human Rights and Freedoms, MacCormick notes that "[t]hrough a sequence of highly newsworthy and controversial decisions, the Irish Court and the ECJ succeeded in avoiding a direct conflict."[53] What is interesting in this instance is that member-state institutions and European institutions can divide normative power within a single legal order despite a lack of convergence on some norms or agreement on a hierarchy of norms.

---

51. Case 6/64 Costa v. ENEL 1964 E.C.R. 585. *See* THE RELATIONSHIP BETWEEN EUROPEAN COMMUNITY LAW AND NATIONAL LAW: THE CASES (Andrew Oppenheimer ed., 1994).

52. Imelda Maher, *Community Law in the National Legal Order: A Systems Analysis*, 36 JOURNAL OF COMMON MARKET STUDIES 237–254 (1998).

53. MacCormick, *supra* note 45, at 111.

The key points in all of this are (i) interaction is best explained as interaction *between institutions*, and not between systems, and (ii) there is no need to suppose that the institutions are hierarchically ordered. We can also observe that when interaction fails, it fails between institutions. As Julie Dickson notes, the European Court of Justice's view on the relation between national law and European Community law is

> unequivocal: owing to the special nature and purpose of the EC legal order, EC law has primacy over national law in cases of conflict, and this is so whether the national law in question is prior or subsequent to the EC measure, even as regards potential clashes between EC norms and norms in national constitutions, and even if this requires significant alterations in past national constitutional practice as regards, for example, whether the judicial suspension and disapplication of primary legislation is legally possible in the jurisdiction in question.[54]

Yet while the ECJ's view is clear, many member state courts take a different view. The German federal constitutional court offers an instructive example. Dickson writes

> Even in the present more co-operative chapter in this tale, the federal constitutional court and the national constitutional order more broadly has reserved to itself the right to determine whether the EU legal system is continuing to fulfil the conditions that the German constitutional order has imposed.[55]

To the extent that such disagreement over where legal supremacy lies is carried out in practice, and particularly in the form of conflicting legal decisions and legal uncertainty, it would show failure of interaction between the German federal constitutional court and the European Court of Justice, but not necessarily between German and European Union legal orders, which are comprised of several other institutions besides their respective courts.[56] Indeed, to contemplate constitutional crisis on the basis of rival supremacy claims made by

---

54. Dickson, *supra* note 40, at 23 [author's notes omitted].

55. *Id.* at 24 [author's notes omitted].

56. This is not to say, of course, that a persistent failure to interact between the German Court and the European Court might not trigger a web of failures of interaction among several other associated institutions. Notice, though, that if such widespread failure emerged, the failure of legality between Germany and the European Union would be attributable to widespread

member-state courts and the European Court of Justice is to ignore the thick web of established integrated legal-normative practices of trade, currency, and employment that exist across states in the European Union. Once again, it is a profound mistake, as we argued above and in the last chapter, to believe that the activities of any particular institution, court or legislature, determine the foundation, identity, and borders of a legal system.

So, although we are sympathetic to MacCormick's approach, it becomes increasingly less clear what meta-theoretical value is to be gained by holding onto the idea of legal system in understanding the European Union. Legal systems which no longer claim to be comprehensive, supreme, and open are far removed from the dominant analytical understanding of legal systems as state legal systems, and further, focus on legal systems draws attention away from, albeit inadvertently, the nature and diversity of *interaction between institutions*. We suspect that what is more interesting in thinking about supra-national legality such as European Community law is the nature and force of emerging interaction between the various European Union and member-state institutions. Once legality is seen to depend upon non-hierarchical practices of institutions interacting with each other across old state boundaries, talk of separate legal systems seems only more and more distracting.

2.4.2 Trans-State Legality Revisited
The distorting effects of reliance on the idea of legal system as a comprehensive, supreme, and open normative system with determinate edges can be seen in its application to supra-state normative phenomena. Yet the mischief created is perhaps greatest in its application to trans-state normative practices of non-state actors. We suggested in the Introduction that the inadequacy of an official, state-centered view of legality and legal system, in which normative practices have the nature of law only to the extent to which they are incorporated by systems which claim to be comprehensive, supreme, and open, is usefully illuminated in its distorting explanation of prima facie legal phenomena. The example of trans-state legality we identified was

---

inter-institutional failure, and not simply the failure of interaction between the two high courts.

drawn from the context of ocean resource governance: the Greenland Conservation Agreement, signed by the Atlantic Salmon Federation of North America, the North Atlantic Salmon Fund of Iceland, and the Organization of Fishermen and Hunters in Greenland on the basis of recommendation by the Scientists of the International Council for the Exploration of the Sea, provides for a seven-year moratorium on commercial salmon fisheries in Greenland's territorial waters, beginning in 2007, effectively continuing an existing moratorium from 2002. The agreement represents collaboration of three avowedly non-governmental organizations and an expert organization with the devolved government of Greenland to develop an enforceable obligation regarding harvesting of a natural resource. The location of the natural resource within Greenland's borders is a key yet temporary part of a cycle in which the resource is sometimes located beyond Greenland's borders, within the borders of the home states of the non-governmental organizations. Two of the non-governmental organizations are harbored in Greenland, yet the other is a sort of transboundary hybrid. The Atlantic Salmon Federation explains itself as

. . . an international, non-profit organization that promotes the conservation and wise management of wild Atlantic salmon and their environment. ASF has a network of seven regional councils (New Brunswick, Nova Scotia, Newfoundland, Prince Edward Island, Quebec, Maine and Western New England). The regional councils cover the freshwater range of the Atlantic salmon in Canada and the United States.[57]

It is worth noting that in this specification of transboundary members between Canada and the United States, the federation does not purport to map precisely to legal boundaries–its regional councils include one in "Western New England," a geographically and resource-driven delineation which maps to no extant legal jurisdiction, since Western New England is comprised of several states. The Home Rule Government of Greenland, which is to enforce the agreed obligation, is a statutory entity of the state of Denmark, a product of the Greenland Home Rule Act 1978.[58] That act provides

---

57. "New Atlantic Salmon Conservation Agreement—Safer Ocean Migration Ensured", http://www.asf.ca/news.php?id=99. (Last visited July 27, 2007).

58. Act No. 577 of 29 November 1978 THE GREENLAND HOME RULE ACT http://www.stm.dk/_p_12712.html (last visited Oct. 30, 2009).

Greenland with status as a "distinct community" enjoying "home rule" over specified affairs.[59] Those specified affairs include via s. 8(1) those natural resources which include the fisheries: "The resident population of Greenland has fundamental rights in respect of Greenland's natural resources."[60] Fundamental rights and devolved powers are limited, but not by fiat from the central authorities in Denmark. Rather, although the central authorities retain jurisdiction over foreign relations including agreements regarding use of natural resources,[61] in situations in which exercise of that jurisdiction affects Greenland interests, central authorities are obligated to consult with Greenland home rule authorities.[62]

As we noted in the first chapter, an official, state-based analytical theory of law explains the legality of the Greenland Conservation Agreement in a distinct way. It is only law to the extent that the officials of Denmark, Canada, and the United States recognize and practice it, or to the extent that their legal systems are open systems capable of supporting its practice. In other words, while the NGOs and the council of scientists played a key, constitutive role in bringing about the practice of a peremptory norm against fishing salmon in a region of the North Atlantic, their formative role only amounted to the creation of a social practice capable of being supported or incorporated into the law of any of the parent state legal systems. We are now in a position to see more clearly why such an explanation is inadequate, since it distorts the contributory role of the NGOs in the

---

59. S.1(1) "Greenland is a distinct community within the Kingdom of Denmark. Within the framework of the unity of the Realm, the Greenland home rule authorities shall conduct Greenland affairs in accordance with the provisions laid down in this Act." http://www.stm.dk/_p_12712.html (last visited Oct. 30, 2009)

60. Id.

61. Section 11: (1) The central authorities of the Realm shall have jurisdiction in questions affecting the foreign relations of the Realm. (2) Measures under consideration by the home rule authorities which would be of substantial importance for the foreign relations of the Realm, including participation by the Realm in international cooperation, shall be discussed with the central authorities before any decision is taken.

62. Section 13: Treaties which require the assent of the Folketing and which particularly affect Greenland interests shall be referred to the home rule authorities for their comments before they are concluded.

formation of a peremptory norm. We contend that, without a determinate functional explanation of the borders of law-applying institutions, of the kind Hart and Raz purport to offer, it is unwarranted to conclude that the practice of the Greenland Conservation Agreement by the NGOs are simply constitutive of a non-legal social agreement, as opposed to constitutive of a legal agreement practiced by law-applying institutions which sit at indeterminate borders between state legal systems. Yet it seems equally unwarranted, we think, to suppose that their normative practices may not in fact constitute a new legal order on its own, detached from their state legal systems' authority altogether. The agreement, after all, aims to govern by deliberate act and practice the Greenland salmon fishery, and does so by using norms generated from civil society groups informed by a scientific expert institution rather than state institutions.

The Greenland Conservation Agreement, while unique in some respects, is certainly not unique as an example of non-state transboundary activity that ought to count as legal phenomena and so is deserving of theoretical attention. Outside analytical legal theory, trans-state law-like practices enjoy growing theoretical attention.[63] For example, in *Bottom-Up International Lawmaking: Reflections on the New Haven School of International Law*[64] Janet Koven Levit provides three illuminating case studies of international law—on trade and export subsidies, climate change regulation, and corporate social

---

63. For excellent accounts, literature surveys, and case studies, *see, e.g.*, Steve Charnovitz, *Nongovernmental Organizations and International Law*, 100 AMERICAN JOURNAL OF INTERNATIONAL LAW 348–372 (2006), Harold Hongju Koh, *Transnational Legal Process*, 75 NEBRASKA LAW REVIEW 181–208 (1996), Paul Berman, *A Pluralist Approach to International Law*, 32 YALE JOURNAL OF INTERNATIONAL LAW 301–330 (2007), Paul Berman, *From International Law to Law and Globalization*, 43 COLUMBIA JOURNAL OF TRANSNATIONAL LAW 485–556 (2005), Janet Koven Levit, *Bottom-Up International Lawmaking: Reflections on the New Haven School of International Law*, 32 YALE JOURNAL OF INTERNATIONAL LAW 393–420 (2007), Robert B. Abdieh, *From Federalism to Intersystemic Governance: The Changing Nature of Modern Jurisdiction*, 57 EMORY LAW JOURNAL 1–30 (2007), and Roger Cotterrell, *Transnational Communities and the Concept of Law*, 21 RATIO JURIS 1–18 (2008).

64. Janet Koven Levit, *Bottom-Up International Lawmaking: Reflections on the New Haven School of International Law*, 32 YALE JOURNAL OF INTERNATIONAL LAW 393–420 (2007).

responsibility—to challenge the following three prevalent assumptions about international law: (i) states, and their executives in particular, create international law; (ii) treaties are the primary form of international law; and (iii) international law is a "*deliberate* process that political elites carefully choreograph from the top down."[65] In each case Levit shows how normative practices giving rise to new international legal norms can emerge as concrete rule-oriented practices of private, industry-based or lobby-based actors pursuing common aims. Most interesting, in the case of climate change regulation, there is evidence that the joint normative practices of non-governmental organizations, trade associations, investment funds, and intergovernmental organizations have served to bind and alter the behavior of multinational corporations and state governments in the United States. So not only is international and transnational legality emerging from the practices of non-state actors, i.e., *actors who are precisely not to be understood as system representatives*, non-state international and transnational legality often comes to shape future practices of states, which as a result may have to relinquish their self-identity claims of comprehensiveness, supremacy, and openness.

This chapter and the last have attempted to show two things: first, there are several new problems for analytical legal theory to face, which emerge from consideration of several forms of non-state prima facie legal phenomena which have become too pervasive to ignore any longer. Second, we have attempted to display the central shortcomings as we see them in Hart's and Raz's contributions to general jurisprudence when assessed in functional explanation of the nature and borders of both state and non-state legality. Although each sought to provide a truly general jurisprudence, their commitments to explaining the characteristic features of the law-state, with its associated ideas of legal officials, legal system, and hierarchy, have rendered their theories unbalanced in various ways and incapable of carrying out their purported tasks and reaching beyond the law-state to investigation of prima facie novel forms of legality. In the next chapter we propose to return to some of the basic aims of analytical jurisprudence, through exploration of meta-theoretical goals that have fallen out of sight, as we begin to lay out the features and commitments of our positive view.

---

65. *Id.* at 398–399.

3. META-THEORETICAL-EVALUATIVE MOTIVATIONS

Much of the work of preceding chapters might be characterized as predominantly negative, finding where others have, in our view, come up short in their explanations of legality. This chapter begins significantly more positive argument, exploring meta-theoretical considerations that motivate our provision of the next chapter's inter-institutional account of legality. We are particularly concerned here with the way analytical legal theorists have sought to identify what they claim are necessary features of an admittedly contingent concept of law, and the meta-theoretical-evaluative virtues appropriate to such an explanation. In discussion below of Hart's and Raz's explanatory departure from the perspective of the ordinary person's experience of the law-state, we explore how their attempts to provide a robust explanation of the necessary features of that contingent concept has become so bound up in the particular jurisprudential problems of the social situation it explains that more basic problems have been overlooked. These issues include: the problem of knowing when sufficient phenomena of the right kind have been examined, warranting assertion that a conceptual explanation has been provided, and the further problem of specifying conditions under which a contingent concept changes or must be changed, and some one or more of its necessary features jettisoned. These basic problems loom large when an admittedly contingent concept meets a challenge to its adequacy, as the state-based explanation of the concept of law meets a challenge from the phenomena we have advanced in the Introduction, as well as phenomena at least anticipated by analytical theorists. In the second part of this chapter we identify and explore elements of a response to these problems, while leaving complete response until the close of the next chapter's provision of the inter-institutional theory.

Here we advance an adapted and extended ordinary person's perspective to meet the new phenomena, and although we leave state-based analytical approaches to legality mostly behind us, we investigate the merits of other largely descriptive-explanatory approaches to gathering and responding to changes in social phenomena informing explanation of the necessary features of a contingent concept. This discussion opens the way to our advocating what we call a "narrative concept of law" suited to interests of the adapted and extended perspective we advance, and the way the inter-institutional theory elaborated in the following chapter, Chapter 4, responds to changes in the phenomena of legality—capturing, we hope, the kind of interplay or circulation between phenomena and concept promised but not delivered by prior analytical theory fixated on the steady-state version of law-state.

3.1 PERSPECTIVE, PHENOMENA, PROBLEMS, AND METHOD

A useful introduction to question of perspective in analytical legal theory can be drawn from Isaiah Berlin's views on the task of philosophy:

> The perennial task of the philosophers is to examine whatever seems insusceptible to the methods of the sciences or everyday observation, e.g. categories, concepts, models, ways of thinking or acting, and particularly ways in which they clash with one another, with a view to constructing other, less internally contradictory, and (though this can never be fully attained) less pervertible metaphors, images, symbols and systems of categories . . . This socially dangerous, intellectually difficult, often agonizing and thankless, but always important activity is the work of philosophers whether they deal with the natural sciences or moral or political or purely personal issues. The goal of philosophy is always the same, to assist men to understand themselves and thus operate in the open, and not wildly, in the dark.[1]

Berlin's conception of philosophy has plenty to offer the sort of philosophy of law that claims that explanation of the concept and practice of law is a worthwhile activity, battling misleading metaphors and systems of categories famously derided by Bentham as "fictions," and aiming to assist the self-understanding of readers of philosophy of law who intend to "operate in the open." Just what it means to "operate in the open" using a theory of a practice is of course

---

1. Isaiah Berlin, *The Purpose of Philosophy, in* THE POWER OF IDEAS 35 (H. Hardy ed., 2000).

controversial, involving as it does a range of meta-theoretical-evaluative commitments and virtues.

3.1.1 The Ordinary Person's Perspective and a Contingent Concept

Hart and Raz have done spectacularly well in stating and operating according to a group of commitments and methods suited to bringing the practice and problems of law "into the open" for contribution to elucidation of a particular, contingent concept of law. Their theorizing from the departure point of the ordinary person's perspective on law has guided a collection of social phenomena relevant to the expansion of the concept of law contingently held in that perspective. That perspective has further guided identification of particular jurisprudential problems arising in social phenomena collected, while clarifying the nature of the methods brought to bear on problems. Yet this success has come with two odd costs. First, elucidation of a socialized contingent concept, approached from a particular perspective, has required such intensive work to characterize the necessary features of that concept, that the concept's contingency has been little investigated, and the particular state-, and legal system-focused concept arising from Hart's and Raz's approach has been mistakenly viewed as a universal descriptive-explanatory account useful as the mark and measure of all legality. The second, associated odd cost is found in method: although Hart, Raz, and others have bootstrapped their explanations of necessary features of the contingent concept they elucidate (official, rule, adjudication, etc.), their use of this method has not been accompanied by explanation of the basis on which they know that the contingent concept has been bootstrapped from a sufficiently broad range of phenomena and possible explanatory categories, Nor, we shall argue, has the bootstrapped relation between description and category been reviewed with appropriate frequency to ensure that the concept really is responsive to the social phenomena. Put bluntly, we are offered a renewable concept and the tool for its renewal, but no account of what triggers operations of a renewal process.

What is odd about all of this is that an avowedly contingent concept, contingent precisely because perspective and phenomena may vary, has become so clearly static, a result perhaps better explained by sociology of the profession than any reason to do with the nature of legal theory. The static picture of the steady-state modern legal system has unfortunately taken analytical legal theory to the point where what was once seen as admirable clarity in depiction of legality is now derided as a view hobbled by failure to adapt. Jeremy Waldron's recent work is a treasure trove of sharp observations on this score, taking analytical legal theorists to task for their failure to engage international law, and most recently criticising the immobility of the structural dimension of analytical legal theorists' contingent concept of law: "there is some effrontery in the positivists' insistence that every legal system contains a rule cast in terms that represent the positivists' own jurisprudential position!"[2] What is even more odd than the ossification of the contingent concept is the fact that two key parts of their meta-theoretical-evaluative commitments are quite clearly usable, with appropriate supplementation, in efforts to respond to the challenge of characterizing legality beyond the stable, modern law-state. The perspective driving Hart's and Raz's accounts of a contingent concept of law can be varied, as they have made clear, and as we explore further immediately below. Similarly, the bootstrapping method they have applied to elucidate features of legality prominent in the law-state from which they depart is equally capable of being applied to other features of legality prominent from a different perspective and departure point. Changes to these two parts of their explanatory approach tend to transform what a renovated approach will regard as the most compelling jurisprudential questions. The exposition in Chapter 4 of the inter-institutional account will be needed to explain how to face some of those problems. What is more interesting as a meta-theoretical-evaluative matter, however, is that analytical legal theory's aim to provide a descriptive-explanatory account of law as it is, responsive to changing phenomena and enabling its hearers to "operate in the open," need not be abandoned as too-closely tied to the experience and fate of the modern law-state. Since we propose to provide an adapted and extended perspective of the sort we think adequate to the task of facing the new prima facie legal phenomena that extant analytical approaches seem unable to handle, it is worth exploring further the perspectival approach we attribute to Hart and Raz and seek to modify.

---

2. Jeremy Waldron, *Who Needs Rules of Recognition?*, in THE RULE OF RECOGNITION AND THE U.S. CONSTITUTION (M.D. Adler & K.E. Himma eds., 2009).

Berlin's understanding of the purpose of philosophy provides a useful backdrop to examination of Hart's conception of the perspective offered by his philosophy of law. Where Berlin saw philosophy providing conceptual categories enabling the self-understanding of actors seeking to live and act free of external and self-imposed deception, Hart's philosophy of law famously departs from the point of view and knowledge of the ordinary man in a typical—and clearly not every—modern municipal state. This limited starting point was clearly not merely a reflection of a commitment to ordinary language analysis or a sort of deflationary pragmatism about characterization of law. As Hart makes clear later in discussion of the separation thesis, theorizing from a point of view is at least partly a result of having come down on one side of the constrained choice left open to legal theorists between a wide, positivist concept of law, which includes as law morally evil laws and legal systems, and a narrower, natural law concept of law, which excludes from law morally evil laws and legal systems.[3] He writes:

> If we are to make a reasoned choice between these concepts, it must be because one is superior to the other in the way in which it will assist our theoretical inquiries, or advance and clarify our moral deliberations, or both . . . It seems clear that nothing is to be gained in the theoretical or scientific study of law as a social phenomenon by adopting the narrower concept: it would lead us to exclude certain rules even though they exhibit all the other complex characteristics of law. Nothing, surely, but confusion could follow from a proposal to leave the study of such rules to another discipline, and certainly no history or other form of legal study has found it profitable to do this. If we adopt the wider concept of law, we can accommodate within it the study of whatever special features morally iniquitous laws have, and the reaction of society to them.[4]

Where Berlin saw philosophy seeking categories better adapted to enabling men to live in the open, Hart in the narrower context of philosophy of law chooses here a wide concept of law characterized by its capacity to assist in theoretical inquiries or moral deliberation or both. Hart's explicit "choice" of concept is shaped by more than considerations weighing for and against "wide" and "narrow" concepts.

---

3. *But see* JOHN FINNIS, NATURAL LAW AND NATURAL RIGHTS 26–8 (1980) for a correction to this misinterpretation of natural law theory.

4. H.L.A. HART, THE CONCEPT OF LAW 209–210 (1994).

This choice of concept is located in the era-, experience-, and purpose-specific nature of the problems salient from Hart's departure point in the modern, typical law-state experienced by the ordinary man. As Hart puts it: "I hope it has enabled people both to take a wider view of the nature of law and problems that arise in the running of the legal system and it has given them a kind of sensitivity to accuracy, clarity of expression, and detail."[5] Hart did not delve deeply into the limits of his approach, yet the fact that he took care to state its perspective and purpose and to mark it as a choice indicates his awareness that his view is limited, and ought not to be taken as providing a universal account or addressing the only salient problems for analytical legal theory. There is room left, in Hart's meta-theory, for other perspectives motivated by other problems. Beyond simply leaving room for other perspectives, there is positive evidence of his acceptance that other kinds of explanation, driven by different perspectives, might actually be needed rather than just possible. In his 1968 remarks on Kelsen's examination of the relation between state and international law, Hart writes:

> The effort of criticism of these difficult doctrines is, I think, rewarding because it brings to light at least two things. First, it shows that there is a good deal of unfinished business for analytical jurisprudence still to tackle, and this unfinished business includes a still much needed clarification of the meaning of the common assertion that laws belong to or constitute a system of laws, and an account of the criteria for determining the system to which given laws belong, and of what individuates one system from another. Secondly, the examination of certain features of Kelsen's doctrine takes us to the frontiers at least of the logic of norms and their interrelationships, and perhaps points beyond the frontiers to the need for something more comprehensive than the present familiar forms of deontic logic.[6]

Not only, it seems, is there room for variation amongst perspectival approaches to analytical jurisprudence, but extension of methods beyond the norm-focussed approach to "something more comprehensive" is allowed as a possible need, all in aid of addressing the

5. Interview with David Sugarman, *quoted in* N. LACEY, A LIFE OF H.L.A. HART: THE NIGHTMARE AND THE NOBLE DREAM 357 (2004).

6. H.L.A. Hart, *Kelsen's Doctrine of the Unity of Law, in* ESSAYS IN JURISPRUDENCE AND PHILOSOPHY OF LAW 310 (1983).

"unfinished business" of jurisprudence. These observations are far from the view gathered by many readers from *The Concept of Law*, that the basic framework for understanding of law is in hand and all that remains is to specify its details, as Raz might be thought to have done in examining the concept of legal system. It is particularly noteworthy that Hart's 1961 rejection of Kelsen's view of international law seems to be reconsidered later, and in the spirit of Hart's own move to reconsideration, we aim to take up tasks at the "frontiers" Hart once thought closed.

Joseph Raz, with the benefit of time to view the debate over Hart's legacy, is acutely aware of the meta-theoretical commitments, virtues and limitations of his own position, and has taken steps to combat misinterpretation of it. Although it is convenient for those seeking a comprehensive, monolithic view of law to suppose that Raz's conceptual explanation of "law" and "legal system" expresses necessary and sufficient conditions for application of those concepts, seen, for example, in his assertion that municipal systems embody claims to comprehensiveness, supremacy, and openness, this is not in fact his view. In his 1998 article *Two Views on the Nature of the Theory of Law* he offers four arguments against the utility of the explanatorily thin "necessary-and-sufficient-condition view of conceptual explanation,"[7] and follows those arguments with some intriguing observations regarding the nature of explanations appropriate to law and inquirers into law:

> There is no uniquely correct explanation of a concept, nothing which would qualify as *the* explanation of the concept of law. There can be a large number of correct alternative explanations of a concept. Not all of them will be equally appropriate for all occasions. Appropriateness is a matter of relevance to the interests of the expected or intended public, appropriateness to the questions which trouble it, to the puzzles which confuse it. These vary, and with them the appropriateness of various explanations. The appropriateness, aptness, or success of explanations presupposes their truth. But the truth of an explanation is not enough to make it a good explanation. To be good it also has to be appropriate, that is (a) responding to the interests of its public and (b) capable of being understood for what it is by its public (should they be minded to understand it).

---

7. Joseph Raz, *Two Views on the Nature of the Theory of Law: A Partial Comparison, in* HART'S POSTSCRIPT 10 (J. Coleman ed., 2001).

> The relativity of good explanations to the interests and capacities makes them ephemeral and explains why philosophy has a never-ending task. It also helps explain away the impression that philosophy is forever engaged in a fruitless debate on unsolvable questions.[8]

Where Hart sought a "wide" concept of law appropriate to expansion of the ordinary person's understanding of law, Raz offers a still more detailed argument in a very similar vein, with interesting echoes of Berlin's conception of the nature, purpose, and limits of philosophy and philosophical explanation. Although Raz does not specifically stipulate a starting point in the understanding of the ordinary person, he is still committed to a perspectival approach in which the "appropriateness" or "aptness" of an explanation is relative to inquirers' purposes.[9] Those purposes vary over time, and, echoing Berlin, the task of philosophy of law is accordingly never-ending even while those explanations that are accepted as "apt" or "appropriate" are constrained by the need to be composed of true propositions. Raz later points to facts weighing against Austin's explanation of state sovereignty, showing that Austin's view fails on the truth of its propositional content, independent of questions of internal coherence, "aptness" in the eyes of readers, and so on. This view is not unique to Raz amongst contemporary analytical theorists. Jules Coleman, using a notion of "our" concept which we have previously criticized as obscure, takes pains to identify a possible cause of revision to "our" concept while insisting that even the changeable concept he elucidates is best characterized in terms of what is necessary to that concept, however temporary it may be:

> Having emphasized the conceptual or descriptive projects of jurisprudence, several points should be noted. The descriptive project of jurisprudence is to identify the essential or necessary features of *our* concept

---

8. *Id.*

9. Raz emphasizes elsewhere his generally perspectival approach which takes seriously the task of providing the basis for self-understanding: "[i]t is a major task of legal theory to advance our understanding of society by helping us understand how people understand themselves" JOSEPH RAZ, ETHICS IN THE PUBLIC DOMAIN: ESSAYS IN THE MORALITY OF LAW AND POLITICS 237 (1995). *See also* Joseph Raz, *Can There Be a Theory of Law?*, *in* THE BLACKWELL GUIDE TO THE PHILOSOPHY OF LAW AND LEGAL THEORY (M.P. Golding & W.A. Edmundson eds., 2005).

of law. No serious analytic legal philosopher—positivist or interpretivist—believes that the prevailing concept of law is in any sense necessary: that no other concept is logically or otherwise possible. Nor do we believe that our concept of law can never be subject to revision. Quite the contrary. Technology may someday require us to revise our concept in any number of ways. Still, there is a difference between the claim that a particular concept is necessary and the claim that there are necessary features of an admittedly contingent concept.[10]

Coleman's view is especially interesting as a continuation of Hart's and Raz's assertion of the contingency of the concepts they elucidate. Where Hart and Raz write quite generally about the circumstances under which a contingent concept might need modification, Coleman is rather more specific. Technology, he says, "may someday require us to revise" our concept. Yet even this is quite unspecific. What ought we to look for in technologies to see whether they are the ones that might force revision of the concept? And when ought we to look? And how are we to conduct revision of a concept whose necessary features have been so painstakingly examined and explained? This gap between contingency and triggers for revision warrants exploration of how analytical legal theorists have generated at least the first version of their contingent concept of law, associated with characterization of the modern law-state.

A recent statement by Coleman about the relation between conceptual analysis and descriptive sociology is a useful entry into understanding an analytical approach to the relation between a contingent concept and the empirical evidence on which it is grounded:

... investigation of [common] usage serves to provide us, in a provisional and revisable way, with certain paradigm cases of law, as well as helping us to single out what features of law need to be explained. Descriptive sociology enters not at the stage of providing the theory of the concept, but

---

10. Jules Coleman, *Incorporationism, Conventionality, and the Practical Difference Thesis*, 4 LEGAL THEORY 381, 393, n.24 (1998). For analysis of the idea of "our concept," *see* John Oberdiek & Dennis Patterson, *Moral Evaluation and Conceptual Analysis in Jurisprudential Methodology*, 10 CURRENT LEGAL ISSUES: LAW AND PHILOSOPHY 60–75 (2007), and Brian Leiter, *Beyond the Hart/Dworkin Debate: The Methodology Problem in Jurisprudence*, and *Postscript to Part II: Science and Methodology in Legal Theory*, in NATURALIZING JURISPRUDENCE: ESSAYS ON AMERICAN LEGAL REALISM AND NATURALISM IN LEGAL PHILOSOPHY (2007).

at the preliminary stage of providing the raw materials about which one is to theorize.[11]

At least three things are worth noticing here, bearing in mind Coleman's suggestion above that "technology" might "someday" require revision of our concept. The first is Coleman's assumption rather than argument for the existence of an available sense of "common" usage that captures rather than presumes the evidential basis for explanatory categories including, as we saw in Chapter 1, hierarchically-ordered "legal officials" whose determinate practices constitute the existence and content of legal systems as well as their borders. Second, although Coleman is right to recognize the importance and place of descriptive-sociology as a stage of semi-pre-theoretical data collection, he and others say very little about how we are to know that we have begun with an adequate collection, and that we have a method for systematically adapting our view to new or changing phenomena. Third, what is still missing, as it is in Hart's and Raz's views, is an account of how events such as technology introductions trigger a repeated rather than preliminary and one-off reference to "descriptive sociology"—whose status as a body of facts, a method, or something else is unclear. This apparent absence or omission is not just a matter of our needing to read more deeply in the analytical legal theory literature. The omission seems rather to be a function of the way analytical legal theory's departure from the perspective of the ordinary person has driven both its bootstrapping strategy and its conception of successful, complete bootstrapping ending at a rich yet static account of the modern law-state.

3.1.2 Bootstrapping in Analytical Legal Theory

Analytical legal theory's attachment to bootstrapping has deep roots: the core of the approach is visible in Austin's assertion that it is "only the systems of two or three nations which deserve attention since it is only a few systems with which it is possible to become acquainted, even imperfectly."[12] The immediately preceding claim

---

11. JULES COLEMAN, THE PRACTICE OF PRINCIPLE: IN DEFENCE OF A PRAGMATIST APPROACH TO LEGAL THEORY 200 (2001).

12. JOHN AUSTIN, THE PROVINCE OF JURISPRUDENCE DETERMINED 373 (Prometheus Books, 2000) (1832).

is key: "From these, however, the rest may be presumed." Austin urges explicitly what is implicit in the arguments of Hart and other analytical legal theorists: a rejection of the epistemic closure principle and adoption of bootstrapped explanatory categories. The nature and application of this principle is usefully summarized by Luper. The principle expresses the view that:

> we can extend our knowledge by recognizing, and accepting thereby, things that follow from our knowledge. The qualifications embedded in the following principle (construed as a material conditional) seem natural enough:
>
> K: If, while knowing p, S believes q because S knows that p entails q, then S knows q.

As Williamson (2002) notes, the idea that we can extend our knowledge by applying deduction to what we know supports a closure principle that is stronger than K. It is a principle that says we know things we believe on the grounds that they are jointly implied by several separate known items. Suppose I know Mary is tall and I know Mary is left handed. K does not authorize my putting these two pieces of knowledge together so as to know that Mary is tall and left handed. But the following generalized closure principle covers deductions involving separate known items:

> GK: If, while knowing various propositions, S believes p because S knows that they entail p, then S knows p.

Proponents of closure are likely to accept both K and GK, perhaps further qualified in natural ways. By contrast, Fred Dretske and Robert Nozick reject K and therefore GK as well.[13]

This passage provides the germ of an explanation of why Hart, Raz, and Coleman provide so little explanation of the connection between their conceptual explanations and the empirical phenomena to which these explanations purport to be responsive. They may be committed to denial of the epistemic closure principle to the extent that general q propositions of general jurisprudence have *not* been advanced as justified in virtue of their being entailed by p. Rather, general q propositions have been gained from something other than knowledge of p. In Austin's case, q propositions have been gained via a combination of specific observed propositions regarding named legal systems, and an unexplained operation of "presumption." Austin's motivation

---

13. http://plato.stanford.edu/entries/closure-epistemic/ (Last visited Feb. 2008).

for his at least implicit denial of the epistemic closure principle is clear: he supposes it is not possible to "become acquainted with" more than a few legal systems. This seems on its face to be an empirical limitation driven by a shortage of observed evidence regarding other systems, and not an objection driven by epistemic concerns regarding, e.g., limits to the epistemic accessibility of practices of cultures very unlike one's own. The plausibility of this motivation need not be taken up immediately, since there is the more interesting and pressing matter of the epistemic operation of presumption. Even if knowledge of further legal systems were available, Austin appears to argue, that further knowledge is not necessary when the method of presumption is available to expand q knowledge claims from some limited p claim. As the passage from Luper indicates, if Austin is indeed one of the opponents of the principle of epistemic closure, he is in good philosophical company as contemporary luminaries such as Nozick and Dretske have taken up the battle against the epistemic closure principle, offering reliabilist and other alternatives. Subsequent analytical work from Austin to Coleman might be read, in light of this view of their epistemic commitments, as not just having but *needing* very little connection to a thoroughly specified body of "descriptive sociology." The claims of Hartian and post-Hartian general jurisprudence are epistemically bootstrapped from a few readily available examples of legality and law-states—or in Raz's case "all intuitively clear" instances of municipal legal systems. Those claims regarding the typical, characteristic availability of an official-based rule of recognition are explicitly and intentionally *not* conceived as q entailments of some knowledge claim p that scopes across all, nearly all, or even something like a representative sample of the social situations which q propositions of general jurisprudence are eventually taken to capture. These q claims are bootstrapped: as Rescher puts it, "Any *experiential* justification of a truth-criterion must pull itself up by its own bootstraps . . ."[14] A thoroughly post-Austinian analytical legal theorist might lean on the bootstrapping approach to explain the epistemic status of truth claims made in a general jurisprudence: they are indeed general claims intended to scope over

---

14. NICHOLAS RESCHER, METHODOLOGICAL PRAGMATISM: A SYSTEMS-THEORETIC APPROACH 28 (1977).

all but outlier phenomena of the law-state and legality, and the claims are indeed drawn from limited experience, yet that limited basis is sufficient since truth of these kinds of claims is properly assessed in terms of reliability or some other truth criterion that includes rejection of the epistemic closure principle.

Rejection of our concerns regarding circularity and indeterminacy is relatively easy for a view whose major claims are supported by bootstrapping. Where we allege circularity, there is instead only pseudo-circularity, the appearance of circularity on the assumption that q claims must be underwritten by knowledge of p, where bootstrapping allows q claims on less than full knowledge of p. The indeterminacy objection suffers a similar fate. Where we see indeterminacy an advocate of a bootstrapped set of q claims of general jurisprudence sees exactly the kind of conceptual imprecision to be expected. Those claims do not map back to some known p, and accordingly once assembled together present something like a "picture" of law whose adequacy is assessed not by its having the right kind of retrospective evidentiary links, but by its explanatory value with respect to a wide range of social situations, including those well beyond the experiences from which bootstrapped q claims were gathered. Bootstrapping is arguably a superior way to begin to generate general conceptual accounts of some complex social phenomena whose amount and variety outstrip our descriptive capacities, while we nonetheless want to get on with the business of constructing illuminating general accounts of those phenomena. Apparent indeterminacy of bootstrapped accounts of these phenomena is simply an expected outcome of accounts that aim to have probative explanatory value over complex, incompletely described phenomena, and whatever indeterminacy might be evident in the absence of the "positive criteria" we demand is resolved in practice as courts with a duty to bring finality in delivering decisions that make clear what was unclear. To ask more of our general jurisprudence is to ask for unavailable and unnecessary precision.

This line of response to our objections is perhaps intuitively satisfying, yet it still seems to us to be wanting, but not on the epistemic grounds that seem to be an attractive locus for discussion of the precise nature of the explanatory claims of an analytical general jurisprudence. Rather, we may accept the probative value of bootstrapping (or for that matter Coleman's pragmatism that "recognizes *explanation by embodiment* as a legitimate form of philosophical explanation of a practice"[15]) and still claim that circularity and indeterminacy are found in the approaches surveyed above. Bootstrapping is of course not unconstrained, and similarly Coleman's explanation by embodiment finds principles not just anywhere but embodied in particular practices. Both approaches are only as plausible as their point of departure in practice allows. A return to Austin is again instructive. Austin was explicit in his identification of the data that form his departure point and offered an availability-based reason for not having looked at further examples of systems of law that might *not* bear close resemblance to familiar systems. Austin's explicit statement of the course of his bootstrapping is very helpful to subsequent jurisprudes holding data from more extensive social science description. Austin's depiction of the limits of his starting point leaves later investigators a much clearer sense of which aspects of his general jurisprudence might lack reliability insofar as they are rooted in an excessively limited experiential basis. The same may not, unfortunately, be said of Hart despite his readiness to criticize Austin's general jurisprudence in light of its functional failings insofar as the command theory misrepresented law within democratic political systems. Hart's sometimes universal ambitions for his theory are not clearly underwritten by explanation of the experiential basis from which he draws, and as we have seen in the arguments of later analytical legal theorists, reference to an experiential basis is charitably assessed as tacit or incomplete. The trouble then with the response to our objection is not bootstrapping itself or rejection of the closure principle, but the way in which bootstrapping is conducted—the initial choice of explanatory categories to be bootstrapped from a particular swath of social facts, and just as importantly for a method informing a contingent concept, when those facts are to be revisited. It is not clear just why many analytical theorists have been satisfied with putting their efforts toward increasingly sophisticated depictions of the details of the necessary features of the contingent concept of law associated with the modern law-state and its jurisprudential problems. Such effort has allowed the contingent concept to become static, failing to represent the key analytical meta-theoretical-evaluative

---

15. Coleman, *supra* note 11, at 8.

virtue of systematic—i.e., more than accidental—intuitive responsiveness to new phenomena driving new categories at the "frontiers"
Hart recognized yet failed to face. Perhaps, as Joseph Raz has said,
problems regarding the necessary features of a particular contingent
concept have received attention, while the relation of that contingent
concept to problems of identity and continuity simply fell out of fashion. In *Two Views on the Nature of Theory of Law* Raz suggests that
successful criticism of Kelsen and Austin has left gaps in explanation
of key features of legal life, gaps that remain and are tolerated. Raz
writes, ". . . the problem that their mistaken doctrines were meant to
explain, namely the problem of the identity and continuity of legal
systems, lost its appeal to legal philosophers, who do not mind leaving it unsolved. Interest has shifted elsewhere."[16]

Yet now these questions are very much back *in* fashion. As our
examples in the Introduction show, and as Waldron has reminded us,
it is something of an embarrassment that international law is so little
examined by analytical legal theory. It is equally an embarrassment
that a phenomena-responsive, contingent concept of law has become
static even while its advocates defend as one of its core merits its contingency, and the availability of a phenomena-sensitive method of
concept-elucidation likely to allow that contingent concept to be
highly adaptable to the changing interests of inquirers using it. It is
no longer enough to be open to change: more must be done to be
clear about the range of data the concept captures from the "preliminary stage," and better yet, explicitly stated, actually operating mechanisms for adjustment of the concept in light of novel or mistakenly
omitted data. This call for greater attention to the evidenciary base
supporting bootstrapped explanations is not simply cautionary
emphasis on steps analytical theorists are already committed to
taking: it is identification of an actual imbalance between structural
and functional aspects of analytical explanations of law.

Although the preceding argument may seem a damning indictment
of the shortcomings of the analytical approach, it must be remembered
that we have identified a silver lining to the problems: the perspective
that drove descriptive-explanatory focus on particular explanatory

---

16. Joseph Raz, *Two Views of the Nature of the Theory of Law: A Partial
Comparison, in* HART'S POSTSCRIPT: ESSAYS ON THE POSTSCRIPT TO THE
CONCEPT OF LAW 10 (Jules Coleman ed., 2001).

categories can be varied to meet new phenomena and new categories, and the method used to flesh out categories can be better used. We shall return later in the chapter to adaptation and extension of the perspective, and the way that change of perspective changes the slate of jurisprudential problems central to elucidation of a concept of law apt to the interests driving the perspective. A better use of bootstrapping, capable of facing changing phenomena and categories, will be introduced in the next chapter. For the moment, however, it is worth turning to examine the merits of other descriptive-explanatory approaches to legality that have sought to avoid the distorting effects of presumption of the priority of the law-state as the model of legality, while remaining responsive to novel phenomena. Even while analytical theory has been preoccupied with a state-focused contingent concept of law, investigation of new phenomena has gone on, so we must be mindful that the analytical clarity and phenomena-responsiveness of a revised analytical approach might well learn some useful lessons from other approaches.

3.2 RECENT APPROACHES TO THE PROBLEM OF PERSPECTIVE

3.2.1 System and Set

Hart, in our view, was perhaps unintentionally prescient in pointing to the future of analytical legal theory by seeing international law as a "set" and not a "system," recognizing the possibility of non-systemic forms of legal order, whose relations to the contingently dominant systemic form of legal order need specification. Here, as in many other aspects of our argument, we follow for at least a few strides in the footsteps of Neil MacCormick, who observes that Hart's conception of the rule of recognition opens the way for a sort of legal pluralism to the extent that officials might choose to incorporate into their system the norms of some external source, while nonetheless withholding from regarding that external source as a binding source of law.[17] This explanation enables a Hartian approach to capture the interaction of at least independent legal systems, and likely the

---

17. Neil MacCormick, *Beyond the Sovereign State* 56 THE MODERN LAW REVIEW 1–18 (Jan. 1993).

interaction of legal system with other legal orders. As MacCormick summarizes the explanatory virtue of this approach, "[w]here systems overlap, neither is necessarily a part of the ultimate reason for the validity of the other, nor do we have to presuppose some common reason for, or ground of, validity external to them both."[18] The same goes, ceteris paribus, for overlap between a legal system and another form of legal order such as the set of international laws. And yet, MacCormick observes, "[d]espite the pluralistic or polycentric potentialities he points to in developing his theory, pluralism remains more a potential than an actual virtue of his own work."[19] We have argued above that these potentialities of renovated use of an official-operated rule of recognition likely cannot be made actual, yet valuable lessons may nonetheless be derived from Hart's entanglement with "set" and "system." However one works out or rejects the reasons for even attempting to work out the "polycentric potentialities" inherent in Hart's work, Hart's talk of set and system serves as an alert to the danger of rooting a perspective to law in the experience of the systemic law-state. The addition of "set" to "system" diminishes the analytical centrality of system at very least by adding another explanatory category and its explanation to our tasks, and given the contingency of our concept of law and historical contingency of our practices allows for a "polycentrism" in which legal system is but one form of legal order amongst others. MacCormick, however, cautions against excessive enthusiasm regarding a polycentric view that renders currently obscure "frontier" legal orders into familiar cousins on equal family standing with legal system within our concept of law. MacCormick argues that the potentialities apparent in Hart's argument must be made actual in a way that does not abandon the notion of legal system. MacCormick writes:

> As Joxerramon Bengoetxea points out, the idea of system functions as itself a regulative ideal within legal discourse. Accordingly, in order to make sense of how we argue and discourse about law, we do need to think of system as a concept contained within or encapsulated within our thought and partly regulating or structuring it. Just for that reason, since thought shapes action to some extent, and action establishes structures in the world, the discourse of law can contribute to the existence in the social

18. *Id.* at 9.
19. *Id.* at 9.

world of some at least partly systemic or even systematic orders of behaviour and conduct. But the actualities cannot be expected to reproduce the ideal perfection and structure that belongs to system as a regulative ideal.

System is, then, an idea which any rhetorical or other cognate analysis of law would have to keep prominent in its analysis of the rhetoric of law and is worthy of study for its special rhetorical force. So we cannot get rid of it, though we may put it in its place.[20]

MacCormick is surely right that legal system is an idea that cannot simply be in some sense rejected: it has too great a grip on our every-day talk of law, our special rhetorical talk that helps us to establish even temporarily boundaries between law and non-law, as a regulatory ideal whose aspirational standards have probative and practical value as we try to organize and navigate through the range of kinds of norms purporting to bind us in various ways. Yet MacCormick is surely also right that while indispensable, the idea of legal system may need to be put in its proper place. This is no easy task, and a brief return to MacCormick's own institutional theory of law, examined in the last chapter, will serve to show why. As we saw, MacCormick shares the concern to reduce the role of state law in theorizing about the nature of law, motivated by commitment to explain the nature of many kinds of law, including but not restricted to state law:

The law of the state is for many people, particularly for most legal profes-sionals and law-students, the law that matters most to them. But it is not the only kind of law. International sporting organizations, confederations like the European Union, treaty-based inter-state entities like the Council of Europe, or NATO, and many others, exhibit institutional normative order in their own way too. So do churches and various kinds of religious and charitable organizations. So does the international community as such, certainly since at least the establishment of the Permanent Court of International Justice (whose Statute was adopted by the General Assembly of the League of Nations in 1920) and all the more so since the foundation of the United Nations, the adoption of the UN Charter, and the establish-ment of the International Court of Justice.[21]

In MacCormick's view, law exists wherever there is a set of practiced norms that articulate an ideal for social practice, supplemented by

---

20. *Id.* at 10.

21. Neil MacCormick, INSTITUTIONS OF LAW 2 (2007). *See also* MacCormick, QUESTIONING SOVEREIGNTY 114 (1999).

distinct institutional agencies that serve to settle disputes, create by deliberate act new rules, and enforce decisions and rules.[22] As we will see, MacCormick's view is closest to ours, but there remain some relevant differences in application and emphasis. The most important is his commitment to remain in state-based legal theory: "I make no apology for giving priority to expounding a theory about law in its state and state-like contexts."[23] There is of course nothing objectionable in such priority, so long as the state-based theory is carried out successfully with appropriate attention to the possible limitations of state-based theory. Similarly, our criticisms of the theories of Hart and Raz are not fundamentally criticisms of the project of a perspective-driven, bootstrapped account of legal officials, hierarchy, legal system, comprehensiveness, supremacy, openness, and so on. Rather, our objection is to an approach that amounts to a one-off bootstrapping of those explanatory categories with insufficient attention to the possibility that perspectives and inquirers' interests may change, phenomena may change, and the contingent concept must be adapted accordingly if it is to amount to an evidence-responsive explanation of a concept. MacCormick's comparatively broader theory of law as institutional normative order may in fact succeed where Hart's and Raz's theories did not, addressing a broader range of phenomena using a broader range of explanatory categories while attending to the law-state at the same time. However, there are certain risks. First, in our view MacCormick unduly restricts the range of phenomena addressed: to inter-state unions, and in particular, the European Union. This runs the risk of generating a distorting view of legality in general. Indeed, as we saw in the last chapter, MacCormick's account of the European Union seemed to rely unduly on a conception of hierarchical state legal systems, such that European Union law can only be viewed as a set of dueling hierarchies. Second, by focusing on institutional normative orders such as the European Union, which already enjoys a high degree of systematicity notwithstanding the claim evident in *Van Gend en Loos* that a novel form of legal order is fostered by the European Union, there is a risk of relapsing to a commitment to the systemic law-state view that supposes that legality

---

22. MacCormick, Institutions of Law, *supra* note 21, at chs. 1 and 2.
23. *Id.* at 2.

only exists in well-established, normatively ordered communities with settled institutions. MacCormick assumes this risk when he supposes, in application of his state-based approach, that the law of modern constitutional states is constituted by the practice of "distinct public institutions—"institution-agencies" let us call them—charged with legislative functions, with adjudicative functions, executive-administrative functions, and with law-enforcement functions."[24] Earlier argument about the ability of analytical legal theory to provide a non-circular, determinate account of the identity of legal officials certainly applies to the descriptive responsiveness of an appeal to "distinct public institutions," so MacCormick owes at least an account of how these might be identified.[25] Yet more importantly, by supposing the epistemological priority of state law, a highly institutional form of legality, there are doubts about the theory's capacity to capture inchoate forms and emerging forms of legality as they emerge, for which a general jurisprudence ought to be able to account. The risk associated with presuming that law only exists when a sufficiently developed system of institutional normative order exists also brings with it a danger of leaving under-explained what connects various institutions of law and institution-agencies together into a system. On MacCormick's account, a system exists when there is a sufficiently practiced institutional normative order, understood as

---

24. *Id.* at 35. MacCormick is not the only institutionalist theorist to risk collapse into state-based legal theory by accepting its epistemological presumptions. Peter Morton writes: "The Organizations within the complex include the executive, the armed forces, enforcement agencies, government departments, and a host of bodies associated with them. Clearly, it may be difficult to determine whether an agency is part, or an 'emanation,' of the State. For the purposes of institutional theory, the only test is the extent to which they are, by express constitutive provisions, subject to executive control, i.e., the structure of the State. The difficulties of the agencies on the borderline need not be discussed here; our concern is with the central constituents of this form." [author's notes omitted]

25. Later in *Institutions of Law* he claims that public officials are to be identified by two necessary conditions: (i) their duty is to act in the public interest and (ii) they have power to act unilaterally. Whether we can find such persons is an open question, as is the appeal to any notion of public or common interest (*see, e.g.*, BRIAN TAMANAHA, LAW AS A MEANS TO AN END: THREAT TO THE RULE OF LAW, (2006)).

a collection of shared beliefs, values, and ideals.[26] Yet what exactly shows that institution-agencies form a system? How can we detect the systematicity of institutional normative order, which must exist beyond the mere sharing of beliefs, ideals, and values that is possible by disparate peoples and institutions? These are of course not insuperable difficulties, but they do provide a motivation to find a way of facing legality that follows MacCormick's lead by recognizing the possible plurality of forms of legality in addition to the systemic law-state, yet is free of the tendency his view exhibits, toward a sort of accidental re-emphasis of the law-state as the mark and measure of legality.

As we face this challenge in the next chapter's explanation of the core of our inter-institutional theory, we should be conscious of two dangers accompanying an attempt to broaden the reach of an analytical theory of legality. These dangers arrive from outside analytical legal theory, in sociological and political science approaches to some of the phenomena left unexamined by analytical legal theory since the time of its intensified focus on structural, norm-level aspects of the modern law-state. The first danger is found in the use of social network analysis to capture relations between social actors, and the second is found in the attempt of some international relations theory to associate legality with efficacy and in turn with power.

3.2.2 Network Theory

Our inter-institutional approach owes something to network theory, the sociological method used to characterize the "density" of enabling and disabling flows of resources among social actors.[27] The method allows construction of "maps" depicting these flows, and identification of actors who are comparatively more connected to particular parts of

---

26. MacCormick, Questioning Sovereignty, *supra* note 21, at ch. 1.

27. On network theory and some of its uses, *see* Manuel Castells, End of Millennium (2000), G. Mulgan, Communication and Control: Networks and the New Economics of Communication (1991), Rethinking the Masters of Comparative Law (A. Riles ed., 2001), M. Goodale & S.E. Merry, The Practice of Human Rights: Tracking Law Between the Global and the Local (2007), and S. Burris, P. Drahos, & C. Shearing, *Nodal Governance*, 30 Australian Journal of Legal Philosophy 30–58 (2005).

the network. The method is particularly useful for contrasting official or diplomatic accounts of inter-actor relations, against actual operations of actors. Political economists sometimes use network theory for tasks such as identification of innovators and innovative collaboration patterns within extant organizational structures such as firms, universities, and governments.[28] The method's great attraction, apart from its tracking actual rather than planned or purported interactions, comes with its being not merely relevant to the phenomena as a good theory of the typical may be, but thoroughly *responsive* to the phenomena such that the map changes as relations change. Yet this sensitivity to empirical phenomena comes at a price. When used contrastively to distinguish actual resource flows from theoretically or organizationally predicted flows, the method relies for its probative value on the prior availability of the prediction or organizational mandate against which it is contrasted, and that departure point embodies a particular conception of the network of actors under analysis. The trouble with social network analysis then, is that its responsiveness to phenomena comes at the cost of the need for *prior* (even if revisable) demarcation of relevant data for analysis—borders of the sort the official- and rule of recognition-based account of law could not provide without generating the range of problems we have surveyed. Analysis of systems whose edges are not marked in advance is problematic to say the least. Further problems arise when the social network method is applied to dynamic social situations. Social network analysis and rule of recognition-based approaches are somewhat similar in their response to change in the practices of those actors whose conduct they capture: where the rule of recognition captures change via the assertion that officials' varying practices are in principle nonetheless part of a constant albeit internally varying rule, social network analysis captures time-slices of difference in "density" of relations amongst actors, a little like animated films are composed of separate slightly varying pictures carrying the changing story of the film. Both views might be reproached for a rather thin explanation of *why* change has occurred, what changes are internally motivated and what others compelled by external forces. Nonetheless, it is noteworthy that social

---

28. P.W.B Phillips, Governing Transformative Technological Innovation: Who's in Charge? (2007).

network analysis takes seriously the difference between organizational claim and organizational reality: in its responsiveness to data it seeks to capture the dynamics of social situations, a useful goal in situations such as those faced by legal theory where we must attempt to explain not just steady-state situations such as the modern law-state, but variations and transitions between forms of legal order such as law-states integrating into a novel legal order, devolving, undergoing revolutions, and so on.

3.2.3 International Relations Theory

The key virtue of social network analysis is its responsiveness to the phenomena it portrays, a virtue undeniably attractive to analytical legal theorists seeking a descriptive-explanatory approach to law that seeks a structurally and functionally balanced account of legality that illuminates rather than distorts the phenomena of legality. A similar motivation is evident in a branch of international relations theory that struggles to find a conceptual basis for capturing and distinguishing international legality, associated with determinate, effective legal-normative practices, from merely aspirational and other sorts of standards. In talk of "legalization" scholars in this area often struggle to mark the transition from political argument to legal determinacy in social life, tending to decry vagueness and simplicity as signs of institutional immaturity, and tending to valorize apparent concreteness, complexity, and institutional interconnection as signs of successful legalization. Along the way, despite typical assertions of recognition of the difference between legality and efficacy,[29] the drive to distinguish the determinate, the concrete, and the reliable in legality from the variability of politics often leads into talk of "hard" versus "soft" law on a spectrum or "continuum" of legality.[30] Interestingly, even

---

29. As a particularly noteworthy example co-written by well-known scholars in this area *see:* K.W. Abott et al., *The Concept of Legalization*, 54 INTERNATIONAL ORGANIZATION 402 (2000). "Note that we have defined legalization in terms of key characteristics of rules and procedures, not in terms of effects. For instance, although our definition includes delegation of legal authority (to domestic courts or agencies as well as equivalent international bodies), it does not include the degree to which rules are actually implemented domestically or to which states comply with them."

30. *Id.* at 404, 407.

amongst leading authors, there is often an unresolved tension between the aim of distinguishing and addressing legal phenomena, and a wish to do so without becoming entangled in jurisprudential debates over the nature of law. Abbott et al. attempt this move in their introduction to a special issue of *International Organization* focused on "legalization":

> Our concept of legalization is a working definition, intended to frame the analytic and empirical articles that follow in this volume as well as future research. Empiricist in origin, it is tailored to the phenomena we observe in international relations. We are not proposing a definitive definition or seeking to resolve age-old debates regarding the nature of law or whether international law is "really" law. Highly legalized arrangements under our conception will typically fall within the standard international lawyer's definition of international law. But many international commitments that to a lawyer entail binding legal obligations lack significant levels of precision or delegation and are thus partial or soft under our definition.[31]

Analytical legal theorists may see with some alarm that the method of definition is unflinchingly grasped as the sort of thing appropriate to resolution of debates regarding the nature of law. More alarmingly, Abbott et al. get around the problem of specifying at least some basic understanding of legality sufficient for talk of "legalization" by three unlikely means. (1) Abbott et. al. attempt to reduce the need for a theoretical component of "legality" by naturalizing their view via assertion that their understanding is fundamentally a reflection of empirical phenomena ("tailored to the phenomena"). (2) They appeal to a sense of legality as a matter of usage rather than explanation of a concept, through reference to some unspecified "standard international lawyer's definition." (3) The risk of inadvertently screening out relevant phenomena from analysis by application of an excessively narrow conception of legality is mitigated by stretching the concept of law into "hard" and "soft" versions.

There are of course ready objections for each of these three tactics, and those objections tend to show not just that these authors have run into difficulties, but that there is a place for analytical legal theory not fully occupied by international relations theorists in our long absence. The objections to these tactics are so familiar as to need

---

31. *Id.* at 403.

only quick rehearsal. The first tactic does not do away with the concept of legality so much as it presupposes without explanation a particular interpretation of the concept and set of application conditions for gathering of data for analysis. The second tactic is liable to Dworkin's "semantic sting" arguments urged mistakenly against Hart's views;[32] and the third tactic amounts to a kind of epistemic promiscuity that chooses to place under the same conceptual umbrella even phenomena so different as to warrant quite different treatment as the category's subdivision into "hard" and "soft" indicates, with a resultant failure to distinguish law from politics. It is likely useful to view these criticisms less as a knock-down of an alternative approach to prima facie international legality, and more as a reminder of the need for structurally and functionally balanced accounts of legality—where at least these prominent scholars of international organization demonstrably need a structural account of legality to match, guide, and reflect their empirical findings. An equally important reminder is evident in these scholars' use of the term "legalization" to capture a dynamic process that they depict on a continuum. Although there certainly are social situations that amount to "steady-state" legality, others are dynamic, and a structural account of legality responding to those phenomena must be capable of explaining their dynamic nature qua legal phenomena and not just as effective or powerful norms, and for the purposes of a particular set perspective and not simply the purposes of "international lawyers" whose definition of law and need for determinate propositions of law for professional purposes seem to drive some theorizing about international organization.

This last observation, regarding disparate purposes pursued by legal theorists and theorists of international organization, deserves consideration from what might be called the extended perspective on analytical legal theory offered by Joseph Raz. In addition to Raz's denial of the possibility of a uniquely correct account of the concept of law, his objections to "a necessary-and-sufficient-condition requirement for good explanations" include a reminder that even good

---

32. Ronald Dworkin, Law's Empire, ch. 2 (1986). For a reply, see Timothy Endicott, *Herbert Hart and the Semantic Sting, in* Hart's Postscript 39–58 (J. Coleman ed., 2001).

explanations are not islands: their meaning is gained in part from their place in a larger "web." As Raz puts it:

> Conceptual explanations not only explain the conditions for correct application of a concept ('an act of torture is an infliction of pain or suffering for its own sake or to obtain some benefit or advantage') but also its connections with others ('torture is worse than murder'). We explain concepts in part by locating them in a conceptual web. These aspects of conceptual explanations can be said to be statements of conditions for the application of the concept only by stretching the idea of condition for application.[33]

To say that explanations of concepts are driven by perspective and sit in a web may seem like a step toward Tamanaha-style relativism, so it is worth remembering that Raz also insists that good explanations are composed of true propositions whose relation to evidence must be specified. Yet even "apt" explanations capable of tracking changing objects of explanations are explanations within a broader conceptual context, as torture is understood in connection with murder, and law is understood in a conceptual web whose membership changes, with recent noteworthy additions including "globalization," "transboundary" and "cyberspace." So not only is there no one uniquely correct explanation of the concept of law, but even an explanation suited to the interests of a particular perspective will need adjustment over time to remain useful and comprehensible to its hearers, and that adjustment may be driven by developments external to philosophy of law.

3.3 RENEWED PERSPECTIVE

We are now ready to return to the task of extending analytical legal theory to face the novel phenomena identified in the Introduction, taking the remainder of this chapter to set out what our analysis reveals as the meta-theoretical-evaluative desiderata to be satisfied by the inter-institutional theory of legality set out in Chapter 4. The first task is to offer a renewed perspectival departure point for a descriptive-explanatory account of a broader range of prima facie legal phenomena and the particular jurisprudential problems the phenomena pose.

---

33. Raz, *supra* note 16, at 10.

The fact of novel prima facie legal phenomena looms large in our renewed perspective, which owes a great deal to both Hart and Raz and is intended to be a continuation of their views. Our perspective is that of the ordinary person in the developed world, a world of interconnection and interdependence. Our ordinary person travels much more than Hart's citizen ever did, and our ordinary citizen finds norms in families, or perhaps bunches or clusters, operated by institutional owners of varying authority, from schools to Greenpeace to the British Airport Authority to the U.N. Security Council and Disneyland. Legality and legal norms certainly have a particular practical force in our ordinary person's life, but their nature and force is not well-represented by metaphors of ladders or chains of authority. Rather, a spatial metaphor seems better suited: in the complex web of norms of various kinds encountered by citizens, legal norms represent a kind of upwelling of normative force, especially forceful standards clustered around particular kinds of life events, relatively stable normative reference points in a context of constant competition amongst norms. To be sure, the distinction between legal and non-legal norms is still of interest to this perspective, but it is focused primarily on the fact of clusters of emerging, continuing, varying, and declining legality and their interaction with one another, from business start-up laws at home to manufacturing, labor, and materials sourcing laws far away, and what data privacy means in each place and in between, possibly even in cyberspace. Our account of legality aims to depart from and expand upon this starting point, providing an interpretation that makes sense of those citizens' experiences in ways comprehensible to them as they experience upwellings of normative force in clusters of norms, in the familiar situation of the law-state, and in intra- and extra-state forms, often in systemic fashion, and sometimes in the form of what at least appear to be other kinds of legal order.

From this perspective, familiar with and often dwelling within modern law-states, the problems of jurisprudence associated with those states are present yet receding. As Neil MacCormick puts it, "it is time to escape the tyrannical grip of geo-centric jurisprudence."[34]

---

34. Keith Culver & Michael Giudice, *Introduction*, 2 PROBLEMA: ANNUARIO DE FILOSOFIA Y TEORIA DEL DERECHO 5 (2008).

From our ordinary person's perspective, the borders between law, morality, and coercion remain important, yet Hart's problems are transformed into the problem of understanding the nature and form of legal orders beyond the law-state and *their* relation to morality and coercion, from international humanitarian law penetrating and constraining the notionally sovereign state, to the First Nations Tax Commission we noted in the Introduction. Raz's problems of existence, identity, and continuity of legal systems is likewise transformed: we must now find the mark of legality uniting diverse forms of legal order including yet not limited to legal system. Existence and identity become characteristics of entities whose characteristically and relatively firm border with non-legal norms now includes a further characteristic of relatively vague interpenetration with other legal entities and orders whose changing nature is captured by ideas such as "legalization" and talk of "failed states." In a phrase, our transformed problems are those of "commonality" of the mark of legality across diverse legal orders, and "continuity" of legality in emergence and dissolution— from integration in the European Union to devolution of Scotland and Wales, and the roiling normative chaos of Somalia.

What then will an "apt" descriptive-explanatory account do in response to these transformed problems? It is no small task to get clear of the tyranny of geocentric tyranny, and on to the view from Hart's glimpsed new "frontiers," all while avoiding problems of circularity, indeterminacy, and hierarchy. A structurally and functionally balanced account of legality needs new analytical categories likely to capture without distortion the range of phenomena regarded and spoken of as legal, and those categories must be responsive to a changing set of evidence as legal orders wax and wane, changing interests on the part of the ordinary person to whom the explanation ought to be comprehensible, and developments in explanations of surrounding concepts. Choice of a legality-marking concept to wield against evidence is of course very difficult if the central available guidance beyond general meta-theoretical-evaluative considerations comes in the form of the imperative to avoid too-narrow bootstrapping of familiar experience of the modern law-state into an explanation of steady-state legality. The problem of continuity interacts with the problem of commonality as we face the task of identifying or rejecting as instances of legality certain social phenomena representative of an unfamiliar legal order. In Chapter 4, we develop an understanding of legal

institutions that departs from our ordinary person's typical experience of legal norms in functionally-united clusters whether within
the law-state or elsewhere, yet although this device, suitably developed, may track legality, it does not on its own respond to the problem
of characterizing continuity of legally orders in whatever forms we
may find them, whether systemic or otherwise. MacCormick is certainly aware of these difficulties, recognizing in *Norms, Institutions,
and Institutional Facts* that legal institutions and their constituent
practices are in a sense parasitic upon social institutions whose onto-
logical and practical status as social institutions is logically prior their
emergence as legal institutions. MacCormick writes that:

> A constitution defines a state as a legal entity. But it is not only a legal
> entity. In an important sense it is a political and social entity before it is a
> legal one; or at least it is an effective legal-institutional reality only to the
> extent that it is a politico-social reality. Politics is about the exercise and the
> control of power in its factual sense. Power concerns what people can be
> made or induced to do. Political power includes and requires ultimately
> the ability to use physical force to overwhelm direct opposition, but, short
> of that, and much more visibly most of the time, it depends on much else,
> including popular support and endorsement, democratic legitimacy, psy-
> chological pressure, economic inducements . . . rhetorical mastery, skill in
> the media of communication, exploitation of public pomp and ceremony,
> personal charisma, traditional respect, and (through all the others) control
> of public agendas.[35]

But this is not all that must be said about the relation of social institutions to legal institutions: there is what Dick Ruiter, interpreting
MacCormick, calls "a certain space of time between the moment at
which a certain institutional legal concept is admitted to the legal
system and the moment of creation of its first instance."[36] It makes

---

35. Neil MacCormick, *Norms, Institutions, and Institutional Facts*, 17 Law
and Philosophy 301, 328 (1998).

36. Dick Ruiter, *Structuring Legal Institutions*, 17 Law and Philosophy 215,
216 (1998), commenting on this passage: "Just because we are dealing with
abstract institutional concepts and facts, the institutional concept must be
logically prior to any factual instance of the concept. If my understanding
is correct, Plato thought that the idea of beds was logically prior to the existence of any particular bed; but that has always seem to me a singularly
implausible view in relation to brute facts; but at least the world of legal institutions is a world safe for Platonists; whether that is good or bad publicity for

some sense to say, then, that the distinctively legal normativity of an institution is something like an emergent property of an institution, conditional on a number of other institutional facts holding together in a kind of narrative regarding that legal institution, and recognizable only once the institution is "in play" within a legal order—and in particular a legal system, on MacCormick's analysis. This sense of legal institutions as conditional on the occurrence of certain other institutional facts including non-legal institutional facts certainly accounts for the common experience of a moment of anxiety as various institutive rules are operated in the hope that certain consequences, particularly legal consequences, will occur. Indeed, the emergence of legal consequences as expected is the final indication that operation of certain institutive rules really has been operation of legal rules. Here MacCormick is a useful analytical pioneer yet perhaps hobbled by his commitment to the modern law-state as the object of his institutional theory. MacCormick's aim to explain the nature of modern state systems via an institutional approach is valuable to the extent that it explores the relation between institutions and underlying social facts in a process of emergence of legality, yet since the modern state's systemic character is taken as an achievement that marks mature and typically ongoing legality, his argument stops short of consideration of the problem of characterizing interaction between legal orders. There is nonetheless an instructive insight to be taken away from MacCormick's rooting his conception of legal system on an argument regarding the "normative coherence" characteristic of a legal system as a combination of legal institutions (themselves complex institutional facts). A legal system is *systematic* in the sense that all member norms of the system have "a common ground of formal validity" in criteria of recognition;[37] *purposive* in the sense that "norms belonging to a system can be envisaged as determinations of particular values or principles;"[38] and have synchronic or

---

the world of legal institutions I should not care to say, but it is clear that the institution as a concept is logically prior to the existence of any instance of it."; MACCORMICK AND WEINBERGER, AN INSTITUTIONAL THEORY OF LAW 54 (1986).

37. MacCormick, *Time, Narrative, and Law, in* TIME, LAW, AND SOCIETY. ARSP III, 119 (Jes Bijarup and Mogens Blegvad eds., 1995).

38. *Id.* at 120.

momentarily unified character that is logically prior to and the ground for any ascriptions of diachronic coherence to what is purported to be a system of legal norms.[39]

As much as this picture of legal system deserves praise for its attempting to engage an aspect of the problem of continuity, it deserves criticism rightly leveled by Gerald Postema. MacCormick's argument understands the life of a legal system as a set of continuous instances of momentary validity, with each "moment" "guaranteed by the fact that it is rooted in the practice of official recognition."[40] Postema counters that: "A legal system is not a sequence of sets of valid norms, any more than a melody is merely a sequence of pitches. Law's *modus operandi* is to offer guidance and a framework for the interaction of rational self-directing agents. This requires at minimum a kind of normative coherence *over time*." Not just any coherence will do, according to Postema:

> Time is essential to law's distinctive normativity. Law is capable of offering effective normative guidance to rational self-directing and socially inter-acting agents only if it is sufficiently congruent with their social lives and the activities and practices that structure them through time . . . Thus, the systematic nature of modern law cannot be conceived simply in terms of some formal norm of validity realized in the law-applying practices of officials.[41]

The hallmark, then, of legal system and in turn a chief characteristic of legality is the actual guiding role played by legal norms in the lives of the citizens they claim to govern over time, as represented by the continuity problem. As Postema adroitly summarizes it, "On the picture Hart and MacCormick offer, modern legal systems, like inverted pyramids, are complex sets of norms balancing on the point of the rule of recognition. But, if we take the temporal dimension of law's distinctive normativity seriously, we must put the pyramid back on its social base."[42]

---

39. *Id.* at 119, 124.
40. Gerald J Postema, *Law's Melody*, 7 ASSOCIATIONS 236 (2003). *But see* more recent Gerald J. Postema, *Melody and Law's Mindfulness of Time*, 17 RATIO JURIS 203 (2004).
41. 238.
42. *Id.* at 238.

Postema's "pyramid" metaphor is helpful, yet stops short of telling us what a properly seated pyramid contains by way of explanation, and whether other architectural forms are possible beyond the pyramid—whether legal systems are but one form of legal order. A return to direct explanation is advisable at this point since the metaphor points to insight rather than fleshing out the insight. Postema's call for legal theory to take seriously the temporal dimension of law is consistent with our proposing to begin from an ordinary citizen's view of law as occurring in functional clusters with and without clear connection to state authors, as these clusters are experienced in diachronic terms—from contracting to purchase a house or leasing a car to meeting commitments of employment.

A deepened account of the nature of legal institutions will be provided in Chapter 4, and that account will enable us to tackle problems of commonality and continuity within and amongst interacting legal orders including legal systems and novel non-systemic orders. A particular sort of descriptive-explanatory account of the concept of law will emerge, enabled by this set of categories and evidence bootstrapped from a broad evidenciary base. It might be called a narrative concept of law: narrative in the sense that the resulting account of the concept of law is an interpretation of a specified set of social phenomena operating within and over a specified time, distinguished from a mere history of linguistic usage by imposition of the next chapter's core explanation of institutional legality onto the prima facie legal social phenomena gathered for examination. The narrative concept of law amounts, then, not to a set of necessary and sufficient conditions for application of the concept of law, but a demonstration that an account of institutional legality best faces the problems of commonality and continuity when challenged to explain the legality or non-legality of prima facie legal phenomena. Clarity, descriptive-explanatory accuracy, and comprehensiveness all count as important meta-theoretical-evaluative virtues, but in the end our narrative concept will be successful not as a final resolution of those problems, but in its receipt by our audience as an "apt" way of categorizing those phenomena as a conceptual backdrop to understanding the role of law in contemporary social life.

4. AN INTER-INSTITUTIONAL THEORY

This chapter presents our inter-institutional theory of legality, and applies it to the most prominent example of legality: the systemic law-state. The next chapter, Chapter 5, takes the inter-institutional approach from this especially salient instance of legality to the remainder of the prima facie legal phenomena surveyed in the Introduction: non-state legality within states, transboundary legality, legality among groups of states as exemplified by the European Union, and Waldron's "issue of the hour" super-state legality. In both chapters we will rely on Chapter 3's elaboration of our meta-theoretical priorities, which mark our view as continuous with prior analytical theory while bringing new elements to it. That chapter set out our meta-theoretical priorities in generally positive terms, to which we might now usefully add, for this chapter's purposes, some cautionary introductory emphasis about what our approach is not, together with a synopsis of the inter-institutional view.

Much meta-theoretical debate over approaches to legality has focused on support of system-based and particularly state-based approaches, perhaps reaching their apogee in Kelsen, or contrasting norm-based approaches as found in the arguments of Hart and Raz. Our view is neither top down nor bottom up; we aim instead to depart from the perspective of the ordinary citizen encountering institutionally-operated norms in functionally-oriented clusters, whose legality or other normative status is often difficult to discern. In departing from the middle, our view is not state-based. We take pains to avoid presuming the systemic law-state as anything like an "ideal type" or central instance of legality, while taking seriously the prominence of the systemic law-state and international law as experiences of law and objects of theory. As we proceed in explanation of the elements of the contingent prominence of the systemic law-state, we seek to mark the elements of that contingency in a way which allows us to characterize as legality even those of its instances occurring in situations in which the intensity of legal-normative interaction amongst norm-subjects is far less than that typical of the systemic law-state, and more importantly, varies over time. The resulting theory is not an essentialist recipe for what law is. Rather, our explicitly stated meta-theoretical priorities and choices enable elucidation of general aspects of intense manifestations of legality such as the systemic law-state, *and* provide the explanatory basis for various non-state types of legality. In our view, then, low-intensity legality can bear the mark of non-optionality over time, no less than high-intensity mutually referential systems of legal norms. The narrative concept's sensitivity to low-intensity phenomena marks it apart from the static rule of recognition approach that asserts rather than explains that the content of the rule of recognition varies as it serves as a marker of legality and its borders in a given social situation. As a concept responsive to both changes in its phenomena and changes in inquirer interests, the narrative concept is dynamic yet not unconstrained: changes in phenomena of life under law are typically relatively rapid when compared against the relatively slow change of inquirer interests, allowing the narrative concept to navigate a middle path between state essentialism and pluralism about the nature of law.

A synoptic overview of the elements of the inter-institutional view will be helpful to introduce some potentially unfamiliar explanatory ideas. We begin with a discussion of legal-normative powers to determine, alter, and enforce legal-normative situations utilizing the familiar idea of norms as content-independent peremptory reasons for action, adding to that discussion an understanding of institutions of law as functional clusters of legal norms operated by various kinds of norm-subjects wielding legal-normative powers to use institutionally-owned norms. Institutions of law as we understand them, e.g., the institution of contract, are typically found in various formations within legal institutions, purpose-oriented agglomerations of institutions of law, most plainly evident in institutions such as ministries or departments in modern municipal states, or in other agglomerations such as commissions or treaty organizations. In the most prominent legal orders, legal institutions are connected in various ways, sometimes amounting to systemic interaction, and all usefully characterized in terms of mutual reference and intensity of relation. In contexts in which systemic and other forms of legal order are evident, legal institutions engage in mutual reference of varying intensity, from framework agreements to memoranda of understanding to joint enforcement activities to Web site links directing citizens to further sources of authoritative knowledge, as legal institutions intentionally communicate normative claims to one another, as commands, obligations, permissions, and so on. In some social situations such as that of the modern law-state, the pattern of intense mutual reference amounts to a system of legal institutions, and in characterization of the modern law-state we re-use the only content restriction Hart places on the cluster of norms at the heart of an enduring legal system—the minimum content of natural law. The resulting view enables us to capture the primus inter pares nature of the law-state as a manifestation of legal order, while allowing nonetheless for the legality of non-state bodies claiming authority to issue peremptory, content-independent norms with respect to other areas of social life. We shall add to this depiction of the systemic law-state a final element borrowed from Raz, recognition that some law-states claim comprehensive, supreme yet open normative control over a specified social situation, often but not necessarily associated with a particular geographical area.

Notice in this sketch that officials play no special role: although officials can and do exist in various legal situations, in our view, they are only one contingently prominent wielder of legal-normative powers. Similarly, although the modern, systemic law-state is within the explanatory reach of a combination of elements present in our view, it is a contingent combination of elements of legality, as is the systemic law-state claiming comprehensive, supreme, and open normative control—a situation which, for example, is contingently evident in unitary law-states yet almost certainly not present in federated law-states containing fundamental divisions of authority. Hierarchy amongst norms and officials is handled in a similar way in our view. Although it is certainly conceivable and in fact evident in some legal situations that officials are organized hierarchically, and the identity of a legal order and form of life are assessable by reference to a chain of validity, our view is designed to capture clusters as well as chains. In clusters, non-hierarchical mutual reference at varying intensity focuses legal institutions on shared, overlapping, or simply agreed divisions of normative tasks in deployment of institutions of law. As we set out the elements of the theory in succeeding sections of this chapter, it will become evident that the imbalance between structural and functional elements in contemporary analytical legal theory is redressed here: analytical legal theory's rich norm-level account of law is supplemented with our exploration of institutions of law, and legal institutions operating in intense, mutually referential configurations whose change over time is characterized as a changing combination of elements of legality explored in the structural side of our account. In characterization of the systemic law-state of the sort many readers live within, between, and among, all of these elements are deployed; yet as we press on to the non-systemic legal order of international law, contingent elements of legality will be shed without loss of legality, as we demonstrate that the content of legal-normative claims and the precise nature of their mutual relation is what distinguishes systemic state law from international law—not anything fundamental to the legality of each situation. The next chapter, Chapter 5, will take up the less familiar facts of plural legal order within states and between and among but not over all law-states, and we will take up there our demonstration of the narrative concept of law as a descriptive-explanatory tool in service of inquirers' evolving purposes, not a political concept or state-valorizing ideology, contra pluralist misinterpretations of the scope and limits of analytical legal theory.

4.1 ELEMENTS OF LEGALITY

4.1.1 Content-Independent Peremptory Reasons for Action

As we noted in the Introduction, analytical legal theory offers rich norm-level accounts of law. Our criticisms of previous analytical legal theories do not extend to these accounts, but only to their near exclusive focus on individual norms at the expense of greater attention to the nature of legal systems and other forms of orders and the relations between these. In this way, we intend to keep a central place for Hart's notion of a legal norm as a content-independent peremptory reason for action in understanding law. In Hart's view, content-independent peremptory reasons for actions are those norms requiring conduct that are capable of being identified and serving as reasons for action independently of consideration of their underlying purposes or justificatory reasons.[1] Although such norms typically do not

---

1. *See* Hart, ESSAYS ON BENTHAM 243–268 (1982). For developments of Hart's view, *see* JOSEPH RAZ, PRACTICAL REASON AND NORMS, (1990); JOSEPH RAZ, THE AUTHORITY OF LAW (1979), and Joseph Raz, ESSAYS IN THE PUBLIC DOMAIN 210–237 (1995).

exist in isolation from other norms, on their own they represent one of the core elements of legality. In our view, where they exist, legality exists.[2]

4.1.2 Legal Normative Powers

In previous chapters we have also argued that several features of state-based analytical legal theory suffer from growing descriptive irrelevance. Among these are the explanatory commitments to officials, hierarchies, and comprehensive, supreme, and open systems at legality's foundations. The idea of legal officials has been used to meet the indeterminacy problem in explaining the function of the rule of recognition, and legal officials have been identified as those norm-subjects whose practices determine the existence, content, and borders of legal systems. Yet as we saw in Chapter 1, the official-based approach likely cannot overcome the indeterminacy problem: the range of normative powers in modern legal systems is too diverse to be divided successfully into official and non-official exercises of law. And as we saw in Chapter 3, once we are meta-theoretically committed to avoidance of the distorting effects of presumption of the systemic law-state as the basic experience of legality, and aim instead to elaborate a concept of law useful to inquirers facing legality in institutional homes within and without the law-state, we become sensitive to the need to provide a deeper account of the way officials and non-officials use legal norms in systemic and other kinds of legal order. Part of the picture of their use of legal norms involves depiction of the

---

2. It is important to note that, like Tamanaha, we do not want to exclude forms of indigenous, natural, and customary law that are not institutionalized to any significant degree. Their possession of content-independent peremptory reasons for action is enough to include them within the subject matter of a general jurisprudence. We do not say very much about them since our particular focus is on the various forms of emerging practices (trans-state, intra-state, supra-state, and super-state) that have other core elements of legality, including institutions (in the sense of interconnected norms and normative powers) and social institutions (in the sense of organized actors). These elements are explained below. In other words we want "legality all the way down" to un-institutionalized norms, but our book focuses primarily on certain kinds of "new" legality that are currently most puzzling in state contexts as well as contexts beyond the state.

normative powers exercised in operation of institutions of law, such as contract.

The first step is to display the types of normative powers and their variable force. Within the dimension of type and focusing on familiar legal-normative powers, we follow Joseph Raz in asserting three overlapping but conceptually distinct categories of normative power used by a range of norm subjects including but not limited to those conventionally identified as legal officials[3]:

(i) *Powers to determine legal-normative situations.* These powers enable authoritative findings of law and legally relevant facts, and enable resolution of disputes. Powers of this kind include the powers of courts, tribunals, arbitration (both voluntary and mandatory) and mediation boards, police officers, and university petitions committees.

(ii) *Powers to alter legal-normative situations.* These are powers to introduce, repeal, modify, debate, etc., legal norms or legal arrangements which form part of a legal situation. Powers of this kind include the powers wielded by legislatures, public servants, courts, and citizens in, e.g., assertion of constitutional rights contra infringing legislation.

(iii) *Powers to enforce legal-normative situations.* These are powers to compel compliance with laws or alert others to the need to enforce laws. Powers of this kind are exercised by, among others, state security services, private security services, police officers, and citizens.

Legal-normative powers also exhibit a second dimension, that of force, usefully analyzed in terms of three categories.

(i) *Scope.* Powers differ in their scope to the extent that they extend variably over the members of the class of norm-subjects within a given legal system. Although two private citizens can each change his or her own and the other's legal rights and obligations by means of a contract (and sometimes they can change the legal-normative situation of specific third parties, such as when one names an executor in a will), legislatures are able to affect the legal-normative situations of entire political populations. Between these two extremes there are

---

3. Joseph Raz, *The Institutional Nature of Law, in* THE AUTHORITY OF LAW (1979).

many gradations. For example, university presidents and petitions committees are able to affect the legal-normative situations of students at their universities, but not beyond.[4]

(ii) *Duration.* Powers to affect the legal-normative situations of persons also differ in terms of their period of exercise. Powers of citizen's arrest, for example, cease once police officers arrive,[5] and so are momentary only, whereas the powers of police officers exist so long as the officers remain in standing. Similarly, powers of elected officials exist in definite durations, as for example, the maximum duration of a federal Parliament in Canada is five years.

(iii) *Assertion of Institutional Force.* Analytical legal theorists have long recognized that legal norms are not, contrary to Dworkin's claims in *Taking Rights Seriously*, necessarily understood as simply applying or failing to apply to a given situation.[6] Rather, legal norms have some degree or amplitude of institutional force. In systemic law-states, institutional force is often evident in hierarchies of norms and officials: a university petitions committee's decision, for example, neither asserts nor enjoys the same institutional force as a lower court judge's opinion, whose decision in turn neither asserts nor enjoys the same institutional force as an appellate court judge's decision. In other words, the authority of one's decision is relative to one's place as it is determined in the hierarchical practice of legal norms and institutions.[7] Yet varying institutional force of particular norms or indeed institutions is not found uniquely in hierarchical chains of validity or hierarchies of officials. Even where hierarchies are absent, legal institutions may make reference to the institutional force of one another's operations. Consider an example drawn from intellectual property law. The European Patent Office issues patents effective in all European Patent Convention member states, yet enforcement is national, within individual member states. So although the European Patent Convention provisions on validity are substantively identical

---

4. We leave aside the complication that laws affect not only their subjects but also non-subjects. Immigration law is a good illustration.

5. In Canada, see section 494 of the Canadian Criminal Code, R.S.C., c. C-46 (1985).

6. Ronald Dworkin, TAKING RIGHTS SERIOUSLY 14–45 (1979).

7. On the idea of "institutional force," *see* WIL WALUCHOW, INCLUSIVE LEGAL POSITIVISM ch. 3 (1994).

to the United Kingdom's Patents Act, interpretation of those provisions is a complex matter raising the possibility of a conflict between the European Patent Office Technical Board of Appeal and courts in the United Kingdom in the event that a defendant in the United Kingdom responds to a claim of infringement by asserting the invalidity of the patent. In *Symbian Ltd v. Comptroller General of Patents*, a defendant did just that, and the England and Wales Court of Appeal exhibited very clearly both the danger of the conflict, as well as how institutional force may operate in the absence of a hierarchy of binding authority. Writing in the context of the exclusion of programs for computers from the category of patentable subject matter, the Court of Appeal held that:

> Given that there are decisions of this court and of the Board which relate to the ambit of the computer program exclusion in art 52, the right basis for assessing that ambit in this court should be as follows. If the judgments in the Court of Appeal cases give tolerably clear guidance which would resolve the issue on this appeal, then we should follow that guidance, unless it is inconsistent with clear guidance from the Board, in which case we should follow the latter guidance unless satisfied that it is wrong.[8]

Notice that while the Court of Appeal recognizes and aims to find a way around conflict between its decisions and those of the Board, it does not grasp a chain of validity to determine the "right basis" for decisions required to apply article 52 provisions. Rather than looking up a chain, the Court looks both to its precedent decisions, *and* those of the Board, and with a further twist insofar as the Board's clear guidance normally regarded as binding may be disregarded if evaluated by the Court of Appeal as false. Not hierarchy, but truth seems to be at issue here in assessing the relative institutional force of the Court of Appeal and the Board. In this particular case, identification of the greatest institutional force bearing on interpretation of article 52 is somewhat complicated by the presence of an only partially relevant European Patent Office precedent, and the fact that the Enlarged Board of appeal has not yet heard a case bearing directly on the issue in *Symbian*. In facing this particular circumstance the

---

8. Symbian Ltd v. Comptroller General of Patents [2008] E.W.C.A. Civ 1066 ¶ 36.

Court nonetheless takes the opportunity to engage the more general question of the relation between the institutional force of the two adjudicative bodies, reinforcing and extending the non-hierarchical nature of that relation:

> It is, of course, inevitable that there will be cases where the EPO will grant patents in this field when UKIPO should not, at least so long as the view in *Pension Benefit* and *Hitachi* is applied by the Board and is not applied here. The fact that the two offices and their supervisory courts have their own responsibilities means that discrepancies, even in approach or principle, are occasionally inevitable. However, the fact that such discrepancies have been characterised as "absurd" by Nicholls LJ, and the reasoning in [3] of *Conor* emphasise the strong desirability of the approaches and principles in the two offices marching together as far as possible. This means that there is a need for a two-way dialogue between national tribunals and the EPO, coupled with a degree of mutual compromise. More directly relevant to the present appeal, it means that, where there may be a difference of approach or of principle, one must try to minimise the consequent differences in terms of the outcome in particular patent cases.[9]

The court's desire to avoid "absurd" discrepancies drives not an appeal to an extant hierarchy of officials or norms, nor to a program of building such hierarchies, but instead to practices of "two-way dialogue" and "mutual compromise" intended to minimize outcome variations between the two bodies. Institutional force, then, may vary within hierarchical arrangements *or* within less precisely delineated overlaps, intersections, and points of integration, and in these non-hierarchical situations the relations of intense, mutual inter-institutional reference we have sketched in earlier chapters are plainly evident.

Analysis of legality in terms of legal-normative powers leads to a kind of matrix view of the interaction of those legal-normative powers. This view recognizes the very wide range of possible combinations of legal-normative powers of several types and varying force. For example, a power to alter the legal-normative situations of others might carry little institutional force while bearing nonetheless on the legal-normative situation of a large number of norm-subjects, as may be seen in the case of individual votes in a referendum on unilateral secession of one part of a state from the remaining part. Other combinations of

---

9. *Id.* ¶ 61

type and force might have quite different effects. Consider, for example, the limited power of an executioner to enforce legal-normative situations, which exists only at certain clearly specified times, yet represents great institutional force in determining absolutely some dimension of the legal-normative situation of the small number of norm-subjects to whom the power applies. As the various possible combinations are considered, it becomes clear that the matrix generating combinations of powers and force is set within a broader web of non-legal norms, ethical, aesthetic, and so on; and further that the matrix of legal and non-legal normative powers is operated by a range of norm-subjects extending well beyond the class of officials. Once again, it seems that the distinction between officials and private citizens does very little explanatory work and the danger of circularity is significantly reduced by focusing on what occurs in characteristically legal situations—wielding of legal-normative powers with respect to peremptory content-independent norms—rather than the identity of those wielding the powers. What is of greater interest is the distinctive character of legality in the context of institutional ownership and deployment of particular combinations of legal powers and varieties of peremptory, content-independent norms. Let us turn now to exploration of that institutional context.

4.1.3 Institutions of Law

The first step toward development of a useful understanding of law's institutional nature is to clarify the sense of "institution" we use, distinguishing it from its general sense in ordinary language and multiple senses in law and legal theory. Neil MacCormick has made sustained use of the idea of institution in explaining practices characterized as *institutions of law*, such as contract, declaratory judgment, and criminal law.[10] An institution of law, in MacCormick's view, may be viewed as encapsulating a legal doctrine comprised of a cluster of related norms which united serve a single or limited number of purposes. This institutional cluster of norms may be used in various areas of life under law, often within organizations confusingly labeled "legal institutions," which persist over time while operating some

---

10. NEIL MACCORMICK & OTA WEINBERGER, AN INSTITUTIONAL THEORY OF LAW: NEW APPROACHES TO LEGAL POSITIVISM (1986) and NEIL MACCORMICK, INSTITUTIONS OF LAW: AN ESSAY IN LEGAL THEORY, (2007).

range of social functions recognized as "institutions of law." Both quite different uses of "institution" rely for their intelligibility on reference to wider social notions of institutions. For example, the "institution" of contract and the "institution" of queuing at bus stops share reliance on shared conceptions of a desirable social function performed by coordinated practices with generally recognized prompts and responses enabling operation of the function. Similarly, the idea of institution as a normative, function-oriented *organization* incorporating a cluster of complex normative practices, such as contract or queuing, transfers readily to the legal context from additional social contexts. Courts are readily understood as normative, function-oriented institutions, as are primary schools, the Red Cross, and the Scouting movement.

Gathering up MacCormick's remarks from our survey in this and prior chapters, it is clear he has an understanding of the social preconditions for institutions of law, and has an account of how institutions of law are distinguishable from social institutions; yet he has said relatively little about the legal institutions in which families of mutually enabling and regulating institutions of law dwell most prominently. For example, after providing a sophisticated account of institutions of law in terms of institutive, consequential, and terminative rules, MacCormick says this about social institutions:

> Tedious though the reasoning which leads to the definition [of institutions of law] is, it is important that we should have defined the term clearly. For there is another use of the term 'institution' which is also of great importance in relation to the law, but which is quite different from the well-established lawyer's notion of a 'legal institution' which I have just explicated. There are certain types of social system or sub-system, such as universities, schools, hospitals, orphanages, libraries, sporting organisations and the like, to which we often refer as 'institutions.' These are organisations of people which retain their organisational identity through time even though their personnel may change, because they are getting on with some job, and getting on with it in an organised way. Such I shall call 'social institutions.' To this class it is obvious that courts, parliaments, police forces, civil service departments, the Faculty of Advocates, and the Law Society, all belong. These are of course, social institutions which exist to perform legal functions, hence the possibility of confusion with the concept 'institution of the law.'[11]

---

11. MacCormick & Weinberger, *supra* note 9, at 55–56.

There is much of interest in the second sense of social institution, and by extension, "legal institution" qua "social system or subsystem," and much depends on its explanation and identity conditions as an explanatory tool amounting to more than a synonym for "system." In particular, if we are to take the performance of families of legal functions understood as institutions of law as the criterion for distinction of legal institutions from among the wider class of social institutions, several questions then need answers: what is it about the "organised" performance of legal functions understood as institutions of law that gives rise to legal institutions? Can legal institutions overlap via shared institutions of law? How can we assess the edges or boundaries of legal institutions? Admittedly, some of these questions concern atypical instances of legal institutions, so we need not answer them all immediately. Yet even a rudimentary inter-institutional account of legality and legal system must engage the central question of how core or typical legal institutions amount to a legal system or other legal orders, so we now turn to that question via a deeper account of legal institutions and their interaction.

4.1.4 Legal Institutions

It is tempting to define a legal institution by following one of the usages reported in *Black's Law Dictionary*—and consistent with MacCormick's view identified in the quotation above—which characterizes a legal institution such as a government department as an agglomeration of institutions of law. On this understanding, a legal institution represents topic-specific deployment of institutions of law peculiar to its legal-institutional focus, together with supporting institutions of law capable of use in various legal contexts yet given specific content and distinctive practice in application to the legal institution's topic-specific purposes. For example, in Canada the federal Department of Fisheries and Oceans qua legal institution deploys institutions of law specific to fisheries management, yet additionally uses in special form institutions of law with multiple forms of application given special expression in the context of fisheries and oceans, e.g., injunctions. As a description of legal institutions and their use of institutions of law this sketch is likely unobjectionable to many analytical legal theorists to the extent that it is more or less a re-description of elements of the analytical account, albeit at a higher level of organization. Preceding discussion of legal-normative powers, peremptory content-independent norms, institutions of law, and legal institutions does a great deal to explain the daily experience informing the perspective of our inquirers, who encounter legal and other normative claims in functionally oriented clusters. Yet the account is insufficient as a general account of legality for reasons familiar from our criticisms of approaches rooted in the rule of recognition. Our account of institutions of law is rooted in an explanation of use of legal-normative powers addressed to peremptory, content-independent norms, departing from the ordinary person's view of legality as emanating from institutional owners of clusters of institutions of law, and although this explanation gets out from beneath the problems of an official-based approach, it does little to address the problems of identity and continuity of legal systems or other legal orders. A variety of the problem of indeterminacy is also evident: even an account willing to ascribe legality to glimmerings as well as high-intensity instances of inter-institutional legality falls short of doing more than simply asserting the existence and utility of a descriptive-explanatory category called "legal." More must be done to explain how legal institutions relate to one another in a legal order, and in that relation constitute an identity over time, discernibly different from adjacent and distant separate legal and non legal-orders and institutions.[12] MacCormick's conception of institutions of law is certainly on the right track in identifying the operational nature of law as a plurality of norm-subjects engage one another in solving coordination problems, using law to support and advance moral goals, and so on, but as Postema points out, this recognition of legality's temporal dimension stops short of the fuller account needed to take seriously the role of clusters, orders, and even systems of legal institutions in protecting norm-subjects' expectations over time. We must, as Postema puts it, find a way to "invert" the explanation which results in seeing modern legal systems as balanced on the point of the rule of recognition, placing the explanation back in its social roots.

---

12. Consider, for example, how legal institutions applying legal norms regarding parole interact with civil society institutions providing norm-guided conditional support for parolees.

4.1.5 Mutual Reference and Intensity

In thinking about unifying relations amongst legal institutions, a debt is owed to MacCormick's recognition of the operational nature of institutions of law as complexes of multi-norm, interactive practices. Yet what MacCormick leaves incomplete is an account of how legal institutions combine to produce the complex institutional formations our ordinary citizen encounters in the globalizing world of the twenty-first century. MacCormick's reliance on the organizing category of legal system perhaps holds him back here, and we must be cautious to develop an explanatory device that captures systemic arrangements of legal institutions without being bound by the distorting presumption that where elements of legality are beyond glimmers, they must be systemic arrangements.

For our purpose in providing a contribution to the general part of a theory of law, it is useful to choose, as legality-tracking characteristics of legal institutions interacting over time, the fact that those institutions are typically part of a composition of inter-dependent institutions related by *mutual reference* occurring at some level of *intensity*. Mutual reference is here understood to cover a wide range of types of interaction amongst legal institutions. Instances of intense mutual reference familiar from the context of Hart's explanation of the systemic law-state include "vertical" reference in chains of validity such as lower courts' deference to the opinion of higher courts, expressed with intensity measured by those lower courts' regular citation of and deferral to higher courts, guidance by related yet less institutionally forceful courts as, e.g., a Canadian provincial court of appeal court might be guided by a decision on point from the Australian Supreme Court. Less familiar yet still prominent instances of intense mutual reference include situations like that explored by the England and Wales Court of Appeal in *Symbian*, where adjudicative bodies in separate hierarchies engage one another outside those hierarchies.[13] Still further instances may be found in divisions of power or authority, shared claims to issue binding directives, communication of standards and expectations, exchange of personnel, information, and techniques, and adoption of norms. Our account is deliberately broad, and meant to cover well-known relations such as constitutional or statutory requirement and authorization, deference

---

13. *Supra* note 7.

to binding authority and inclusion of guiding authority in the balance of reasons for action, as well as less well-known relations such as legal transplantation, transnational norm-sharing, and recognition of joint or divided sovereignty.

What our ordinary person recognizes as familiar legal institutions are familiar in part because of their relative centrality to life under law. The most familiar legal institutions characteristically possess many points of intense mutual reference with other legal institutions, and the operation of legal powers by these institutions tends to have particularly significant institutional force whose actual efficacy results in a particular degree of intensity in inter-institutional interaction as legality's claims are in fact practiced in various ways. Institutions at legality's borders tend to have fewer relations of mutual reference with other legal institutions, with less institutional force carried in each legal institution's most forceful operations of legal powers with respect to institutions of law, resulting in less actual efficacy in legality's claims being reflected in practice with a particular intensity over time. Consider, for example, the difference between an appellate court and an institution such as the recently disbanded Law Commission of Canada. Appellate courts are typically established, modified, and eliminated by provincial or federal statute. Their operations, including determinations of law, are normative reference points for a range of legal institutions and institutions of law, from persons within government departments charged with administration of acts of parliament whose application conditions are authoritatively determined by appellate courts using their determinative power, to government and private lawyers for whom courts are normative reference points. Even civil society organizations may gain special intensity for their normative claims against the Canadian legal system when they enter into a relation of mutual reference by appearing as *amicus curiae* to inform the court of issues and arguments deserving of the court's consideration. Mutual reference between appellate courts and these and other legal institutions occurs with varying intensity over time and in individual instances where normative communication carries particular institutional force. For example, in the wake of the Supreme Court of Canada decision in *Marshall* regarding aboriginal fishing rights,[14] the federal Department of Fisheries and Oceans, Attorney General for

---

14. *R. v. Marshall*, [1999] 3 S.C.R. 533.

New Brunswick, and other legal institutions referred to the decision whose institutional force required considerable changes to the views and actions of those legal institutions, including the Department of Fisheries and Oceans operating its legal power of enforcement in a particular way in administering institutions of law for which it is responsible. The pattern of continued mutual reference with the normative intensity delivered by assertion and regular observation of peremptory, content-independent norms supplies legality over time and with the character of a particular order achieving a particular set of social outcomes. Notice that the particular pattern of legality evident from legal institutions' operation of the matrix of powers available to them will constitute a pattern of inter-institutional interaction that may vary significantly over time, leaving each legal system or order with a uniquely variegated pattern and record of intense legality. In those variegations retaining a particularly inter-institutional variegation over time we find the phenomenal basis for identification and distinction of legal orders. This narrative picture of legality is admittedly a reflection of institutional facts visible only after particular variegated arrangements of legal institutions have in fact interacted in mutually referential ways with varying intensity; but this ought to be expected from a descriptive-explanatory approach which aims at responsiveness to phenomena as a meta-theoretical-evaluative virtue, and seeks to avoid presumption of the centrality of any particular systemic or other arrangements of legal institutions in delivering a descriptive-explanatory account not to be mistaken for a "political concept of law." More will be said regarding the variegation characteristic of the systemic law-state, so for the moment we may continue to consider an example of mutually referential, intense inter-institutional legality rather further from the contingently prominent situation of appellate courts in systemic law-states such as Canada, treading now toward legality's borders.

The nature and role of a legal institution such as the Law Commission of Canada, eliminated in 2006 while similar bodies remain elsewhere, e.g., England, is much different from the role of appellate courts. While the Law Commission of Canada was a statutorily established body composed of lawyers, legal academics, and former government officials, its findings, reports, and recommendations were not characteristically understood to be institutions of law or exercises of powers of alteration, determination or enforcement of institutions of law. Indeed, its activities are best understood not as making claims *within* or *on behalf of* the legal institutions whose particular kind of inter-institutional relation constitutes the Canadian systemic law-state, but rather *to* that legal system. During its existence, the Commission's function was to investigate the merits of existing laws, legal practices, and legal concepts, and to offer suggestions for reform or improvement.[15] It was not part of its nature to issue, or even claim to issue, legally-binding directives. It is of course possible that this or some other legal system's law commission might well warrant being regarded as a legal institution in light of its development of sufficiently intense mutual reference with other legal institutions such as legislatures, departments charged with policy formation, judicial bodies, and so on. Yet as the Law Commission of Canada in fact operated, the intentionally and actually limited scope of its powers—no determinative or law-altering powers are evident—warrants explaining the commission as a non-legal advisory social institution. The Law Commission might be well analyzed instead as a social institution that docked with or was integrated into the operations of the legal institutions of the Canadian legal system while remaining a non-legal institution. Analysis of the Law Commission using the suite of legality-detecting and legality-characterizing tools we have developed leaves us with a clear statement of the nature of the relation between the non-legal Commission and the legal institutions of the Canadian legal system, a statement which accepts and explains integration and docking without recourse to confusing and incomplete statements about a fact of "adoption" unsupported by explanation of how "adoption" is not the same as incorporation into "membership."

A final example drawn from oceans governance will help to demonstrate the utility of our view at legality's shifting borders. At legality's borders, evidence may come from relatively unusual places—in

---

15. Article 3 of the Law Commission of Canada Act, c. 9 (1996) states: "The purpose of the Commission is to study and keep under systematic review, in a manner that reflects the concepts and institutions of the common law and civil law systems, the law of Canada and its effects with a view to providing independent advice on improvements, modernization and reform that will ensure a just legal system that meets the changing needs of Canadian society and of individuals in that society . . ."

this case, an August 2008 Ministerial Statement from Canada's
federal Department of Fisheries and Oceans:

> The Honourable Loyola Hearn, Minister of Fisheries and Oceans, today
> issued the following statement:
>
> I want to extend my personal congratulations to the Association of Seafood
> Producers, who after almost two years of hard work have seen the north-
> ern prawn trawl fishery become the first Canadian fishery certified by the
> Marine Stewardship Council.
>
> In addition to being the first in Canada, I am proud to note that this is
> the largest MSC certified shrimp fishery in the world.
>
> Our government has made important investments to ensure responsi-
> ble and sustainable management decisions are taken by the Department
> of Fisheries and Oceans (DFO), but government is only one part of the
> big picture. That's why it's so important to recognize efforts by private
> industry and independent third parties who share our commitment to
> conservation and sustainable use of the fishery.[16]

What can the inter-institutional view make of this? It is likely best
explained as a matter of low-intensity mutual reference, where a non-
governmental organization, the Marine Stewardship Council, has
engaged in extensive norm-formation and assertion with a degree of
institutional force. The Canadian federal government has acknowledged this activity in a low-intensity reference identifying government as "one part of the big picture" in which parties "who share our
commitment" can participate in norm-guided and norm-governed
fishing. It of course remains possible that the Canadian federal government might displace the Marine Stewardship Council's activities,
but this possibility is a familiar matter of one normative system out-
weighing another normative order in terms of institutional force.
Until such an event occurs, which seems unlikely in this instance so
long as the Council's norms are satisfactory to the Canadian government and relieve the government of a difficult task, the shrimp
fishery is governed by two overlapping normative orders, each with
more or less institutional force capable of changing over time. Yet for
now, the overlap remains, and bordering normative orders appear to
have reached a stable interrelation.

---

16. Canada's First Marine Stewardship Council Certified Fishery, http://
www.dfo-mpo.gc.ca/media/statement-declarations/2008/20080819-eng.
htm. (Last visited November 27, 2008).

As these examples tend to show, by introduction of the ideas of mutual reference and intensity the inter-institutional account of legality puts Postema's pyramid metaphor on its head, as Postema supposes a properly socialized theory of law must do. The inter-institutional approach marks and measures legality in a way which does not presuppose any particular form or order of legality as the central case of legality, using instead in an era of plural forms of legality the ideas of content-independent peremptory norm, institution of law, legal institution, legal-normative powers, and mutual reference and intensity to try to "screen in" for examination rather than "screen out" instances of legality whose characterisation as particular orders of legality can be encountered later as inquirer interests and purposes discipline choice of identity conditions for particular forms of legal orders. This approach supports the view that identification of discrete legal orders is the result of post facto choices of explanatory category applied to particular variegated patterns of intense mutual reference among a particular set of legal institutions. We have avoided, then, the distorting effects of presupposition of the centrality of the experience of the systemic law-state to explanations of legality in the context of contributions to general jurisprudence. We are not, however, released from the task of explaining how the admitted prominence of the systemic law-state can be characterized within this view in a way which gives due recognition to that contingent yet significant fact.

4.2 THE SYSTEMIC LAW-STATE

4.2.1 Minimum Content of Natural Law

Our explanation of the systemic law-state involves all of the preceding elements of legality we have surveyed, and adds to them some contingent yet presently prominent aspects of systemic state legality—a legal order whose familiarity should not blind us to its relatively recent existence, as a creature of the post-Westphalian era. Our first step in characterization of the "state" aspect of the systemic law-state is to employ a radically underutilized feature of Hart's view of legal system: the minimum content of natural law thesis.[17] We propose

---

17. H.L.A. HART, THE CONCEPT OF LAW 193–200 (1994).

using Hart's minimum content of natural law thesis as it was intended, as a generally observable feature of a certain kind of legal system which identifies the core[18] subject matter or content of that legal system. Hart famously argues that given certain logically contingent but naturally necessary features of human and social life, any legal system must include basic rules restricting the free use of violence, securing property, and enforcing promises. Without such content, a legal system cannot hope to persist or provide support for any other rules. There are at least two reasons why the minimum content of natural law thesis has not served, as we think it can, as a general feature in identification and distinction of the systemic law-state from other legal systems, legal orders, and non-legal normative social situations. First, attention has been unfortunately concentrated on the question of whether Hart's admission of a minimum content of natural law reveals that his legal positivism is untenable, despite his argument to the contrary.[19] Second, Hart misleadingly avoids describing the thesis as a conceptual claim about the "modern municipal systems" central to his investigation, opting instead to characterize it as a "natural necessity." Talk of "natural necessity" has distracted readers whose central interest has lain with the relation between law and morality, not on a descriptive-explanatory account of legality including legal system. Understood in its broader context, a generalized descriptive-explanatory account of the salient features of modern municipal systems of law, the claim is evidently not a universal assertion about human society so much as it is a conceptual claim about the factual nature of municipal legal systems. It is only a fact about modern municipal systems, because of the nature of humans and social life as they are, and so it is conceptually possible to imagine legal systems which do not need such content.[20] Put in its proper place, then, the role of the thesis in an explanation of legality embodies contingency in two senses. First, it is a claim about a feature of legality which is contingent on the facts of human life being as they are, such that we are unable to continue for long without protection against the free use of violence, control over property, and control of

---

18. Though by "core" we do not mean to deny that the necessary rules may and do themselves vary in particular content.

19. *See, e.g.,* LON FULLER, THE MORALITY OF LAW 154–5 (1964).

20. Consider, for example, a global system of cyberlaw.

the making and breaking of promises. Second, the thesis itself is a contingent part of a conceptual theory of law, a theory which as we have argued in Chapter 3, following Raz, need not be composed solely of necessary or conceptual truths about law. On this reading of the minimum content of natural law, it captures conceptually the typical yet contingent facts of legality in the restricted ambit of the modern municipal state, whose relevance to a general jurisprudence is further restricted by its being but one kind of legal order. Put in this broader context, it soon becomes clear that the typical core content of such legal orders is of rather less theoretical interest than the way those orders conceive of themselves as systemic in more than ethnocultural ways, and how that conception of a systemic nature affects systemic law-states' relation to other legal orders.

4.2.2 Comprehensiveness, Supremacy, and Openness

The second element of our explanation of the systemic law-state is drawn from Raz. Here, just as a modified version of Hart's analytical commitment to the minimum content of natural law can be used in a modified way to explain another contingent part of the "state" aspect of the systemic law-state, Raz's conception of the key claims made by the systemic law-state—claims to comprehensiveness, supremacy, and openness—can be used. We will omit here detailed discussion of the nature of these claims since we have examined them in another context in section 2.2 of Chapter 2. There we noted additionally their dependence on presumption of the social nature of legal systems, and Raz's intention to capture only those characteristics universally evident in municipal legal systems—perhaps evident in international law also, Raz says, but that question is beyond the scope of his investigation. As elsewhere in our argument, it seems to us that the analytical reach of comprehensiveness, supremacy, and openness is useful but incomplete. These ideas certainly capture the claims characteristic of some situations where legality is evident, yet in addition to Raz's self-imposed limitation to the reach of these ideas via his assumption that his analysis aims directly at municipal states only, a further specific limitation must be imposed to recognize that only some states make all of these claims.[21] Consider, for example, that it

---

21. Even those states making these claims do so in tandem with subjection to international treaties, conventions, and similar agreements entered into

seems to invite charges of inventing a distorting fiction if a comprehensive claim to authority is attributed to some federations. Although there is clearly an available, comprehensible sense in which Canada claims comprehensive authority over social situations within its borders, this sense is inadequate for more than loose, metaphorical usage. Even in the hands of ordinary citizens the notion of a comprehensive Canadian claim to authority is soon set aside as masking the interdependent character of federal, provincial, and territorial governments. Although the federal Parliament is superior to provincial legislatures in many ways, as a matter of constitutional law, these bodies have separate powers and obligations, firmly separated by constitutional measures including the provinces' exclusive power to amend their own constitutions, and areas of exclusive jurisdiction such as provinces' authority over education.[22] So although it is perhaps momentarily plausible to represent the federal government in Canada as the source or seat of Canada's claim to comprehensive authority in the context of disputes over Canada's physical borders, the constitution of Canada explicitly rules out anything like a concentrated single source or seat of comprehensive authority for Canada as a whole. A similar case may be made against the supremacy claim, as, for example, even if there is such a thing as a Canada claiming comprehensive authority, in the context of First Nations land claims, the accompanying claim to supremacy is not just challenged but the challenge is recognized by federal and provincial governments. As the federal Department of Indian and Northern Affairs summarizes the nature of "comprehensive claims" to land on the part of First Nations, "Comprehensive claims deal with the unfinished business of treaty-making in Canada. These claims arise in areas of Canada where Aboriginal land rights have not been dealt with by past treaties or through other legal means."[23] Although it seems clear even on Raz's broad notion of typical municipal legal systems that Canada is indeed within the range of legal systems his view ought to reflect, this

---

voluntarily, and *jus cogens* norms of international law, as Hart observed in argument contra Austin's denial of the possibility of international law.

22. The Constitution Act, 1982, being Schedule B of the Canada Act, 1982, UK, s. 45.

23. "Land Claims," http://www.ainc-inac.gc.ca/al/ldc/index-eng.asp (last visited Nov. 2008).

"unfinished business" seems a powerful challenge to the idea that legal systems claim supremacy. Here it is not only that a claim to supremacy is ineffective, but that it is not made. We might also consider the fate of the openness claim in this context, but it seems there is little merit in doing so. Once we have identified some typical municipal legal system whose interaction with other legal orders is not one of a kind of communication between a comprehensive and supreme system and another such system, talk of such systems as exhibiting "openness" as a style of adoption of norms without thereby certifying them as members seems to obscure rather than illuminate the nature of those systems and their claims relative to other legal orders. That is, once we see that comprehensiveness and supremacy, at least, are not just contingent characteristics of legality, but contingent aspects of the systemic law-state, we encounter again the questions at which we arrived after consideration of the contribution of the idea of a minimum content of natural law to an understanding of the systemic law-state. We are drawn away from characterization of the systemic-law state in isolation, and toward questions about the interaction of systemic legal orders with other legal orders, contingent variations of forms of the systemic law-state. Also, as we are freshly sensitive to the possibility of a plurality of legal orders amongst which the systemic law-state is only one, the old problems of continuity and identity of legal systems and other legal orders are seen in a new light. We shall take up non-state legal orders in Chapter 5, and discussion of the problems of identity and continuity will appropriately accompany that discussion's engagement of variations in identity and development of state and non-state legal orders. It remains here to take up the idea of system, which has done so much work for state-focused legal theory in the past, yet is in need of renovation to face the possibility that for a law to be a law, it may, but need not be a member of a legal system—an expanded analysis made possible and demanded by rejection of Raz's early assumptions regarding the probative value of a theory restricted to universal features of typical municipal legal systems viewed as social systems.

4.2.3 System

Even as we are skeptical of the possibility of characterizing typical instances of legality as systemic in the way Raz's early work demands, we recognize nonetheless the explanatory value of the idea of system, if only as a "regulative ideal" as MacCormick has put it.[24] The question is just how some particular conception of "system" might be useful to characterizing that social situation. We have given extensive attention to the shortcomings of Hart's "single rule of recognition approach," which specifies and ranks diverse sources of law, allowing a detached observer to assess the membership of any putative member-rule of the system by pulling on a chain of validity. Raz's apparently more robust explanation is ultimately no less fragile, even with its acceptance of a plurality of rules of recognition in individual legal systems exhibiting claims of comprehensiveness, supremacy, and openness. At best, Raz's view might be modified to capture the range of extant municipal legal systems regarded as typical, and not dismissed as borderline cases. Those typical cases remain the most prominent instances of legality today, even when their claims and function overlap with non-systemic legal orders from First Nations' land claims to peri-systemic legal orders such as international humanitarian law. Our view here is yet again an echo of our handling of the minimum content of natural law as a contingent element of the systemic law-state as a form of legal order, and the equally contingent status of claims of comprehensiveness, supremacy, and openness to explanation of both legality and the systemic law-state. Although a claim to or exhibition of a systemic character might be a core part of the nature and claims of the law-state, legal system is but one legal order. Ascription of a systemic nature to a particular legal order may well help understanding that order and is certainly part of a contribution to a general jurisprudence whose understanding of legality includes identification of various legal orders. The ascription of a systemic nature will almost always, however, be incomplete as a descriptive-explanatory account of legality in a given, typically complex social situation. Given, however, the recent prominence of non-state phenomena, we might now be forced to reject as obsolete Raz's view (discussed in Chapter 2) that "It would be arbitrary and pointless to try to fix a precise borderline between normative systems which are legal systems and those which are not. When faced with borderline cases it is best to admit their problematic credentials, to enumerate their similarities and dissimilarities to the typical cases, and leave

---

24. *See* our discussion in 3.2.1.

it at that."[25] More must be done to understand legal system not just as an independent phenomenon and object of study, but in its relation to the plurality of other forms of legality which can no longer be ignored. To be fair to Raz, he has been very clear in later work explored in Chapter 3 that he does not suppose there is any uniquely correct explanation of the concept of law, seeking instead "apt" explanations suited to the purposes of inquirers; and as novel prima facie legal phenomena emerge, we might well, on grounds we have provided, revisit his early assertion in *The Authority of Law* that a theory of legal system must come hand in hand with a theory of the state, as the two are "intimately interrelated."[26] Neil MacCormick has perhaps done the most to take novel phenomena seriously, attempting to escape the distorting effect of state-based jurisprudence while still remaining, in our view, too much in its thrall and equally in the thrall of the distorting presumption of legal system. In *Questioning Sovereignty* he writes in almost Hartian tones about the challenge posed by extra-state legal phenomena such as the European legal order, here characterized as a system, and the challenge they pose to the methods and categories of legal theory:

> The interlocking of legal systems, with mutual recognition of each other's validity, but with different grounds for that recognition, poses a profound challenge to our understanding of law and legal system. The resources of theory need to be enhanced to help deal with a challenge full of profound and potentially dangerous implications for the successful continuation of European integration. We have come to the frontier of the problem of legal pluralism, and have to reflect on solutions to the difficulties for practice implicit in the very idea of pluralism.[27]

Much like Raz, MacCormick offers a carefully qualified view about the nature of ascription of "system" to particular legal situations, and carefully qualified not as a minor matter following presentation of his central argument, but at the outset:

> A proper representation of a legal system may reasonably take one or another of several forms, depending on one's practical concerns of the time. Material which is characterized in one way in a dynamic perspective takes a different shape when viewed in a momentary-judgemental

25. Raz, *supra* note 3, at 116.
26. Raz, *supra* note 3, at 99.
27. NEIL MacCORMICK, QUESTIONING SOVEREIGNTY 102 (1999).

perspective. There is no single uniquely correct reconstruction of the raw material of law into a single canonical form of 'legal system.'[28]

Raz and MacCormick differ with respect to issues of method, and the nature of legality, in non-trivial ways as MacCormick's view is rooted in an account of law as an institutional social order, and Raz's view is rooted in an account of practical reason. Despite these differences Raz and MacCormick offer remarkably similar views on the limits of their accounts of legal system: Raz in 1998 rejects the idea of a single uniquely correct concept of law, and even in earlier work takes care to limit his theory to municipal legal systems, and MacCormick similarly rejects a "unique" "canonical" idea of legal system while reaching rather further into the phenomena of legality to identify the possibility of legal systems other than municipal systems. Further similarities arrive in analysis of the limitations of both views. Raz's conception of legal system, when allied with ideas of comprehensiveness, supremacy, and openness, seems to encounter difficulties in characterizing the phenomena well within its self-declared limits of intuitively clear instances of legal system, well prior to encountering phenomena such as international law. MacCormick's institution-based approach does rather better in encountering non-state-based phenomena, but even MacCormick recognizes that "interlocking" of legal systems, never mind non-systemic legal orders, poses "a profound challenge" to not just our understanding of law, but legal system as well.[29]

---

28. *Id.* at 11.

29. Notice, however, that MacCormick's analysis goes no further than acknowledging this challenge. His handling of the European legal order remains framed in terms of "system": "The legal systems of member-states and their common legal system of EC law are distinct but interacting systems of law, and hierarchical relations of validity within criteria of validity proper to distinct systems do not add up to any sort of all-purpose superiority of one system over another. It follows also that the interpretative power of the highest decision-making authorities of the different systems must be, as to each system, ultimate" *Id.* at 118. The plausibility of this view can be disputed on conceptual grounds regarding the choice of 'system' to characterize the supra-state legal order of the European Union, and on factual grounds of the sort we have demonstrated above in our discussion of *Symbian*, where the ultimacy of highest decision-making authorities is clearly challenged by practices of

Our response to the profound challenge can accept the idea of legal system as a regulative ideal currently most prominent in systemic law-states, as MacCormick does, while preferring an inter-institutional account of legal system as a particularly prominent manifestation of legality, typically encountered with contingent demonstration of the minimum natural law content of a legal system, and claims to comprehensiveness, supremacy, and openness. Moreover, we can do so while retaining our ability to encounter phenomena Raz simply does not examine while he asserts without argument that certain distinctions between legal systems and other normative systems are likely pointless and arbitrary, phenomena examined only partially and incompletely by MacCormick in his state- and European Union-focused approach. This virtue seems particularly valuable, and not a pointless and arbitrary exercise, in an era of increased interrelation between states as opposed to increased assertion of sovereignty and separation.

In the era of increased interrelation, the systemic law-state as one order amongst others can of course be explained to some extent via a single- or multiple-rule of recognition approach, whether inhabited by dynamic social institutions of MacCormick's argument or special practical reasons of Raz's argument. Yet a more apt explanation than either is one which accepts the contingency of the law-state, and its constituent elements, as a form of legality, and recognizes the place of the law-state in changing social circumstances where, e.g., systemic legality might briefly endure while the minimum content of natural law has been trampled, and where comprehensiveness, supremacy, and openness were never claimed. This does not amount, however, to a "mix and match" view of legality; it is an acknowledgement of the contingency of even prominent forms of legality such as the systemic law-state, and the contingency of particular combinations of the elements of that prominent form of legality. Meta-theoretical recognition of contingency may seem to be damaging to the project and problem of determinacy with respect to the borders of systemic law-states, but once that problem is reformulated as a problem of interrelation, continuity, identity, and transition between

---

mutual reference "laterally" between legal institutions of nominally separate systems.

forms of legal order, the identification of various forms of legal system in the systemic-law state is ultimately freeing. Once legality is separated from the state as the mark and measure of legality, the way is open to fuller characterization of legal phenomena beyond the state, the task to which we turn in the next chapter.

4.3 THE NARRATIVE CONCEPT OF LAW AND THE PROBLEMS OF CIRCULARITY AND INDETERMINACY

As we turn away from the systemic law-state, and toward other forms of legality, we must return for a moment to the question of the kind of concept of law we are offering, and how that concept of law fares when faced with the problems of circularity and indeterminacy which stood at the center of our discussion in Chapters 1 and 2 of official-based accounts of legality. We asserted in Chapter 3 that our view amounts to a narrative concept of law that reflects changes in inquirers' interests, and changes in the phenomena of legality whose characterization contributes to a picture of law satisfactory to those interests. Elements of that account have now been set out. We have assembled a picture of legality that includes legal powers to operate institutions of law, which are themselves housed in legal institutions whose interaction in legal orders we have explained using the ideas of mutual reference and intensity.[30] We have characterized the systemic

---

30. Our sensitivity to law's situation in time borrows most obviously from Postema's criticism of Hart, yet it owes a debt to MacCormick and Kelsen as well, drawing inspiration from MacCormick's characterization of part of Kelsen's argument in Chapter 5 of THE PURE THEORY OF LAW, (trans. Max Knight, 1967). In QUESTIONING SOVEREIGNTY 10–11, MacCormick writes:

> Law conceived as an institutional normative order can thus come to be constitutive of a law-state. However, as Kelsen pointed out, there are two possible ways to conceive and represent the order as a working system. One way is a dynamic way. Here, the process of change through time is central, including the way in which legal provisions themselves set the terms for valid change. . . .
>
> The other way is what Kelsen called a 'static' representation. Here, we represent the order by individuating rules or norms prescribing duties, or conferring rights either permissive or beneficial. Sometimes, in an even more microscopic way, we simply individuate particular duties and rights,

law-state, the most prominent form of inter-institutional organization, as exhibiting a particular variegated pattern of inter-institutional interaction together with institutional provision for protection of the minimum natural law content of this systemic arrangement of legal institutions.

Our argument is aligned with Raz's meta-theoretical view that there is no uniquely correct explanation of the concept of law, and his associated argument against a necessary and sufficient condition account of the concept of law. It would be a serious misunderstanding of our view, then, to see it as offering a set of necessary and sufficient conditions for legality as might be sought in a state-focused account of legality. Instead, our account is meant to operate in radar-like fashion, identifying markers or indicators of legality that combine in various ways to form legal orders in emerging, settled,

---

depending on the current focus of attention. But this 'static' conception proves to be misnamed. For it concerns not stasis, but rather momentary normative judgement, whether the judgement envisaged is that of a court seeking to determine a litigated question, or that of a citizen engaged in practical judgement what to demand in a given setting, or indeed that of a scholar trying to produce a coherent representation of some branch of the law. The recognition of rights and duties in this practical-judgement setting is in any event an intellectual procedure different from that of seeking guidance about the valid exercise of normative power within a normative order dynamically conceived; the two interact and overlap, but are not the same. Law as a normative order has two aspects: the dynamic and the momentary. H.L.A. hart sought to draw these together into a single structure of 'primary and secondary rules,' but there is a notorious difficulty about the interconnection of his 'rule of recognition' with 'rules of change' and 'rules of adjudication.'"

We have discussed MacCormick's remarks following this passage in the context of his meta-theoretical views regarding explanation. It is useful now to have these preceding remarks in hand as a marker of his sensitivity to the temporal dimension of law Postema accuses him of lacking, and his sensitivity to the problem faced by Hart's attempt to capture momentary and dynamic aspects of legality. Our inter-institutional view has a different role for officials and does not face the problems Hart found in entanglement of a theory of adjudication with a general theory of law. We recognize nonetheless that our encountering the temporal element of law as we have is a matter of taking up a problem Hart flushed out for consideration, taken up by MacCormick in ways we suppose are ultimately too limited, and taken up in our view.

and decaying forms including but not limited to the law-state. In avoiding presupposition of the state as the mark and measure of legality we aim to contribute to a balanced structural and functional explanation of legality, gathering for scrutiny all candidate phenomena and accepting the possibility of the existence of forms of legal order significantly different from the model of the state. This view's virtues include its capacity to capture the strikingly variable forms of legality beyond the state, and the fact of their change over time.[31] These virtues are, however, only part of the case for the plausibility of our view. It might still naturally be asked at this point how our structurally and functionally re-balanced theory overcomes the problems of circularity and indeterminacy we identified in Chapter 1.

The problems of circularity and indeterminacy are fundamentally problems for official-based accounts of legality needing non-circular accounts of these norm-subjects whose activities track the reach of legality and in a state-system-focused account demonstrate the borders of that system. Our view is not reliant on officials, viewing them as one group amongst many users of legal powers. Yet our escape from circularity relies less on this aspect of our view than on our analysis of the problem as really one of pseudo-circularity. Hart, Coleman, and others did in fact rely on some empirical evidence from which their general jurisprudential claims regarding officials were drawn, so their view is not straightforwardly circular. Rather, the problem lies in their bootstrapping from too little evidence, and lacking specification of when bootstrapping ought to be repeated or expanded to track changing or novel evidence. Our response to the problem lies in what we do with the bootstrapping method, whose constant liability to the

---

31. On the meta-theoretical importance of this virtue *see:* PETER MORTON, AN INSTITUTIONAL THEORY OF LAW 4 (1998): "The most striking feature of [the institutional] world is its state of continuous change. In the world of social interaction nothing stands still; new activities emerge as new techniques are developed and new inventions are made; old activities die out or are merged with others; practices are rendered obsolete; new procedures emerge or are instituted; relationships between agencies are renegotiated; and so forth. All objects in this world are, in differing ways, vulnerable to incremental change or subject to deliberate destruction and reform. The vocabulary of the types of changes in this Heraclitean world makes the vocabulary of geomorphological or biological change seem poverty-stricken." [author's notes omitted]

charge of circularity can at best be adequately mitigated. By tracking mutual reference and its intensity in interaction between legal institutions, without presupposition of the centrality of the law-state or its characteristic hierarchies of norms and officials, our view is both inherently change-tracking and less likely to omit consideration of prima facie legal phenomena potentially relevant to a general account of legality. Our view is nonetheless a matter of choices of conceptual tools in response to dynamic normative phenomena, so there is always a possibility of a gap between our narrative concept and the phenomena it seeks to explain. Use of the ideas of mutual reference and intensity aims to mitigate the effects of that gap, while we recognize its possibility and adjust accordingly the nature of our claims for the merits of our view. At least some of the merit of our view, then, in addition to its meta-theoretical-evaluative virtues, lies in our attempt to be self-conscious regarding the limits of our explanation. Bootstrapped theories of complex social phenomena are a particular kind of theory, with particular benefits and risks, and confidence in those theories should be in proportion to those benefits and risks.

The problem of determinacy, as we have argued in Chapter 3, is transformed by our adoption of a novel point of departure—that of the ordinary person encountering norms in clusters or clumps, often with readily observed institutional authors—and our separation of legality from the state. In a theory focused on legality in its forms beyond the law-state, the problem of determinacy is no longer that of finding legality's hard borders at the edges of systemic law-states. The new problem of determinacy lies in characterization of relations between legal orders: interpenetrating of legal orders as might be occurring between international law and systemic law-states, overlap as might be occurring among North American Free Trade law-states, and what MacCormick has called "interlocking" legal systems in the context of the European Union. This book does not provide the local jurisprudence which would result from descriptive-explanatory theoretical account of these situations. It does, however, attempt to demonstrate the importance of these situations for an inquirer- and phenomena-responsive general jurisprudence informed by a broader range of particular, local investigations, and the need for jurisprudence to recognize these relations as core and not peripheral to the project of general jurisprudence. In the next chapter we move from the systemic law-state to these new challenges.

5. AN INTER-INSTITUTIONAL ACCOUNT OF NON-STATE LEGALITY

In this chapter we come full circle, returning to the novel prima facie legal phenomena we identified in the Introduction, and to the problems posed by that phenomena for the possibility of a meaningfully general jurisprudence. As we depart from the previous chapter's account of the systemic law-state to encounter non-state legality once again, we revisit in the first section of this chapter the question of how our view differs from a style of legal pluralism which, if true, may demand abandonment of hopes for a meaningfully general jurisprudence. The legal pluralist challenge to the possibility of a general jurisprudence becomes especially acute when that general approach attempts to explain non-state legality. In addition, then, to reflection on the difference between our view and varieties of legal pluralism, we will press on in the second section to application of our inter-institutional theory to the non-state prima facie legal phenomena presented in the Introduction. That discussion will lead us to the final chapter, which will take up meta-theoretical issues identified at the close of Chapter 4 in discussion of the relation of the systemic law-state to other forms of legality. There we explained how in separating legality from the systemic law-state, our view transforms the problem of determinacy from one of finding exclusionary borders to understanding of overlap, intersection, and other forms of engagement between analytically separate legal systems or orders. In the final chapter we will also take up the associated problems of identity and continuity, transformed, we shall argue, by expanding analytical legal theory's attempt to explain state and non-state legality.

5.1 META-THEORY REVISITED: BETWEEN LEGAL PLURALISM AND GEO-CENTRIC STATISM

In preceding discussion we have marked the challenge legal pluralism poses for analytical theories of law. Legal pluralist approaches are well-positioned to demonstrate the imbalance between structural and functional aspects of analytical legal theory, which ascribes legality only to those social practices and situations that either share the characteristics of the systemic law-state,[1] or are in some way supported by state practice or recognition. Against this approach, which is applied by analytical theorists to phenomena as diverse as public international law and the European Union, legal pluralists advance a combination of novel evidence and argument regarding best explanation of that evidence. Legal pluralists reject state-based legal theory, and on the back of sociologically-sensitive evidence-gathering, urge admission that the forms of legality are simply too diverse—with none more theoretically important than others—to make anything other than a thoroughly "functional" explanation of legality possible. Brian Tamanaha is perhaps the most staunch advocate of this view[2]:

> The long history of failed attempts at articulating an essentialist concept of law should be taken as instructive—there is something wrong with the ways in which the question of what law is has been posed and answered. The source of the intractable difficulty lies in the fact that law is a thoroughly cultural construct. What law is and what law does cannot be captured in any single concept, or by any single definition. Law *is* whatever we attach the label *law* to, and we have attached it to a variety of multifaceted, multifunctional phenomena: natural law, international law, state law, religious law, and customary law on the general level, and an almost infinite variety on the specific level, from lex mercatoria to the state law of Massachusetts and the law of the Barotse, from the law of Nazi Germany to the Nuremberg Trials, to the Universal Declaration of Human Rights and the International Court of Justice. Despite the shared label 'law', these are diverse phenomena, not variations of a single phenomenon, and each one of these does many different things and/or is used to do many things. There is no law *is* . . .; there are these kinds of law and those kinds of law; there are these phenomena called law and those phenomena called law; there are these manifestations and those manifestations of law . . . No wonder,

---

1. Constituted by the collective practice of a determinate and hierarchically-ordered cohort of public or legal officials who claim to govern comprehensively and supremely over some specified population and geography.

2. Others include BOAVENTURA DE SOUSA SANTOS, TOWARDS A NEW LEGAL COMMON SENSE, (2002), and WILLIAM TWINING, GLOBALISATION AND LEGAL THEORY (2000).

then, that the multitude of concepts of law circulating in the literature have failed to capture the essence of law—it has no essence.[3]

Tamanaha's pluralism disarms legality of its special explanatory task and role, and leaves it as just one normative contender among the many norms and normative systems bearing on practical reasoning. Tamanaha's view, interestingly, is not the sort of partial conflict of method and goal seen in contrasts between findings of fundamentally descriptive sociology, and fundamentally explanatory theoretical approaches—whether rooted in sociology, philosophy, or elsewhere.[4] Tamanaha works from a jurisprudential starting point, inquiring into the nature of law from a perspective familiar with and open to the ambitions of general jurisprudence. In questioning the possibility of a unified, general account of law he is engaged in the familiar

---

3. BRIAN TAMANAHA, A GENERAL JURISPRUDENCE OF LAW AND SOCIETY 193 (2001), [original emphasis] We should note that Tamanaha's version of socio-legal pluralism is not representative, rejecting as it does both the idea of essential sources of law as well as the idea that the concept of law has any essential properties. *See* Tamanaha, *The Folly of the 'Social Scientific' Concept of Legal Pluralism*, 20 JOURNAL OF LAW AND SOCIETY 192–217 (1993) and Tamanaha, *An Analytical Map of Social Scientific Approaches to the Concept of Law*, 15 OXFORD JOURNAL OF LEGAL STUDIES 501–535 (1995). Some legal pluralists accept that law's sources are diverse, but reject the claim that law has no essence. For example, Robert Cover argues that while law could be generated by both state and non-state actors, "all collective behavior entailing systematic understandings of our commitments to future worlds [can lay] equal claim to the word 'law'". Robert Cover, *The Folktales of Justice: Tales of Jurisdiction*, 14 CAP. U. L. REV. 179, 181 (1985), *quoted in* Paul Schiff Berman, *A Pluralist Approach to International Law*, 32 YALE JOURNAL OF INTERNATIONAL LAW 301, 307 (2007). We have chosen to focus on Tamanaha's version for two related reasons: first, he begins from within the same tradition as we do, the analytical tradition best associated with the work of H.L.A. Hart, and second, unlike most legal pluralists (including Cover) who focus on particular contexts (for example, a particular post-colonial state), Tamanaha attempts a theory of general jurisprudence not restricted to any particular manifestation of plural legal orders.

4. *See* Kenneth Himma, *Do Philosophy and Sociology Mix? A Non-Essentialist Socio-Legal Positivist Analysis of the Concept of Law*, 24 OXFORD JOURNAL OF LEGAL STUDIES 717–738 (2002), and William Twining, *A Post-Westphalian Conception of Law*, 37 LAW AND SOCIETY REVIEW 199–257 (2003).

business of attempting to liberate jurisprudence from unhelpful fictions, just as Bentham attempted to do.

Even a familiar business, however, may have unacceptable costs. Tamanaha's approach seems to us to give up too easily—and with troubling implications—on the project of constructing an analytical theory of law which identifies core features of legality. In many of the contexts of social life we have identified, for example, there is doubt and worry among ordinary persons and theorists alike over the issue of whether some agreement or practice amounts to or is properly called law or considered a legal system or legal sub-system. If Tamanaha's conventionalist account is correct, these doubts and worries are rendered meaningless or perhaps meaningful only from the standpoint of political analysis tracking uses of power, since there is nothing to doubt or worry about except the use of a conventional label "law" that can be and has been attached to various and in no way essentially characterized phenomena.[5] Yet, if such doubts and worries are not groundless, and so not mere pseudo-disputes about how a purely artificial label ought to be used, work remains to be done to develop theories or theoretical concepts aimed at explaining structural features of legality of precisely the sort Tamanaha thinks misguided.[6]

---

5. Roger Cotterrell writes: "Brian Tamanaha has advocated a further approach which he calls *conventionalist*. It amounts to accepting as law 'whatever people identify and treat through their social practices as "law" (or *droit, Recht*, etc.)': *See* Tamanaha 2001, 166. But this surely combines the worst of all worlds: maintaining a definitional concern with what the concept of law should cover, yet removing from the concept so defined all analytical power." Roger Cotterrell, *Transnational Communities and the Concept of Law*, 21 RATIO JURIS 1, 8, n.6 (2008).

6. While a fuller examination of Tamanaha's rich and voluminous work is beyond the aim of this book, we should note a further worry we have about his view. The worry is about the compatibility of his claim that various kinds of law are simply too diverse to be captured under a single concept of law with the observation that various kinds of law—state, transnational, international, religious, customary, aboriginal, etc.—often conflict. It seems odd to suppose that such phenomena can conflict as often and typically as they do if they are so radically different. Indeed, conflict (and its ever-present potential) seems to suggest a degree of overlap or similarity in form, structure, and content rather than difference.

It seems to us that these doubts need to be taken rather more seriously than Tamanaha takes them. We are deeply sympathetic to his phenomena-driven approach to dominant explanatory tools and categories, and equally sympathetic to his sense that certain intuition-supported fictions need to be examined and put in their place. Yet not all intuitions are misleading. Some intuitions are crucial parts of the "regulative ideals" which, per MacCormick, may need to include even those ideals such as legal system, which upon reflection may need modification with respect to their content or our understanding of that ideal in relation to other ideals. The intuition that "law" and "legality" have at least settled cores, perhaps susceptible to explanatory expansion toward more precise understandings, seems to us to be one of those intuitions which ought to be supported so far as possible since it is a dominant part of the interests of our ordinary person facing clusters of norms while striving to understand and act in these clusters of, e.g., food labels, standards of professional conduct, use of public space, and so on. In addition to the importance of this intuition in daily life where the legal, moral, and political are usefully separated, for instrumental reasons to do with the daily operation of interlocking normative systems in complex societies,[7] there are further meta-theoretical reasons to resist Tamanaha's diminution of the role of general jurisprudence[8] in a broad understanding of legality. One central reason is bound up in the controversial matter of characterizing the metaphysical commitments of analytical legal theory's understanding of legality. We have offered in Chapter 3 a set of arguments against regarding at least Hart and Raz as offering an "essentialist" theory of law of the sort Tamanaha supposes we ought to use as evidence that we have been asking the wrong question about law in the wrong way. Tamanaha might of course reject our reading of Hart and Raz, in which we are far from alone as, e.g., MacCormick, sees in Hart some "polycentric potentialities" enabling escape from at least state-based theorizing and so from at least the sort of essentialism

---

7. See discussion of MacCormick in sec. 4.2.1. above on legal system as "regulative ideal" for his observations on the relation of theory and practice.

8. We should say *general jurisprudence as classically conceived by Bentham and Austin to Hart and Raz*, as a theory of law's core features. Tamanaha of course still envisions a role for general jurisprudence, conceived with different goals. *See* Tamanaha, *supra* note 3, at 195–7, 224, 234–6.

that might be rooted in presuppositions of the centrality of state experience. Yet whatever is said about our reading of Hart, Raz, and other analytical legal theorists, they remain at least the inspiration for our analytically-rooted inter-institutional view. Our view is avowedly non-essentialist in extension of analytical methods to suit expanded analytical goals, reflecting in our narrative concept of law some of the regulative ideals, such as legal system, which give an explanatory shape to our experience of law even as we acknowledge and seek better explanation of the relations amongst its regulative ideals. As a response to legal pluralism this is of course in a sense incomplete, likely because analytical responses to this sort of skepticism are unlikely to come from sheer force of analysis: what matters in the end is whether, as Raz reminds us, our understanding of law satisfies inquirers' interests, in doing so amounting to the best available explanation of legality. Perhaps, then, the best way to enable inquirers to make the inference to our explanation being the best available is to demonstrate what our theory can do to give shape to encounters with particularly puzzling phenomena, such as those presented in the Introduction.

5.2 MEETING THE EXPLANATORY CHALLENGE: BRINGING ELEMENTS OF LEGALITY TO BEAR ON EXPLANATORY PROBLEMS BEYOND THE SYSTEMIC LAW-STATE

In the Introduction we identified four provisional yet intuitively familiar categories of social phenomena we summarized as non-state phenomena. Categorizing those phenomena as we did we were complicit in state-centered legal theory to the extent that our categories were all expressed in terms of their relation to the state—intra-, trans-, supra-, and super-state phenomena. Much of our subsequent argument has been devoted to challenging the merit of attempts to explain relations between these categories as involving "hard" or "sharp" borders. Indeed, as we have suggested in Chapter 4, an analysis reaching beyond the systemic law-state tends to transform the problem of determinacy from one of hard edges between legal systems, legality and no-legality, and so on, into a problem of understanding overlap, interaction, and other quickly-used yet often weakly-specified metaphors. Many borders become points not of fundamental change, but of exchange—as a Briton entering France is no longer simply a stranger to be classified as fundamentally different from a French citizen, but a member of a shared European identity which allows the Briton to exchange at the increasingly porous border a "fully British" identity for a "British and European and French" identity when seeking employment, undertaking education and so on. Seeking hard conceptual borders in these areas seems not just to doom us to increasingly particular jurisprudence, but to ignore the fact of closer interaction notwithstanding nationalistic and otherwise motivated assertions of the enduring meaningfulness of certain borders. All of this inclines us towards deepening explanation of the phenomena raised in the Introduction, not by reasserting and sharpening the edges between those provisional categories, but by revisiting them as a whole. In our view the provisional categories represent legal orders with particular peaks of intensity and mutual reference, and are joined to other legal orders across peaks and valleys of mutual reference and intensity, which nonetheless serve to distinguish distinctively legal normative order from the other diverse orders informing daily life—moral, aesthetic, religious, and traditional.

5.2.1 Intra-State Legality

Intra-state legality of the kind we have discussed is clearly the most indebted to state-based legality, and support or recognition emanating from the systemic law-state from which the intra-state legality is nonetheless meaningfully distinct, at least in the ways it is regarded by ordinary citizens and likely on operational or functional grounds as well. Intra-state legality, then, is a legal analogue of an internal political minority—insiders who nonetheless retain something of their outsider status. In our view, intra-state legality exists wherever there is, within a conventionally determined law-state (whether systemic or not), a legal order demonstrated by the practice of some or all of the following elements of legality at some level of intensity, with a particular kind of mutual reference: content-independent peremptory norms are deployed using normative powers of determination, alteration, and enforcement, institutions of law, and legal institutions that mutually refer to each other with some degree of intensity. Crucially, such an intra-state legal order involves legal institutions which refer to one another yet tend to be relatively isolated from the legal institutions of the surrounding, supporting, and recognizing law-state. Various institutional configurations might occur, from a practice of channeling all communications between the intra-state legal order and its supporting state through a single or a few coordinating institutions, to a configuration of frequent low-intensity references between an intra-state order's legal institutions and the legal institutions of the supporting law-state, all regulated by the comparatively greater institutional force of a particular legal institution or subgroup of institutions within the variegation of mutual reference in the intra-state order. This analytical specification of the nature of an intra-state legal order reflects a wide variety of practices and overlaps between legal and other normative orders, from the "laws" of sports to their overlap where a sporting foul is additionally a criminally actionable assault, and on to components of a federated law-state whose mutual reference and intensity is limited. Our view nonetheless enables some useful identification of points of distinction and exchange between an intra-state legal order and a supporting or recognizing law-state.

In the Introduction we discussed the situation of the First Nations Tax Commission in Canada, a commission which authorizes First Nations to set and apply tax laws in First Nations communities. Why might our inter-institutional theory, rather than an official, state-based theory, better explain the nature of the First Nations Tax Commission? On an official, state-based theory, the legal nature of the institution is indeterminate. The Commission must be understood as either a legal institution that is part of the legal system of Canada because it forms part of a system of norm-applying institutions which claims to be comprehensive, supreme, and open; or the Commission is not a legal institution, and simply a private institution supported by the authority of the state, much as the Red Cross once served in Canada as a non-governmental yet state-supported provider of a public service in maintaining national blood supplies. On this account, the Commission is at best a borderline case of legal institution, perhaps safely left in that status as part of that ineliminable vagueness found at the intersection of normative orders. One problem with this account, however, is that the indeterminacy of the legal nature of the commission is not of the sorites kind of vagueness, where the problem is simply one of drawing a precise line. Rather the indeterminacy is radical, as the account provides no means for *how* any line might be drawn: we have no determinate criteria for either including or excluding the First Nations Tax Commission. Yet a more significant, meta-theoretical problem is that on this account the very problem of indeterminacy itself is constrained as simply one of determining whether the institution belongs within or without the legal system. If we are right in claiming that legality's borders are not always or best determined by searching for a state legal system's edges as these are revealed by officials' practices, then we have good reason to suppose that the problem of indeterminacy is misunderstood if taken to be a problem entirely about the membership of norms in determinately-bordered state legal systems. Here we see precisely the distortion created by existing analytical legal theories and the problem of indeterminacy they suppose in explanation of "borderline" phenomena. On our account, there need be nothing radically indeterminate about the legal nature of the First Nations Tax Commission. It is a legal institution to the extent that its operators practice content-independent peremptory norms via use of norm-creating and norm-enforcing powers in ways that recognize and mutually refer to other similarly-constituted and purposed institutions in Canada. To the extent that there is indeterminacy, it lies not at the level of whether the commission is or is not a legal institution, but at the level of the frequency and intensity of its interaction with other institutions and the degree to which its norms are practiced.[9] Indeed, on our account the question of the membership of the commission in a system whose members are legal institutions and whose non-members are non-legal institutions only detracts from the more important question of the features of legality that the commission does possess and its potentially non-hierarchically-ordered relations with its institutional partners.

This explanation of intra-state legality brings with it the opportunity to explore the extent to which a descriptive-explanatory picture of legality is distorted by a commitment to a hierarchical view of legality, and still further distorted by combining that commitment with a commitment to understanding legality as fundamentally systemic in

---

9. Other non-radical indeterminacies include: indeterminacy in the overlap between norm-applying and norm-enforcing institutions, indeterminacy in the overlap between norm-enforcing and norm-creating institutions, indeterminacy in the overlap between norm-applying and norm-creating institutions, and indeterminacy in the identity of institutional partners.

Raz's sense of a systemic claim to comprehensiveness, supremacy, and openness. Taken together, these commitments put a rule of recognition not just at the tip of a pyramid of validation of legal rules, but at the tip of explanation of normativity in daily life in a given social situation. In scenarios in which legal systems are understood as expressing claims of comprehensiveness, supremacy, and openness, all other norms and normative orders within that social situation are understood as authorized or supported by the legal system, or extant only to the extent of their compatibility with the norms of the legal system. Other normative systems within a legal system, then, are regarded as owing their continued existence to the forbearance of the legal system's officials—often its political officials who in accord with a political philosophy devise certain limits on the reach of law. Intra-state legality demonstrates one shortcoming of this view, to the extent that intra-state legal orders may exist as a form of internal minority State order yet with a sort of robustness which defies plausible characterization as a subordinate, supported, or merely tolerated order.

There is, however, another shortcoming of the pyramidal view, one related to the question of how our inter-institutional view can serve as a radar for legality while avoiding a kind of pluralism of exactly the sort we claim to avoid. The pyramidal view of legal system and its place in daily life is ill-suited to characterizing the social role of non-state social institutions whose norms carry institutional force sufficient to obviate the need for the legal system to address social affairs of some kind, and moreover, do so in a way which imposes limits on the capacity of the legal system to address those social affairs. Consider, for example, the generation of standards by institutions in markets, where those standards displace or obviate the need for state norms. "Non-state, market-driven" phenomena, as they are called, are used in various certification schemes best known in fisheries and forestry.[10] The Marine Stewardship Council, for example, has been very effective in advancing various norms regarding sustainable capture

---

10. B. Cashore, *Legitimacy and the Privatization of Environmental Governance: How Non-State Market-Driven (NSMD) Governance Systems Gain Rule-Making Authority*, 15:4 GOVERNANCE—AN INTERNATIONAL JOURNAL OF POLICY AND ADMINISTRATION 503 (2002). B. CASHORE, G. AULD, & D. NEWSOM, GOVERNING THROUGH MARKETS: FOREST CERTIFICATION AND THE EMERGENCE OF NON-STATE AUTHORITY (2004).

fishery practices, advancing as norms various standards established by the Food and Agriculture Organization of the United Nations.[11] In markets in which consumers support the standards advanced by the Council, producers have little choice but to meet those standards. In situations in which these non-state market-driven norms have institutional force sufficient to make them the governing norms, they are very poorly explained if understood as holding their normative force only insofar as they are recognized or supported by the law-state. These norms are quite unlike, for example, local practices recognized as customary law, or religious institutions of marriage supported by state recognition. Rather, non-state market-driven norms tend to come from outside the state, often engaging in a kind of super-state normative leadership, urging conduct within and between states in

---

11. About the Marine Stewardship Council (MSC):

The MSC is an international non-profit organization that was set up in 1997 to promote solutions to the problem of overfishing. The MSC runs the only widely recognized environmental certification and eco-labeling program for wild capture fisheries. It is the only seafood eco-label that is consistent with the ISEAL Code of Good Practice for Setting Social and Environmental Standards and UN FAO guidelines for fisheries certification. The FAO "Guidelines for the Eco-labeling of Fish and Fishery Products from Marine Capture Fisheries" require that credible fishery certification and eco-labeling schemes include:

- Objective, third-party fishery assessment utilizing scientific evidence;
- Transparent processes with built-in stakeholder consultation and objection procedures;
- Standards based on the sustainability of target species, ecosystems and management practices.

The MSC has offices in London, Seattle, Tokyo, Sydney, The Hague, Edinburgh, and Berlin. In total, more than 140 fisheries are engaged in the MSC program with 38 certified, 86 under assessment, and another 20 to 30 in confidential pre-assessment. Together the fisheries record annual catches of more than 5 million tons of seafood. Of fish for human consumption, they represent more than 42 percent of the world's wild salmon catch, 40 percent of the world's prime whitefish catch and 18 percent of the world's lobster catch. Worldwide, more than 1,900 seafood products resulting from the certified fisheries bear the blue MSC eco-label. For more information, please visit Marine Stewardship Council, http://www.msc.org/newsroom/press_releases/archive-2008/maine-lobster-fishery-seeks-certification-to-msc (last visited Dec. 2008).

accord with specified norms. It is of course possible that the law-state might introduce standards that conflict with the non-state market-driven norms prevailing in some social situation, and so state legality might displace those non-state legal norms. Yet to say prior to conflict that these non-state market-driven norms are in some sense authorized by the state is to indulge a fiction: until such time as a state in fact attempts to supplant these norms, and succeeds, the social fact of the situation is that the law-state's authority simply has not extended to it. What is perhaps most interesting about these non-state market-driven norms is that they may at times have greater institutional force than the institutional force of state legality: sometimes non-state market-driven norms may exceed legal norms in the stringency of the standard they set, outstripping rather than being supported by state legality. In other situations law-states choosing to violate these standards in their domestic affairs may find their fishers or foresters unable to export or sell internally, as the governing norm is not a state legal norm but a non-state market-driven norm. In increasingly common situations of this sort, where law-states are affected by normative claims from without, from *jus cogens* norms of international law to non-state market-driven norms urged by the Marine Stewardship Council, Forest Stewardship Council, and so on, law-states do not in fact function as if making claims to supremacy or comprehensiveness. Indeed, law-states seem in some of these situations to welcome the advance of complementary normative orders solving problems otherwise posing a burden for the law-state. Given the very widespread use of non-state market-driven norms, these phenomena are not borderline or outlier situations plausibly set to one side as a Razian picture of legal system and its claims continues to be maintained. Rather, this evidence shows that it is increasingly unrealistic to hold the Razian view, which requires us to insist on regarding as somehow less than fully legal those law-states in these situations where states simply are not and sometimes perhaps cannot be said to be making claims to comprehensiveness, supremacy, and openness. Indeed, where law-states are perhaps better characterized as being quite satisfied with other formalized normative systems' assumption of regulatory burdens, it seems that legality is increasingly understood by its users not as the top of the pyramid of normative orders, but as a particular tool for particular kinds of social tasks. What is ultimately distinctive about legality as a normative order, then, is not its supremacy over all other normative orders conceived as a hierarchy of orders with internal hierarchies of norms, but the nature of its claims: where legality is evident, peremptory content-independent norms are present, and where distinct legal orders are present, a certain kind of variegated pattern of legal institutions exists, giving life in those areas a distinctive character, e.g., systemic or non-systemic, overlapping with other legal systems in transboundary areas, or relatively independent of such situations.

5.2.2 Trans-State Legality

Our discussion of non-state market-driven norms brings us to their near relations, situations of trans-state legality. Gunther Teubner has provided a useful albeit incomplete explanation of trans-state legality as amounting to "autonomous private legal regimes" notably including the "*lex mercatoria* of the international economy and the *lex digitalis* of the Internet."[12] This explanation brings both troublesome terms and examples. To describe legality in the borders between states as "autonomous" is helpful to the extent that it marks trans-state legality as separable from each of the states it stands between, yet troublesome to the extent that part of the identity of trans-state legality is the fact and nature of its situation between specific law-states, a sort of special situatedness and dependence that amounts at best to a qualified sense of autonomy. Similarly, while talk of trans-state legality as "private" is perhaps useful as a distinction of some instance of trans-state legality from membership in the legal systems between which it stands as a sort of mediator, trans-state legality seems typically to be more than merely private. To the extent that trans-state legality typically aims to govern all specified conduct in a particular trans-state situation, to call it private is only to say that it is not sponsored by a single law-state's system. Whether competing normative orders can supplant trans-state legality is again a question of institutional normative power, not a question of the conceptual or empirical possibility of trans-state legality. Finally, while *lex mercatoria*

---

12. Andreas Fischer-Lescano and Gunther Teubner, *Regime-Collisions: The Vain Search for Legal Unity in the Fragmentation of Global Law*, 25 MICHIGAN JOURNAL OF INTERNATIONAL LAW 999, 1010–1 (2003–4). *See also* Paul S. Berman, *The Globalization of Jurisdiction*, 151 UNIVERSITY OF PENNSYLVANIA LAW REVIEW 311 (2002).

and so-called *lex digitalis* serve as useful examples of non-state law, they are perhaps not especially illustrative of what is distinctive about trans-state legality as opposed to supra-state legality. Our example, from the Introduction, of the Greenland Conservation Agreement is perhaps rather more useful as an illustration of the character of trans-state legality as it is separate from and so not a member of the legal systems of law-states using it, instead mediating between law-states in non-comprehensive fashion, over some limited area of social life, in a coordinative rather than authoritative relation, unlike, e.g., *jus cogens* norms of international law that function as standing constraints on law-states' authority. The Greenland Conservation Agreement is unlike *lex mercatoria*, which addresses law-states generally over a broad range of conduct; rather, the agreement is private in the sense of lacking an origin in or membership in a law-state's legal system, and mediates between those states by asserting a content-independent peremptory norm prohibiting commercial salmon fishing in Greenland's territorial waters. The agreement was signed and is practiced by three non-governmental organizations on the recommendation of a scientific council; its connection to any state recognition or systemic authorization is tenuous at best, as it has only been recognized by the devolved government of Greenland which has agreed to "help enforce it". In the standard analytical picture, then, the agreement lacks legality, since it lacks official recognition by state authorities whose practices create the core and borders of legal systems. In this way, the agreement is not, unlike the First Nations Tax Commission, a borderline case of legality. It simply is a non-legal, private agreement which is capable of being supported by various state authorities, including Greenland, Denmark, Canada, the United States, and Iceland. Yet as we suggested in our initial diagnosis and can now extend via the inter-institutional view, such an account seems to under-emphasize the non-optional nature of the agreement and the character of the norms used by institutions evident in the situation: several institutions have deliberately created and now enforce a content-independent peremptory norm governing the use of natural resources. On our account, the agreement is legal in nature, as it is constituted by the practice of a norm-creating power which is shared amongst and exercised by several institutions which mutually refer to each to such a degree that they have effectively eliminated all licenses to commercial salmon fishing in

Greenland's territorial waters.[13] Notice in this analysis that trans-state legal institutions are not limited to state-based actors: we understand the institutional actors of trans-state legality in a somewhat specialized sense, including both state actors and typically non-state actors such as NGOs, market institutions, multinational corporations, and industry institutions.[14] It might of course be objected that this conflicts with the self-conception of some of these actors, to which we may respond that as a tool for satisfaction of inquirer's interests, including interests of self-understanding, our inter-institutional theory may sometimes bring to the surface inconsistency between intention and action, and observe with respect to this particular objection that it is not always the case that norm subjects recognize fully, in the throes of action, all of the consequences of those actions. It is conceptually and practically possible for norm-subjects acting under the guise of morality, even sincere belief that they are engaging in nothing more than moral agreement and practice, to act in ways which amount to the setting of law—just as those acting under what they believe to be the justification of law can in fact be seen to be acting not under law but according to moral norms. That such a situation might not last long, assuming reasonably self-reflective agents who typically encounter criticism of their views and practices from without, is no objection to this possibility.

---

13. On this score we share a perspective with legal pluralists. E.g., Paul Berman notes the distinct advantage of widening the scope of sources of legal authority: "Accordingly, by taking pluralism seriously we will more easily see the way in which the contest over norms creates legitimacy over time, and we can put to rest the idea that norms not associated with nation-states have no binding authority. As a result, instead of focusing solely on who has the formal authority to articulate norms or the coercive power to enforce them, we can turn the gaze to an empirical study of which statements of authority tend to be *treated* as binding in actual practice and by whom." [original emphasis, author's notes omitted] Paul Berman, *A Pluralist Approach to International Law*, 32 YALE JOURNAL OF INTERNATIONAL LAW 301, 323 (2007).

14. Compare with PHILIP C. JESSUP, TRANSNATIONAL LAW (1956), who includes both state and non-state actors as practitioners of transnational law. For purposes of the division between categories of prima facie legal phenomena, and because we argue that the distinction between state and non-state actors is of diminishing relevance, we see no reason to follow strictly Jessup's or other conceptions of transnational law.

Trans-state legality of this sort—operated by state agents and others—raises another issue associated with the analytical picture wed to a systemic conception of legality with accompanying Razian ingredients. It might be argued from that picture that the Greenland Conservation Agreement cannot be an instance of legality because it neither includes nor identifies law-applying institutions with dispute-settling jurisdiction. On this view, the Greenland Conservation Agreement is at best a borderline case of legality not simply because it lacks membership in a legal system, but because it lacks a necessary institutional characteristic of legality. Unlike the criticism we faced earlier in discussion of intra-state legality, which worries that intra-state phenomena's standing outside the pyramidal hierarchy of norms precludes its being legal, this criticism is in a sense internal to an institution-focused view. Responses to this criticism are useful to both elucidation of the nature of trans-state legality, and to further demonstration of the way an inter-institutional theory depicts and distinguishes the various manifestations of legality evident in intra-state, trans-state, and systemic law-state legality. On one line of response it could be argued that the member institutions, while likely on the state-centered view to be understood as members of particular states' fishing industries, are better conceived as having multifaceted roles associated with their membership, including function as law-applying institutions, since any disputes about the Agreement's application must be settled by them. This response seems persuasive to at least the extent that it saves the Greenland Conservation Agreement from the criticism that it lacks law-applying mechanisms, but it runs the risk of stretching the notion of a law-applying institution unrecognizably beyond its familiar examples of trial and appellate courts in state jurisdictions. A second, better response is to argue that law-applying institutions are only a contingent feature of legality, rather than a necessary feature which relies on presumption that all legality must resemble or be connected to state legality. On our account, mutual reference with a supplementary law-applying institution within the Greenland Conservation Agreement, or mutual reference with sponsoring law-state- or international law-applying institutions, would certainly increase the scope of the Agreement's legality and give that legality a particular character as an association of legal institutions, perhaps increasing its intensity as well; but mutual reference to law-applying institutions is not a necessary condition of the Agreement's legality. So perhaps unsurprisingly, in our analysis, displacement of this trans-state legal institution by law-states would increase the institutional force and intensity of interaction between the Agreement, law-states, and other actors; but even in the event of that displacement and enhancement of institutional force, the legality of the Agreement would remain throughout that process and would not commence at the moment the Agreement gained the sponsorship of a particular law-state.

The relation between trans-state legality and the systemic law-state may appear to be an uneasy one, as the institutional force of trans-state legality as an independent, or "autonomous legal regime" as Teubner puts it, appears susceptible to competition from law-states and from supra- and super-state legality. It may be tempting to view this uneasy relation as evidence against the existence of trans-state legality, choosing in light of this susceptibility to attempt to understand particular instances of trans-state legality as in fact instances of some more familiar category, perhaps a systemic law-state or a set of international legal norms. Yet choosing this interpretive option comes at the cost of ignoring what is perhaps most interesting about the fragility of trans-state legality as a legal order: the reason for its fragility, which is likely not inherent to the concept of intra-state legality, is its place at a shifting border between systemic law-states, supra-state organizations, and super-state international law. That border shifts over time, and the uneasiness of the relation between trans-state legality and the systemic-law state is an indication of the shift in the problem of determinacy from demarcation of boundaries between states, to understanding and specifying the kinds of normative exchange between legal orders, as exemplified by trans-state legality, and the ways even systemic law-states are themselves changing and not just affecting the nature of other legal orders. Trans-state legality as an organizing concept in a general jurisprudence is itself affected by this discussion: it marks a contingent inter-institutional variegation whose identification as that form of legal order is a matter of choice in response to that legal order's particular association of legal institutions relating to one another with specific patterns of mutual reference with some degree of intensity. The same may be said of the phenomena we shall discuss next, first raised in in the Introduction: supra-state legality as exemplified by the rise of the European Union.

5.2.3 Supra-State Legality

The European Union, as an example of supra-state legality emerging from a collection of formerly relatively independent law-states, offers a useful opportunity for further examination of the limitations of analytical legal theory's work on the problems of the identity and continuity of legal systems, and further reflection on what the shortcomings of analytical legal theory can tell us about the task of an improved approach. Those limitations are usefully approached by considering Julie Dickson's recent attempt to assess the applicability of a Razian approach to the European Union. In a recent article she takes the central task of theorizing about the European Union to be provision of "a sound understanding of the character of and relations between legal systems". In working towards such an understanding she makes two commitments: the first is to adopt Raz's understanding of legal system as a normative system which claims to be comprehensive, supreme, and open. The second commitment is to understand the relations between legal systems in terms of norms. As she says, her approach "takes the question of how to think about the legal systems of the EU given the complex interrelations between EU norms and EU Member States' national norms as its central concern".[15] With these two commitments, she then offers and considers evidence for three different views about the nature of the European Union. We might hold that (i) there is a distinct European Union legal system, as the European Court of Justice has made claims to the supremacy of European Community law with considerable success. Or, (ii) we might hold that there remain distinct Member State legal systems, as their supreme courts often make rival supremacy claims, to the effect that European Community law is valid but only because authorized by Member State constitutional commitments. Finally, (iii) we might hold that Member State legal systems and the European Union legal system are not distinct, since European Community legal provisions of "direct effect" may show that European Community law is in fact also part of Member State legal systems. In determining whether a European Community law is part of Member State legal systems,

---

15. Julie Dickson, *How Many Legal Systems?: Some Puzzles Regarding the Identity Conditions of, and Relations Between, Legal Systems in the European Union*, 2 PROBLEMA: ANNUARIO DE FILOSOPHIA Y TEORIA DEL DERECHO 9, 13 (2008).

Dickson adopts Raz's distinction between giving legal effect to non-member norms and applying binding norms which are already part of a system's membership of norms. As Dickson notes, the key to Raz's test is to look to an "accumulation of evidence" about the reasons and attitudes of political actors about the membership of a norm. If courts, legislatures, and citizens view a norm as "their norm", then such beliefs constitute evidence in favor of the norm's membership. If such beliefs are absent, but the norm is viewed as applicable "foreign law", then the norm is not part of the system but nonetheless must be given legal effect.

A central concern of Dickson's article is precisely to offer an account that illuminates how we might attribute a home for European Community laws. Such an approach is no doubt required so long as we are concerned with explaining the discreteness of legal systems, understood as systems of norms which are hierarchically ordered. Yet the motivation for such an approach is open to question. Indeed, if our earlier argument about the diminishing relevance of hierarchy in theorizing about law is sound, we have good reason to resist Dickson's first commitment to Raz's theory of legal system. A concept of legal system which supposes that legal systems are constituted by distinct hierarchies of law-applying institutions tends to force a detached observer to view institutional interaction as a chain of authority leading to some ultimate authority. Yet it might be quite misleading to ascribe these sorts of chains of hierarchy to the thick institutional practices which contribute to the legality of the norms actually recognized and practiced in the European Union, such as the claims of Member State courts or the European Court of Justice. As we demonstrated in our discussion of *Symbian* in Chapter 4, the interactions between law-applying legal institutions in the European Union seem to involve "dialogue" and "compromise" between similarly situated, potentially conflicting legal institutions, not reference to a chain of authority to determine which legal institution holds greater authority.

Dickson's second commitment—to focus on the interrelations of norms—seems equally ill-advised, especially when this commitment amounts to an attempt to determine the home of individual norms which ultimately relies on examining the attitudes of legislators, courts, and citizens. Such an approach certainly faces the now familiar problem of indeterminacy: exactly whose attitudes count?

What if they conflict? What if they overlap? In supposing the existence and borders of law depend on individual attitudes towards norms leaves us little distance ahead.[16]

As Dickson emphasizes, however, her aim in the article is not to settle conclusively one way or the other the precise nature of the relations between legal systems in the European Union.[17] Indeed, toward the end of the article she observes that perhaps part of the problem in determining whether a norm belongs to one system or another is that it assumes a choice must be made:

> [p]erhaps the "rather than" is out of place here, and it is possible that EC norms enforceable in national courts are part of a distinct EU legal system *and* part of Member States's legal systems at the same time. If this is the case, then the simple picture of there being as many distinct legal systems in the EU as there are member states' legal systems plus one, the EU legal system which has a separate relationship with each of the legal systems of Member States again seems to break down somewhat, because when we come to examine which norms belong to which system, we will find considerable overlap in content between the EU legal system and Member States' legal systems simply in virtue of EU norms being applied by national courts. On this view, when a national court applies an EC norm domestically, it thereby renders that EC norm part of the Member State legal system as well as part of the EU legal system, and hence increases

---

16. In our view, explained more fully below, what matters is not the reflective attitudes or reasons legislators, judges, or citizens of Member State legal systems (or a European Union legal system) have in deciding whether norms are or are not part of their legal systems. Nor is the distinction between norms which are given legal effect in a legal system but are not part of the legal system and norms which are binding and part of the legal system of much relevance. What matters is the combination of normative powers which are exercised among member state and European community institutions, the areas of social life they purport to govern, and the intensity of the relations of mutual reference between them, which range in kind from recognition of divided sovereignty, to authorization, to imposing obligations.

17. "It is true that in all of this I have not staked my claim to a conclusive position on the matter of the character of and relations between legal systems in the EU, but as I stated at the outset, my aim in the present discussion is rather to provide a better and more focused understanding of the relevant questions and puzzles as regards this issue by examining them in light of some legal philosophical considerations." Dickson, *supra* note 15, at 45–46.

the overlap between the domestic system and the EU legal system.[18] [original emphasis, author's notes omitted.]

Dickson also notes that the bulk of interpretation and application of EC law is done by Member State courts. She writes,

> This seems to indicate that, when a point of EC law is in play and must be applied by national courts, that those national courts are in effect acting as EC courts, and as part of the EC legal system. Given this level of overlap as regards system norms and indeed system institutions, we may begin to wonder whether it is sensible even to continue to ask questions regarding which norms belong to which system—Member State or EU—although once again, the points mentioned above raised by Raz's work on the nature and limits of legal systems suggest interesting questions remain in this regard, which can be solved only by focusing on various of the attitudes to these systems in terms of their role as part of units of political identification and/or alienation held by, amongst others, Member States' courts and Member States nationals/EU citizens.[19] [author's notes omitted]

It is of more than passing interest that Dickson questions whether it is "sensible to ask questions regarding which norms belong to which system" since so much work at the level of particular jurisprudence seems to be required to provide even a relatively local explanation, owing a great deal to sociological examination of possibly temporary attitudes, and the contribution of that local explanation to a general jurisprudence would likely be slight. It seems more plausible to simply accept that the question that would drive such sociological investigations is no longer a relevant question in light of the kinds of close interactions evident amongst institutions in the European community. Notice, however, that this is not to say that attitudes of political identification are of no importance. They are important, but their importance is separable from Raz's ideas of the importance of the discreteness of legal systems and the relevance of a distinction between given legal effect to foreign norms and applying binding norms of a system. Attitudes of political identification are no doubt part of a politically relevant and sensitive assessment of the motivation and justifiability of allegiance to some norms or institutions rather than others. But issues of motivation and justifiability of allegiance are not determining factors in finding the borders of legality

---

18. Dickson, *Id.* at 43.
19. *Id.* at 44–45.

or even the borders between legal orders. It seems, then, in light of preceding discussion, that a hierarchy-presupposing, authority-tracing view tends to raise as many questions as it answers, and some of those new questions are about the merit of trying to apply that approach to novel phenomena. We do not deny the enduring plausibility of a Razian approach, extended as Dickson suggests, but it does seem to us that it is no longer an "apt" explanation for most inquirers, and is particularly inapt for inquirers within the European Union seeking self-understanding enabling a clearer view of the problems of life under law within such a legal order. Once again, MacCormick's approach seems to us to present a much more useful step toward an apt explanation taking seriously the possibility that the European Union demands jurisprudential tools beyond those associated with explanation of the law-state, and demands explanation in a way which is not preoccupied with systemic identity and continuity.

We have already discussed Neil MacCormick's attempt to characterize the transformation of the post-Westphalian state in the European Union, a task complicated by the need to overcome the double-commitment to the ideas that states are and must be individually and absolutely sovereign, and that legal systems can only be associated with territorially sovereign states.[20] As he notes, these commitments make it impossible for non-state legality, especially of the supra-state kind, to exist. Yet the facts we must examine show otherwise, as Dickson's analysis begins to show, and much as Hart observed in argument contra Austin's sovereignty-dependent view: the objection that the fact of sovereignty is a conceptual bar to the possibility of international law is easily countered by demonstration that at least post-Westphalian states do not in fact hold or assert a mode of complete sovereignty of the sort required by Austin's rejection of the possibility of there being both state and international law. Extending Hart's observation, it seems that what are at least prima facie supra-state legal orders have in fact emerged out of the practices and agreements of several states, often regionally concentrated, as we see in MERCOSUR, NAFTA, and the European Union. These legal orders demonstrate a remarkable transformation in the nature of law-states' borders. Once primarily physical edges in the geo-centric

---

20. NEIL MACCORMICK, QUESTIONING SOVEREIGNTY 117–118 (1999).

state, borders are now both physical and notional points of translation and exchange, as exemplified in matters such as member states' national implementation of Union-wide commitments of the sort we noted in Chapter 4's discussion of the interaction of European and United Kingdom intellectual property law. The European Union as a point of interaction, exchange, and translation of legal norms implemented by meaningfully independent member states leaves the union in a sense continuous with trans-state legality's position between law-states. Perhaps the most interesting difference lies in the increased scope of the European Union's social subject matter beyond the typically limited scope of trans-state legality, and the intensity of mutual reference between European Union legal institutions and member-states whose membership includes a giving up of claims to comprehensive, supreme, and open authority. The nature of member states of the European Union is interestingly transformed, an abandonment of prior claims in favor of a new, possibly better existence as member-states form a nexus of overlapping domestic and supra-state European legal norms. A number of choices exist with respect to the answer to MacCormick's "questioning sovereignty" by the title of his book of the same name. An adaptation of Quebec's once-favored relation to Canada, the notion of "sovereignty association,"[21] is of course possible, as are other categories suited to inquirers' interests, perhaps even as simple as a special category of "European state" which might later be matched by analogous developments amongst "NAFTA states." What is important in the context of elaboration of an inter-institutional theory of law, where legality is shorn from officials, states, and geography, is the diminishing importance of the law-state to an account of legality—even as a political account of law-states' particular institutional composition and patterns of intense mutual reference becomes increasingly important to particular jurisprudence and its intersection with political science. In our view, what distinguishes the European Union as a legal order, contrasted against, e.g., a non-Union systemic law-state with a federal internal order, is perhaps far less jurisprudentially significant than has been thought. Although both of these situations may be politically

---

21. Robert Jackson, *Introduction: Sovereignty at the Millennium*, 47 POLITICAL STUDIES 423–430.

quite different and pursue quite different ideals using quite different legal norms, both are characterized by a concentration of legal institutions for interaction between central and peripheral institutions, e.g., in Europe, overlapping representative institutions such as the European Parliament and the Westminster Parliament and the Scottish Parliament, and in Canada, institutions such as the Council of the Federation.[22] What is most jurisprudentially significant about these situations is perhaps no longer the question of how a group of states forms a supra-state legal order which is distinguishable from a federated law-state, but instead a more basic question about particular versus universal legal orders—what it is that distinguishes particular relatively local variegations of legal orders from claims to super-state legal order found in international law. Once we are oriented toward this more basic question, we are freed from a number of preoccupations associated with the assumption that the systemic law-state carries the mark and measure of legality. Instead we are focussed on understanding a variety of contingencies associated with institutions of law and legal institutions: legality may but need not be state-based, may but need not be geocentric, and need not have any particular content, as there are a variety of ways of achieving the various goals we have in life under law, using overlapping legal orders, and overlaps between state and non-state legal-normative orders.

As we ask this refocused jurisprudential question about varieties of legal orders and their interaction in an "inverted pyramid" style of socialized jurisprudence, a static time-slice view of a momentary hierarchy of legal institutions has very little probative value relative to inquirers' interests, and is inapt given the dynamic nature of the phenomena. An apt explanation takes seriously the dynamic nature of the European Union, from its roots in the European Coal and Steel Community, to its ongoing enlargement process. Unsurprisingly, given the historical origin of the European Union, it contains elements of legality identical in structure to those found in the law-state, albeit varying in content and patterns of intense mutual reference. Institutions of law are evident in the European Union in the form of e.g., European Directives, and particular national implementation of European legal norms. Legal institutions are also evident in the

---

22. http://www.councilofthefederation.ca/ (last visited May 10, 2009).

European Union, from the three central institutions (European Parliament, Council of the European Union, European Commission) to adjudicative and law-applying institutions, all exercising specified legal-normative powers. Unlike law-states of the kind amenable to hierarchical, official-based analytical approaches, the European Union appears to lack the sort of systematic unity visible in the law-state via identification of core institutions responsible for maintenance of the minimum natural law content of the system. Instead this responsibility seems to be distributed amongst Member States, whose implementation of this content is subject to interplay with European institutions such as the European Court of Justice, and the European Court of Human Rights. What gives the European Union its particular character is, then, both the patterns of intense mutual reference amongst its legal institutions and those of Member States, and the particular distribution amongst those institutions of functions familiar from the systemic-law state, yet not present in the same systematic fashion in the European Union, since distribution and horizontal inter-relation and interdependence are as prominent as law-state-like hierarchy. Viewed contrastively against the law-state, and against intra-state and trans-state legality, the European Union amounts to a sui generis form of legal order qua variegation of legal institutions, whose origins in overlapping and intersecting institutions might over time be gradually displaced by pan-European legal norms and legal institutions, much as in common law systems customary law has been gradually displaced by statute and precedent. Here Kelsen's, MacCormick's, and Postema's sensitivity to law's temporally dynamic nature becomes important to adequate explanation of the European Union legal order. It is a relatively recent product, developed over nearly sixty years, and by its own reckoning is far from complete in both its integration of legal institutions already in relations of intense mutual reference,[23] and in its inclusion of other legal institutions via enlargement. The "work in progress" nature of the European Union, and enlargement in particular, underscore the aptness of what at the end of Chapter 3 we identified as a "narrative"

---

23. E.g., transport, banking, telecommunication, research (nuclear research an early example). See http://www.questia.com/library/book/european-institutions-co-operation-integration-unification-by-a-h-robertson.jsp. (Last visited May 2009).

concept of law. There we urged adoption of an understanding of conceptual explanation which gives due regard for the situation of the phenomena under interpretation within a particular temporal scope. In this suggestion we did not so much diverge from other analytical theorists such as Hart, who called for investigation into broadly "modern" municipal systems, but rather we aimed to achieve what Hart and others perhaps did not in excessive focus on the details of a picture of legality without re-informing that picture with new phenomena. The narrative concept of law that emerges from this analysis of the law-state's nearest cousin, the legal order of the European Union, is a concept that finds legality rooted in institutions whose interaction and recombination in varying over time produces, contingently, the law-state, and equally contingently, the European Union. The contingent identity of the European Union as an agglomeration and variegation of legal institutions is emphasized rather than undermined by observation that its roots in systemic state law are being gradually overgrown by European Union institutions of law and legal institutions, which replace comprehensiveness, supremacy, and openness with comprehensiveness, interplay, and overlap, as seen in its relations with less-than-member states whose legal institutions are nonetheless in mutual reference with European Union legal institutions. Associated States, Candidate States, and Potential Candidate States fall into this border zone of less intense yet meaningful inter-institutional mutual reference.

One obvious objection to this view is that it fails to capture and reproduce what makes the European Union a distinct legal order—it fails to settle on one of the three Razian options identified by Dickson. Yet from our stance, this apparent failure is in fact a distinctive feature of our inter-institutional view: in taking seriously the possibility that the European Union represents a novel form of legal order best characterized in terms other than those familiar from the systemic law-state, we avoid what Waldron called the "effrontery" of the analytical theorists' presumption that the only legality of theoretical interest is found in situations usefully captured by a rule of recognition. In our view the European Union can amount to a distinct non-systemic legal order whose special quality relative to the systemic law-state is evident in the union's particular kind of institutional agglomeration which is historically continuous with the law-states whose nature is gradually transformed through their membership in the European Union.

Rather than seeking to draw hard lines where deliberate practice aims to avoid those hard lines, the inter-institutional view tracks and records the intensity of inter-institutional mutual reference characteristic of the European Union legal order, from Member states, to enlargement process categories of "candidate" and "potential candidate" countries. We might of course be faulted on various grounds for having failed to provide here a comprehensive account of the European Union legal order; but since our goal here is to explain why an inter-institutional *approach* ought to be preferred to prior analytical approaches, we may safely leave for future work the task of specifying more precisely the relation between the various kinds of members of the European Union. For now it is sufficient that we have supplied a method and the beginning of its application, sufficient to contrast the general merits of our approach with prior analytical approaches.

5.2.4 Super-State Legality

The final category of prima facie legality we identified in the Introduction is super-state legality. By super-state legality we mean those elements of legality and their combination which often but not always emerge out of the agreement and practice of states and which purport with some degree of success to bind or govern non-party states and their nationals as a step towards creating universal or global law. The best example of super-state legality is international humanitarian law, which attempts to establish universal human rights via prohibitions against, for example, the use of torture and genocide. In international legal scholarship, universal legal norms are often labeled as peremptory norms of *jus cogens* and obligations *erga omnes*.

One way of searching for super-state legality is to locate a central law-applying institution with the jurisdiction to prosecute and apply universal humanitarian law. Existing institutions include the international war crimes tribunals for the former Yugoslavia and Rwanda, and also the more recently created International Criminal Court which has begun investigations but not yet tried anyone at the time of writing. These law-applying (and law-creating) institutions are designed precisely to deal specifically with violations of international humanitarian law and to do so under certain conditions in cases involving non-party nationals.

The successes of the war crimes tribunals for the former Yugoslavia and Rwanda make it difficult to deny their legal nature. Where there are doubts, these are typically about the legitimacy of the tribunals, which are often viewed as selective and highly political in their creation and operation. Doubts about the legality of the International Criminal Court are deeper, and tend to rest on its overt failure to secure universal, compulsory jurisdiction, manifested most clearly with the lack of United States' support. We have suggested earlier, in Chapter 1, that such skepticism rests on an adverse but largely unwarranted comparison with many state law-applying institutions. A successful claim of universal jurisdiction, viewed primarily as a condition of legitimacy, is not a necessary condition of legality. On our account, the International Criminal Court has several structural features of legality: it is composed of several institutions with norm-creating, applying, and enforcing powers, poised to exercise these to prosecute and sentence individual offenders for violent crimes against persons. What remains to be seen is how well it can *function* as a legal institution, requiring as it does relations of mutual reference and support in those places where local, regional, and national institutions' cooperation is needed.[24] The relations of mutual reference between the court and other institutions will no doubt vary in intensity, but they will be detectable in instances where the normative situations of individuals are affected.

Yet on our account a focus on the existence, operation, and effectiveness of international tribunals such as the International Criminal Court is only one means of detecting and understanding the existence of super-state legality. Indeed, super-state legality occurs wherever the norms of international humanitarian law are practiced as norms of international humanitarian law, and divisions of power and authority are struck on the basis of respect for such norms. In this way, the practices of many human rights NGOs, typically described as lobbying or pressuring state governments and institutions, begin to blur the boundaries between lobbying for normative change and securing compliance with international human rights norms.[25]

---

24. *See* MARK DRUMBL, ATROCITY, PUNISHMENT, AND INTERNATIONAL LAW (2007).

25. For example, the International Criminal Court at present requires NGO support, and often appoints NGO officers as ICC delegates. *See*

We can now see clearly why we ought to resist Tamanaha's view that since state law is only one kind of law, others being international law and transnational law, the nature of legality is therefore plural. Tamanaha and other legal pluralists suppose that state law has a unique nature, as a legal system constituted by the collective practice of a determinate and hierarchically-ordered cohort of public or legal officials who claim to govern comprehensively and supremely over some specified population and geography. In this way, legal pluralists and state-based legal theorists oddly share a common (but mistaken) view, that the nature of state law has been correctly explained. Yet once it is recognized that legality within states is constituted not by the activities of the state, or supreme state sources of law, but rather is constituted by institutional interdependence and interaction which may or may not be organized hierarchically, and may or may not rest at the borders with the activities of determinately identifiable state officials, it becomes clear to see that inter-institutional activity can occur at many levels and across many different geographical regions.

B. Schiff, Building the International Criminal Court 149, 155–6 (2008).

6. FRESH PROBLEMS

The bulk of this book has been occupied with a task that is fundamentally positive in spite of its arriving in the midst of a welter of criticism: the task of characterizing novel legal phenomena arriving in system-like and non-system-like legal orders standing within and alongside the law-state. This task has required us to give extended attention to the idea of legal system, and to follow system-influenced conceptions of the problem of continuity, which is bound up in the question of identity. As Raz put the problem,

> Questions of continuity concern the various ways in which a legal system ceases to exist and is replaced by a new system. Does, for example, a revolution, or a *coup d'etat*, or a declaration of independence, terminate the existence of one legal system and signal the emergence of a new system?
> A momentary legal system is a legal system at a particular point of time. The problem of scope is the search for criteria of identity of momentary legal systems, whereas the problem of continuity is the search for criteria providing a method for determining whether two momentary legal systems are part of one, continuous legal system.[1]

As Raz conceives it, the problem of identity is specifically a problem about the identity of *legal systems* (and particularly *municipal* legal systems), in which a criteria-based test is sought for determining all the laws that belong to any particular legal system.[2] Questions about the efficacy of laws ask about the existence of laws within a legal system. Questions about applying existing laws or adding new ones are about the existence or addition of laws to existing legal systems. And as Raz supposes, a view about the relation between law and state is needed because "the identity of a legal system is bound up with that of the state the law of which it is . . ."[3] Yet once one rejects the central focus placed on legal system, especially legal system understood as the legal system of a state, the questions of continuity and identity

1. Joseph Raz, The Authority of Law 81 (1979).
2. *Id.*
3. *Id.* at 99.

become quite different. It is no longer a matter of constructing tests to find homes for laws in established state-based legal systems, but rather a matter of constructing a theory capable of testing for the emergence of legality in the interactions between institutions.

We have given at most incidental attention along the way to the consequences of our rejection of Raz's understanding of the problem of continuity as essentially a problem of succession between legal systems. Relatedly, we have given at most incidental attention to the question of whether our improved bootstrapping and responsiveness to new phenomena has been sufficiently thorough. For example, have we taken seriously the possibility raised by Coleman, that "technology" might compel revision of "our" concept of law? Yet the inter-institutional theory is designed to be responsive to the dips in intensity of mutual reference characteristic of replacement of one legal system by another in situations such as revolution, and just as importantly, as a theory which is not reliant on tracing of hierarchies of officials or institutions to find legality, the inter-institutional view is designed to be responsive to various kinds of failures of succession between systems, and failures of mutual reference within systems. Indeed, a significant part of the value of the inter-institutional theory, even when laid out in preliminary fashion in a short book, consists in its surfacing previously underexamined issues demonstrably needing more thorough consideration.

We will first take up what might, following Hart,[4] be regarded as the pathology of legality, to be followed by brief discussion of novel or emerging phenomena beyond what we have introduced, identifying without resolving, and so leaving for future work, problems made prominent by the inter-institutional view. Discussion of these problems will provide a useful basis for closure of this chapter and the book by way of a return to the meta-theoretical-evaluative issue with which we began: the relation between structural and functional aspects of a descriptive-explanatory account of legality, from the prominent yet no longer dominant systemic law-state, following legality "all the way down" to its pathological forms.

---

4. H.L.A. HART, THE CONCEPT OF LAW 117 (1994).

6.1 PATHOLOGIES OF LEGALITY

The pathology of legality is perhaps especially interesting as a topic whose focal problem illuminates the distance between the theoretical priorities of state-focused analytical approaches, and Tamanaha's style of legal pluralism. From our perspective, the intense mutual reference found in the interactions of legal institutions in the law-state is of theoretical interest because of the distinctive nature of the pattern of interactions characteristic of the systemic-law state; detection of additional legal orders is not so much a disproof of the analytical account of the law-state as it is cause for revision of that account. Indeed, the possibility of other legal orders whose characteristic form of coherence is non-systemic tends to leave us open to the possibility of a diverse range of forms of legality whose diversity certainly need not compel acceptance of a "law is whatever is called law" view because those forms exhibit distinctive forms of intense mutual reference amongst their constitutive legal institutions. Yet challenges remain: how might we best characterize the range of changes to life under law arriving as legal systems change character within as inter-institutional interactions shift, and as legal orders are transformed over time in ways satisfactory or unsatisfactory to participants and onlookers? And how might we conduct this characterization without slipping into presumption of the superiority of some particularly familiar legal order such as the systemic law-state? Can a pathology of legality be developed without presumptions of hierarchies amongst legal institutions and officials or power-wielders within them?

This is perhaps a more difficult task than a first glance reveals. Consider, for example, the difficulties generated by Hart's contrast of "simple" pre-legal societies with the defect-resolving relatively complex systems operating under a combination of primary and secondary rules. Complex modern legal systems are implicitly regarded as superior in that discussion, and with good reason, since they tend to support societies in which norm-subjects' expectations are procedurally and substantively protected. This good reason is, however, a reason supporting a normative judgment regarding the comparative superiority of complex systems as contributors to justifiably desired ways of life. A morally neutral descriptive-explanatory theory cannot, of course, rely on this basis when attempting to develop a pathology of legality—a descriptive-explanatory account must be cautious to avoid prematurely assessing a difference as a defect. Sophistication and complexity are not always, for example, evidence of continuity or persistence of a legal order, and may instead be evidence of a deficit of legality when assessed in light of the legal order's claims and aspirations. One useful illustration of this problem may be seen in the situation of equality law in the United Kingdom, where a 2007 proposal for a Single Equality Act, in place of nine major pieces of legislation[5] and supporting regulations, was justified by Communities Secretary Ruth Kelly as the remedy for an unsatisfactory set of inter-institutional interactions: "For over 40 years, laws have been introduced in a piecemeal fashion and have as a result become overlapping and less clear. So it is right we have this review to ensure the laws which govern how people are treated in their everyday lives are as clear and effective as possible."[6] The Chair of the Commission for Equality and Human Rights,[7] Trevor Phillips, offered a similar assessment, calling extant legislation an "impenetrable thicket."[8] There is here evidence of a decline in intensity of mutual reference—legal powers allocated amongst legal institutions are diplomatically said to be "piecemeal" and "overlapping" by one official, and slightly less diplomatically described as a "thicket" by another.

---

5. As documented in the *Discrimination Law Review* consultation paper: Equal Pay Act, 1970; Sex Discrimination Act, 1975; Race Relations Act, 1976; Disability Discrimination Act, 1995; Employment Equality (Religion or Belief) Regulations, 2003; Employment Equality (Sexual Orientation) Regulations, 2003; Employment Equality (Age) Regulations, 2006; Equality Act, 2006; Equality Act (Sexual Orientation) Regulations, 2007. Several European Directives are also noted: Equal Pay Directive (75/117/EEC); Equal Treatment Directive (76/207/EEC) as amended by the Equal Treatment Amendment Directive (2002/73/EC) (gender); Race Directive (2000/43/EC) (racial or ethnic origin); Framework Directive (2000/78/EC) (disability, religion or belief, sexual orientation and age). *Discrimination Law Review A Framework for Fairness: Proposals for a Single Equality Bill for Great Britain* 28 (London: Department for Communities and Local Government, 2007).

6. "Tackling Discrimination, Modernising the Law", http://www.gos.gov.uk/gosw/news/newsarchive/559077/ (last visited May 20, 2009).

7. (Empowered by the Equality Act 2006).

8. Laura Smith, *Discrimination Law Proposals 'Should Go Further,'* http://www.guardian.co.uk/society/2007/jun/12/equality.discriminationatwork (last visited May 20, 2009).

Detailed analysis is required to understand just what these largely spatially-oriented metaphors aim to capture, but with an ordinary understanding of those terms, there is not just an institutional lack of capacity to achieve institutional goals using assigned powers, but a distinct inability to achieve those goals, caused by inefficient or perhaps counter-productive interactions amongst the very tools meant to enable those institutions. In our terms, this situation seems to be one in which the intensity of mutual reference amongst legal institutions is significantly diminished relative to purpose and expectations, and marks the sort of situation with potential, with further decline, to be part of a larger set of problems eventually associated with a problem of continuity, as mutual reference amongst institutions ceases to the point where a transition to another legal system or form of legal order becomes retrospectively evident. Equality law might not be the most likely locus of inter-institutional failure to start or even continue some chain of events leading to revolution, we realize, yet there is an illustrative value to the example nonetheless. Raz calls for examination of evidence drawn from attitudes and allegiance when attempting line-drawing needed to assess whether legal norms are members or momentarily adopted foreign norms used in a given system, and just that sort of evidence needed for line-drawing seems to us to be relevant to assessment of the internal cohesion of legal systems—whether the sort of cohesion enabling us to say of a system that it is distinct from other systems, or in transition from being a legal system to embodying some other form of legal order. This last issue seems to be particularly troublesome: once we are clear of the Razian presumption that laws are members of legal systems, and the similar (early) Hartian view that the legality worth examining is in modern municipal law-states, our inter-institutional view is responsive to phenomena of legality at various levels of inter-institutional intensity. That responsiveness is only really a virtue to the extent that it maps legality so far as possible, even, perhaps, through transitions between legal orders.

The problem of how to characterize and track transitions is possibly most acute in situations where, unlike the internal change explored above, which is wholly internal to a legal system, a legal system's continuity-failure affects surrounding legal orders, demanding a re-drawing of conceptual borders amongst forms of legality in light of these changes. A particularly intriguing challenge comes from recent exploration of emergencies and the limits of legality. There is a long history of jurisprudential discussion of emergencies of legality, typically conceived as catastrophes within the law-state caused by forces from without, including but not limited to terrorist attacks and natural disasters such as earthquakes or tsunamis. In those emergencies, law-states often operate under special legal norms brought into operation by the emergency's satisfying conditions established ex ante to trigger those special legal norms, or actors within law-states operate to sustain the state's continued existence using extra-legal resources for which later post facto ratification may be sought in various ways. Recent argument suggests that at least some emergencies of this sort ought to be conceived rather differently, with greater attention to the situation of the subject law-states within a global web of legal-normative discourse and practice. Kanishka Jayasuriya, in particular, argues that events such as the September 11, 2001 attack on the United States generated legal-institutional responses best characterized not as internal to a given law-state, but as part of a global state of emergency and response to it. Jayasuriya argues that

> In effect, 9/11 is a global state of the emergency, the distinctive nature of which is the growth of a new jurisdiction of emergency governance layered on to the domains of national and international law. It produces forms of administrative power and regulation pertaining to acts in both the international and national domains of governance that bends and makes elastic the boundaries between state and non-state actors and civilians and combatants. The rigidity of these boundary distinctions has been crucial in shaping conditions of national citizenship. Consequently, changes in these boundaries will determine the way in which the state deals with its own citizens as well as persons outside its territory.[9]

Evidence for the global state of emergency is produced from an amalgam of exercises of legal-institutional powers, from the U.N. Security Council Resolution 1373 "that provides a framework for global administrative law to combat 'terrorism'"[10] to "the Patriot Act

---

9. Kanishka Jayasuriya, *Struggle over Legality in the Midnight Hour: Governing the International State of Emergency*, in EMERGENCIES AND THE LIMITS OF LEGALITY 361 (V. Ramraj ed., 2008).

10. *Id.* at 361.

in the US, a range of anti-terrorism legislation in the UK and the Anti Terrorism Bill 2005 in Australia."[11] Jayasuriya illustrates one particular exercise of such legal powers, observing that:

> In Australia, for instance, the introduction of preventive detention, control orders, as well as specially designed 'rules of engagement,' have, in effect, created a regulatory framework of emergency governance for 'enemy combatants.' The distinctive feature of this emergency governance is not the untrammeled exercise of sovereign decision, but the creation and entrenchment of new forms of administrative power and jurisdiction such as those over the treatment of 'enemy combatants.' The creation of these legal subjects and categories produces a trench of emergency governance in domestic and international law.[12]

Several analytical avenues are opened by Jaysuriya's use of a "trench" metaphor to mark inter-state, inter-institutional response to emergencies by creating newly "elastic" boundaries between actors within and without states. The most interesting, for our present purposes, is his explanation of the trench as a sort of standalone legal order, possibly short-lived, which is nonetheless within the control of the sponsoring law-state whose actions, in creation of the standalone order, express its sharing with other states a political commitment to use very similar legal tools to face shared threats. What seems special about this situation, and in need of further investigation, is the way this "trench" differs from law-states' self-limitation via devices such as constitutions and treaties with other states. The trench certainly needs characterization in its own right as a possibly momentary order of a type which might be expected to recur, and needs further characterization with respect to its knock-on effects for other states. In-state decisions contributed to trans-state co-ordination in response to emergencies affecting one or all states in a cluster of response may be significant consequences for other states and their capacity to frame citizenship and boundaries. These problems need further investigation not just because they are new, but because they do not seem to be usefully understood via current means. It is too easy, for example, to suppose these trenches of legality are simple extra-territorial extensions of state legality, in part because they grow from legally independent actions of separate states, and in part because they may persist

---

11. *Id.* at 367.
12. *Id.* at 367.

even when originating law-states withdraw support for them—e.g., U.S. moves to close the notorious Guantanamo Bay detention facility do not end the existence of the range of preventive orders, U.N. administrative resolutions with respect to terrorism, etc., which initially grew up largely in response to U.S. initiatives. It is also too easy to regard the trench as an international agreement—it is a patchwork product of legal-institutional efforts of politically allied law-states, with consequences possibly unanticipated at the time of loosely coordinated conception. Yet the patchwork beginnings of the trench are irrelevant to the fact of its functioning as a relatively cohesive nonsystemic legal order. How should we characterize this and analogous phenomena using an inter-institutional theory which advertises as a hallmark its responsiveness to novel phenomena? The problems raised by emergencies of legality are likely to be increasingly important to a general jurisprudence that seeks to capture the dominant legal order in the form of the systemic law-state, while taking seriously the way globalization has enabled new intensity of mutual reference amongst legal institutions engaged in global interactions including communications, trade, immigration, pollution control, and many others. A properly pyramid-inverting, time-sensitive jurisprudence must address this phenomena head-on, avoiding premature relegation of the phenomena to familiar explanatory models. To do any less is to let theory drive data, a dangerous "effrontery" we must avoid.

6.2 NOVEL TECHNOLOGIES AND THEIR IMPLICATIONS FOR CONCEPTIONS OF LEGALITY

A final category of challenges for a general jurisprudence, and our inter-institutional theory, comes from a different side of our commitment to data-responsiveness. Information communication technologies—from telephone to the Internet—are increasingly important to the ways we learn, do business, socialize, and govern. One particularly interesting development is the capacity of information communication technologies to retain and apply our stated preferences automatically, for tasks as simple as personal identification for banking, to much more complex tasks limited only by our capacity to develop algorithms to present our preferences in response to particular stimuli. In this way, particular information communication technology applications can serve as proxies for our flesh-and-blood selves. Some software, for example, serves as a stand-in for human memory in the case of simple tasks such as automatic provision of passwords for access to online banking. Slightly more complex software enables automated trading in various degrees of sophistication, beginning with eBay's simple automatic bidding process in which prospective purchasers of an auctioned item can authorize the eBay software to increase their bids as competing bids arrive, with control over increase increments, and peak offered price. It is easy to imagine from this basic example the potential for far more complex tasks to be made algorithmic, and it is equally easy to imagine these tasks being carried out in ways operationally independent of human agency, and for the sake of familiar kinds of artificial persons—corporations, for example. These facts raise the question of whether an artificial legality is possible, independent of human agency. A re-socialized, inverted-pyramid picture of legality in a technology-laden situation might just be a picture of a formal system of rules. If this seems plausible, on what basis is legal theory properly regarded as fundamentally a matter of social theory? This is perhaps exaggerating a little the current prospects for automated law, yet it is not entirely far-fetched, and it allows us to return usefully to the question of the appropriate relations between functional and structural dimensions of analytical accounts of legality.

6.3 RE-BALANCE AFTER IMBALANCE: CONSEQUENCES OF RE-SOCIALIZING A DESCRIPTIVE-EXPLANATORY VIEW OF LAW

Our attention to the technologies we have just mentioned may dismay some readers, who might hold the view that our excursion was too little to do with real human experience of law. Discussions of those technologies, even if ultimately a rejection of arguments for their relevance to legal theory, are part of a commitment to responsiveness to new social data potentially amounting to legal phenomena. Those discussions are also a part of the ongoing consideration of the aptness of a descriptive-explanatory account for its readers. It might well be the case that typical contemporary readers of jurisprudence are skeptical of the effect of novel information communication technologies on legality, although at the same moment the next generation of jurisprudence scholars not only uses some of those technologies, but establishes alternate online identities. Thus in online worlds such as Second Life, "in world" Linden Dollars can be converted to the U.S. dollar, the Euro, and so on for use in the offline, real world. The "trench" of legality established following the September 11, 2001 terrorist attacks on the U.S. may yet have an analogous "trench" in virtual worlds composed of virtual agents whose activities cannot be controlled by the turning off of a switch in any particular state—as the growing debate over governance of the Internet tends to show. This is quick, speculative discussion whose merit is yet to be seen. Its underlying motivation, however, has been demonstrated throughout the book, and even this speculative discussion should at least provide further support for that motivation: to find methods that improve the capacity of a descriptive-explanatory approach to detect and engage all of the social phenomena deserving scrutiny as potentially legal, and so potentially part of the dimension of social life captured by a general jurisprudence. The novel phenomena discussed in this chapter further underscore the importance of incorporating into that jurisprudence elements capable of capturing the dynamic aspect of law, an aspect which may include the need to find new tools enabling distinction of human from artificial legality, perhaps at the cost of generality in a general jurisprudence.

Some of these suggestions will no doubt seem to some readers to be a step too far, yet each step has been generated by questioning the presumption that the law-state's political dominance means that all law-like phenomena must be assessed in light of state experience. However surprising that questioning might be, its time has certainly come, as we demonstrated in our exploration in the Introduction of novel prima facie legal phenomena, and here we have demonstrated if nothing else the possibility of still more novel phenomena. The inter-institutional theory we have developed to face these novel phenomena—and phenomena yet to come—is admittedly incomplete. Yet every theory has a beginning, and ours now has its beginning, with some novel elements, and substantial parts set out in a way intended to be continuous with much of the work available in predecessor theories, and in particular, the institutional legal theory of Neil MacCormick. Our theory, then, is an amplification and extension, not a revolution, but it is sensitive to the possibility that thoroughly phenomena-responsive theories may yet have to become revolutionary if new phenomena outstrip the explanatory capacity of present theory.

INDEX